THE BILLY MEIER STORY

SPACESHIPS
OF THE PLEIADES

KAL K. KORFF

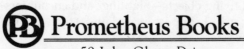 Prometheus Books

59 John Glenn Drive
Amherst, New York 14228-2197

Published 1995 by Prometheus Books

99 98 97 96 95   5 4 3 2 1

Library of Congress Cataloging-in-Publication Data

Korff, Kal K.
    Spaceships of the Pleiades /by Kal K. Korff.
        p.   cm.
    Includes bibliographical references and index.
    ISBN 0-87975-959-3
    1. Unidentified flying objects—Sightings and encounters—Switzerland. 2. Meier, Eduard. 3. Impostors and imposture. I. Title.
TL789.3.K672   1995
001.9'42—dc20   94-46992
                                                                          CIP

Printed in the United States on acid-free paper.

*This book is dedicated with love and respect
to the Jacob family in Switzerland.*

*In the spirit of Hans Jacob, this
work is also for those who wish
to know the truth about the Meier case.*

Contents

Acknowledgments

I would like to take this opportunity to thank the many individuals and organizations who helped make this book possible, in their own unique and various ways.

Organizations and Companies:

Agfa Corporation, South San Francisco, California. Apple Computer Inc., Cupertino, California. BAL Airlines, a subsidiary of Swiss Air, Basel, Switzerland. Capitol Color of Santa Clara, California. Claris Corporation of Santa Clara, California. Carlson Travel Network, Cupertino, California. Steve Diddams, proprietor and president of Diddams Amazing Party Store, Palo Alto, California. NASA/AMES Research Center, Mt. View, California. The Schweiz (Swiss) Meteorologische Zentralanstalt, Switzerland. Schnarwiler Books, Wetzikon, Switzerland. Pan Gas, Winterthur, Switzerland. The non-profit organizations, Mutual UFO Network (MUFON), Seguin, Texas; and the Intercontinental UFO Network (ICUFON), Jackson Heights, New York. The *San Jose Mercury News*, San Jose, California.

Researchers and Associates:

Shirley Anderson, Mr. Walt Andrus, Dr. Michael Arends, Jim Borden, Sussi Cadotsch, Paul Cerny, Joe Chan, Steve Ciacciarelli, Jerome Clark, Ed Corney, Neil Davis, Gina DiBari, Ken Dinwiddie, Roma Donovan, Bill Duvall, Russ Estes, Pamela Ezra, Lucius Farish, Ron Fregosi, Stanton T. Friedman, Thomas M. Gates, Jeff Gottlieb, Dr. Andrew Grotowski, Dr. Richard F. Haines, Jackie Hall, Richard Hall, Dr. Keith Harrary, Richard Heiden, Wayne Heppler, Michael Hesemann, Susi Heussi, Glen Hoyen, Dave Hurlburt, Dr. James Hurtak, Dr. J. Allen Hynek, Ilse von Jacobi, Karl Jentzsch, Philip J. Klass, Harry Lebelson, Greg Long, James Lorenzen, Coral Lorenzen, Dr. Bruce S. Maccabee, Caroline McFarlane, Gary McFarlane, Ernst Meckelburg, Cindy Miller, Garret Moore, Jim Moseley, Josh Moskovich, Dr. Robert Olgilvie, H. Leo O'Neal, Tom Page, Henry Parker, Raj Reddi, Brian Rohan, Helena Rowe, Ferdinand Schmid, Konrad Schutzbach, Karin Schröder, Arnold Schwarzenegger, Max Shafi, Richard Sloan, Jim Smith, Virgil Staff, Ray Stanford, Hal Starr, Ronald Story, Marv Taylor, Jaan Uhelski, Mark Uriarte, Dr. Jacques Valleé, Karl Veit, Marcel Vogel, Illobrand von Ludwiger, Dr. Walter Walker, Jerry Wickham, Ruth Wieser, and Dr. Irwin Wieder.

While I have had the honor of benefiting from so many acquaintances over the years, I would like to take this opportunity to especially thank the following individuals:

My sincere thanks to Mr. David P. Aune, Director of Technical Support at Apple Computer's software subsidiary, Claris Corporation. Mr. Aune has always been supportive of me, and his leadership has been a source of inspiration and encouragement for myself and others. Several of Aune's excellent managerial principles and project management techniques were applied with great success, helping to complete both this book and its related endeavors.

To Ms. Marlene Dingwall, who helped organize and computerize into JPEG and AIFF file formats the hundreds of Meier computer images here on file at TotalResearch. I would also like to thank her for working on the numerous edits of not only this book, but on the wide range of original research material which pours out of here at TotalResearch.

My sincere thanks to Mr. Bruce W. Edwards, my former German instructor and one of my mentors, who always encouraged me to think critically about anything worth studying. I shall be forever grateful for the knowledge, philosophies, and disciplines he instilled in me during the four years in high school that I was lucky enough to have him as a teacher.

In this same vein, I would also like to thank Mr. Robert Sletten, George F. Malone, and Richard Kirchhofer for also being some of my other mentors, men who have made a difference in my life, and many other people's lives.

My thanks to Mr. Carl Finwall and his business partner, Frank Lewis. Both of these men are shrewd and respected business experts who have always supported and encouraged my research and business efforts. I have enjoyed working with them and hope to continue to do so in future business ventures.

Mr. Joseph Bouska, who has been a good friend for six years, and like a true friend, has stuck by me and has always supported my efforts in many ways, including assisting in the making of the Meier exposé video documentary and in supplying various computer components, which turned out to be critical to the completion of this book.

My sincere thanks to Steve Horsch, the professional prop maker who is well known for his work on Paramount Picture's television series "Star Trek," who made the UFO model shells and components used in my experiments during the undercover trip to Switzerland.

A special thanks to Dr. Loren Eskenazi, who allowed us to

use her property during the filming of our Meier UFO model recreations and experiments for the video documentary version of this book. Dr. Eskenazi's place doubled for the mountainous terrain of Switzerland in our experiments. Loren has always encouraged me to move forward with my many projects, even when it seemed there was no light visible at the end of some of those tunnels. Dr. Eskenazi is a very creative, innovative person, and has been featured in the media worldwide for her ground-breaking approaches to medical research. To receive a steady vote of confidence from her over the years such as I have, means a lot to me.

This is also true of Dr. Eskenazi's sister, Diane, who is founder and president of Golden Films Incorporated. Diane has always encouraged me as well, and being a very successful entrepreneur herself, her advice has always carried great weight with me.

My thanks to Don and Marie Carlson, for always supporting me and tolerating my often weird hours and workaholic schedule. Don and Marie are two of the nicest people one could hope to have as friends.

To Mr. Nathan G. Daniel, founder and president of Underground Video, who helped produce and later directed the video documentary of my research into the Meier case on which this book is based. I look forward to continue working with him on the other video projects, some of which are currently in production.

My humble and sincere love, respect, and "thanks" to Mrs. Margrit Jacob, Claudia Jacob, Cornelia Jacob, and Thomas Jacob of Switzerland. The entire Jacob family not only invited this author and Tina Layton to be their guests, but made us feel like we were one of their own family during the ten days we stayed with them. The Jacobs gave unconditionally, their support and time to this project while we visited, and without their generous assistance this book would not be as complete as it is.

My sincere thanks to Mrs. Marylynn Kretchun, a supervisor of mine for several years, starting just before my tenure on Claris Corporation's HyperCard® Development Team and my undercover trip to Switzerland in 1991 (see chapter 2). Marylynn, like the rest of Claris's management, has always been supportive of me, and her advice has always been "top-notch." Marylynn Kretchun is the best supervisor I have ever had the privilege of working under, and I hope our friendship (and an excuse to work together) continues beyond the Claris years.

A special thanks to Dr. Paul Kurtz, chairman emeritus of Prometheus Books, for believing in this project throughout the two years I promised to get it to him. I first discussed this book with Dr. Kurtz at the 1992 American Booksellers' Association (ABA) show in Anaheim, California, where I was demonstrating a touchscreen-based, computer kiosk system called BookBrowser™ that I had helped invent. In literally thirty seconds, Dr. Kurtz expressed both interest and support for this project, and I knew instantly that I had found my publisher. I considered no one else.

Ms. Tina Layton allowed me to persuade her to accompany me to Switzerland to investigate this unusual UFO case. Tina has been a wonderful, close friend

My sincere thanks is also extended to Mr. Richard A. Mead, founder and president of Information Montage. Richard is one of my closest, dear friends, who has hung in there with me these past four years, through thick and thin.

To my editor, Mr. Steven L. Mitchell at Prometheus, who also got behind this book project and managed to fit it into his hectic workload. Steven has always been very supportive, wonderful to talk with on the telephone, and ever so patient. Steven is a real intellectual with a great sense of culture and history.

My sincere thanks to Mr. William L. Moore, who proved to be instrumental in getting the original incarnation of this book published back in 1981. I would also like to thank him for his help on the text of that first edition.

My thanks to Ms. Rajini Ram for inputting a lot of boring file codes for TotalResearch's many case file records. Rajini's work helped expedite the integration of the various computer database libraries in use here at TotalResearch.

My sincere thanks to Mr. and Mrs. Al and Barbara Reed for their continual advice and criticisms over the years, and for their support and friendship during the early 1980s when I first met them. Their love and hard work was critical to the release of my first book exposing the Meier case, and played a big role in the revisions of this manuscript.

My heartfelt "thanks" to Mr. Mitch Plott of Claris Corporation for his continual advice and friendship. Although Mr. Plott and I first became acquainted through events surrounding activities independent of Claris, his assistance in dealing with those issues, and how to manage what has been a very heavy and diverse workload for me these past years, has often been very sound, and certainly appreciated. Like Mr. Aune and Mrs. Kretchun, Mitch Plott helped me focus and "sharpen the saw."

My thanks to Dr. Tina L. Seelig for restoring my faith in the publishing industry and stimulating my long dormant desire to write again. I enjoyed working with Tina on a daily basis during our BookBrowser™ software development project, and the early filming of the Meier exposé video documentary when she was involved. I have enjoyed meeting through Tina the many wonderful bookstore owners, distributors, and editors in the publishing industry. Tina is a fireball of creativity, and some of my best work ever (as well as the work of some of my associates) has come forth when working with her.

Brad and Valerie Sparks, also two of my closest friends, who have hung in there over the years. Brad is (arguably) one of the most brilliant researchers on this planet, and the respect he commands from the professional research community for his academic and legal prowess is well deserved. Even the California Supreme Court has ruled in Brad's favor on issues he has championed! Who could argue with this track record? Brad Sparks is also one of my close research associates, and we have many joint authorship and original research projects we look forward to releasing to the public during the coming years.

Valerie Sparks is the kind of woman that every single male (like this author) wishes he could marry. Loyal, dedicated, heart of gold, her success and the way she has championed various original TV and media-related projects like "Real Heroes" speaks for itself.

My thanks to Nancy Pless, another friend of many years, who has known about this book since 1987. Nancy helped me conduct my very first detailed experiments with helium balloons and UFO models. The results of these experiments later proved helpful in the investigation of this case.

A special thanks to Ms. Angela Stone, yet another editor on the TotalResearch end of the project, whose strong will and determination to fight for what she thinks is right made the decision to work with her more than justified.

My thanks to Mr. Stanley Swihart, President of the Swihart Group in Dublin, California, and a former colleague at Lawrence Livermore National Laboratory in Livermore, California. Stanley provided me with the best geographical, regional, and raw intelligence data concerning the country of Switzerland and the area where Billy Meier lives. Stanley's similar information about Germany, Austria, and Lichtenstein also proved to be invaluable.

My special thanks to Major (Ret.) Colman VonKeviczky for his generosity in allowing me the use of his many Meier-related photos over the years, and for providing great leads for the undercover trip to Switzerland I undertook to investigate the Meier case firsthand.

To Dr. Roger S. Woodward, the brilliant medical genius

who finally figured out what had been ailing me for fourteen years, since my teenage days. Dr. Woodward has helped me walk that fine line between letting my workaholic tendencies get the best of my health (literally!), yet still insure that my research projects and other endeavors get completed.

My sincere thanks to Mr. Bob Kiviat of the Berkeley Group and coordinating producer for FOX TV's popular television show "Encounters" for believing in me also. Bob felt that my research was important enough on the Billy Meier case to be featured on the show, and I am grateful to him for the opportunity he gave me. I never enjoyed filming a studio debate more than during the Meier episodes of "Encounters" that Bob produced.

Along this same line, I would also like to thank television talk show host Larry King of CNN's "Larry King Live!" for having me on his program as well. It was a pleasure working with CNN, Larry, and his production staff of Kerri Stevenson and Linda Wolf. They are true professionals, and I have never been more comfortable during a live, one-on-one television interview than when I was on Larry's show.

My thanks is also extended to another close friend of mine, Mr. Roy Neil, president of Neil Media and Neil Research Laboratories, for being a terrific friend who has always supported and encouraged me with his advice. Roy Neil, like Richard Mead and Brad Sparks, is a true genius and I am proud to count him as one of my closest friends.

To Rick Neil, another great friend and genius, who has always encouraged me in my efforts and has also helped unselfishly whenever the need arose. As is the case with his brother Roy, I never spend enough time with either of them.

To Ms. Betty Neil, one of the sweetest people I have ever known, and someone who has a giving heart that knows no boundaries. Betty Neil, like Rick and Roy, Steve Horsch, and Tina Layton, helped tremendously with the planning and preparations for the undercover trip to Switzerland.

Mr. Kyle MacDonald for helping plan and execute various covert investigative and research operations during the years, and who has provided much needed bodyguard and security services on occasion.

My thanks to Mr. Jonathan L. Walter, a good friend of many years, who helped acquire and later taught me how to use the video equipment I took undercover with me to Switzerland for this investigation. Jonathan has always supported my efforts, and I miss working on multimedia software development projects with him.

Mr. Carl Otsuki, president of Capitol Color in Santa Clara, California, supplied the press pictures for the jacket of this book, the media kits, and other promotional materials. Capitol Color has one of the finest state-of-the-art photographic and digital image laboratories; their work is second to none.

My thanks and sincere respect to Mr. David Eiduson, my present personal manager who decided to represent me based on what he saw in my research. I am honored to be the only non-rock-and-roll artist and musician that he manages. Dave not only handles the ropes in Hollywood for me, but has taught me a lot this past year about how the entertainment business really works.

To Mr. Bob Steiner, who provided invaluable information regarding the background of "Dr." Marcel Vogel. Bob is a very shrewd and thorough paranormal investigator who has done great work exposing frauds where they exist.

My sincere thanks to Ashley, Carol, Rick and Valerie Finwall, Gina Kramer, Donald and Julie Nordenthal, Mark and Mary Vermillion; Thomas, Jeremy, Jesse, and Kyra Bridgeman; Elvira Korff, Erica Korff, Kalvin Korff, Kurtis Korff; Dorothy Toone and Val R. Toone for inspiration and encouragement.

Finally, a heartfelt thanks to my fellow friends and associates at Apple Computer's software subsidiary, Claris Corporation. Many of the people there have always stuck with me and have been very supportive over the past six years, even when my outside distractions, research, and various endeavors managed to intrude sometimes into their lives. Working at Claris has always been a challenge for me, since I feel that I have led for years somewhat of a "dual life" while employed there—computer software support technician and former HyperCard development team member by day; author, historian, lecturer, media personality, multimedia developer, paranormal researcher, UFOlogist, etc., during my "off" hours and so-called "spare" time.

The individuals at Claris to whom I refer are: David Acoba, Sherie Ahmadi, Shane Alexander, Tom Barnum, Cathy Barradas, Betty Beardslee, Steve Becker, Adam Behrens, Dana Berkow, Gregory Bergantz, Karen Billings, Damone Blake, Robert Bogar, Van Bolton, Matthew Bowe, Germaine Brown, Rob Burns, Dennis Cohen, Barbara Crowder, Sergio Cruz, Eric Culver, John Darrah, Nicholas de Paul, Maria Duran, Bob Eddings, Dan Eilers, Michael Ellard, Nydia Estrada, Larry Faulks, Donna Ferrozzo, Janice Fetzer, Amy Fihn, Patrick Fitch, Alexei Folger, April Frederick, Jeff Garver, Lara Golden, Peter Haase, Tom Hammer, Scott Hartman, Dave Heiber, Jennifer Henderson, Lisa Hennig, Geri Hyde, Chris Illes, Sara Johnson, Jimmy Jones, Kevin Jundt, Christina Keith, Steve Kurasch, Jay Lee, Paul Lee, Denise Lejardi, Ken Mahler, Kevin Mallon, Bill Marriott, Linda Meissner, Ben Miller, Chris Nalls, Lydia Nicholson, Francisco Odón, John Michael Osborne, Jon Perr, Lyle Petersen, Karl Pittenger, Keith Proctor, Jamie Pruden, Max Pruden, Tanya Pruden, "Big Red," T.G. Ricker, Ed Rosenzweig, Don Ross, Tony Rotolante, Steve Ruddock, Bill Schissler, Stephan Schwirzke, Mark Seymour, Jeff Songster, Jim Spelman, Mark Stobbs, Eric Sugg, Jill Sullivan, Bill Swagerty, Greg Tanner, Kit Teater, Tex Tyner, Linda Waldon, Ronald Watson, Joe Weese, James P. Weil, Owen West, Michael Whitney, Vince Wood, and David Wu.

Lastly, to Mr. Avtar Singh of the American Cab Company

in Santa Clara, for providing excellent personal service in driving me to all kinds of locations during sometimes crazy hours in order to help me conduct my business and complete this book.

To all of you: Although it may have at times appeared otherwise, I never once *really* regretted listening to your advice and criticisms. While I will not deny that it proved to be sometimes painful, I cannot *thank all of you enough* for helping to lay a foundation upon which I intend to forever build upon.

1

Eduard "Billy" Meier: The Man, the Claims

And how many times has Billy Meier met with the space people?
Kal Korff, in a question to "Simone" at the Meier cult[1]

More than 350 official contacts or times and another 250 contacts
which he [Meier] cannot talk about. They especially visit him on
his [Meier's] birthday.
"Simone," Billy Meier devotee and follower[2]

Eduard Albert Meier, or "Billy" as he prefers to be called, was
born February 3, 1937, in the small village of Bülach, near the
city of Zürich, Switzerland.[3] Purportedly raised as a Protes-
tant, Meier never completed his formal education, dropping
out of school before finishing the sixth grade.[4]

During the next few years, young Meier spent his time
working various manual labor jobs, dodging truant officers,
and having occasional brushes with the law. He would be sentenced, more than once, to such correctional facilities for "trou-
bled boys" as Albisbrunn, from which he repeatedly escaped.[5]
Later, when he was arrested and charged by the police for
thievery and forgery, he was ordered to serve six months[6] at
the Aarburg correctional facility[7] in the town of Rheinau.[8]

23

After one month of incarceration, Meier wrote that he "simply could stay no longer."[9] Hence, after allegedly fabricating a key out of "wood and woolen carpet," he escaped once more, crossing the border into nearby France. Within days he joined the French Foreign Legion, and was transferred to a unit of soldiers stationed in Algeria.[10]

After just a few months in the Foreign Legion, Meier went AWOL.[11] Distraught and determined to "find" himself, he returned to Switzerland and voluntarily surrendered to authorities, and served out the remainder of his sentence.[12]

After the transgressions of his youth, Meier claims he spent twelve years traveling extensively through forty-two countries on the African, Asian, and European continents.[13] Working whenever possible, Meier survived by doing a variety of odd jobs, including chicken farmer, grape picker, nail pounder, snake catcher, truck driver, puppeteer, waiter, German tutor,[14] and ship painter.[15] Once, Meier even tried to present himself as a veterinarian, but was unsuccessful.[16]

On August 3, 1965, in Iskenderum, Turkey, Meier was injured in a bus accident. His left arm was amputated,[17] just above the elbow.

By December of that year, Meier, still recovering from his tragic accident, began the admirable task of trying to adapt to his new handicap. He relocated to Greece.

On December 25, 1965, Meier, now twenty-eight, met and fell in love with a seventeen-year-old girl named Kalliope while attending a Christmas party in the city of Thessaloniki.[18] One month later, the two were engaged. However, because Kalliope's parents objected to Billy Meier as a suitor for their daughter, the two decided to elope. They were married in Corinthos, Greece, March 25, 1966.[19]

The following year, the Meiers moved to Pakistan. On September 20, 1967, Kalliope gave birth to their first child, a girl named Gilgamesha.[20]

In 1970 the couple moved to Switzerland. On August 9, their second child, a boy named Atlantis-Socrates, was born.[21]

When the Meiers arrived in Switzerland, life was not easy. Job stability for Billy proved to be elusive, thus their financial status was marginal. Indeed, Billy's only dependable income came from a small monthly welfare sum paid by the Swiss government because of his physical disability.[22]

By the year 1971, the Meier family was firmly settled in the small town of Hinwill (pronounced hin•VEAL), a twenty-five-to-thirty-minute drive from the city of Zürich.[23]

In December 1973 Meier and his family moved into an old farmhouse, which the town of Hinwill leased to him for a small sum.[24] To help supplement the family's income, Kalliope would sell eggs from the chickens they raised, and Meier would sell occasional birds from a large flock he tended in his back yard.[25]

In the fall of 1974[26] Billy Meier borrowed some money from his friend of several years, Jacobus Bertschinger,[27] to place an advertisement in the prestigious German magazine *Esotera*. The ad solicited anyone who might wish to form a group for discussing and studying "metaphysical" or paranormal subjects. Several people responded, and by the end of 1974, Meier's newly formed metaphysical study group had ten members and met often.[28]

It was during the course of one of these meetings that Meier made a startling announcement. He proclaimed that on January 28, 1975, he had established direct physical contact with a group of aliens from a star cluster known as the Pleiades (pronounced PLEE•uh•dees).[29] The Pleiades are located in the constellation of Taurus, some five hundred light-years away. Although comprised of literally hundreds of stars, only six are visible to the human eye. While historical references to the Pleiades are found among the myths and legends of ancient cultures (they are called the Seven Sisters in Greek mythology, for example), today they are often mistaken by untrained observers for the constellation of the "Little Dip-per" since they are similar in appearance.[30]

The initial reaction to Billy Meier's astounding claim from some of the members of the now-fledgling metaphysical study group was one of skepticism. Billy, however, stuck by his stories of repeated alien contact and soon started produc-ing hundreds of exceptionally clear photographs of the "Pleia-dian spacecraft" as proof that he was telling the truth.[31]

As time passed, Meier's stories began to gain acceptance. Those members who still did not believe him simply left the group, while those who were either "on the fence" or accepted what he said stayed around. But as the number of believers grew, so did the scope of Billy Meier's claims. What began as a simple series of "contacts," with the first allegedly occurring on January 28, 1975, soon evolved into a much more detailed and elaborate scenario complete with religious overtones.[32]

The first prominent UFO researcher outside the ranks of the metaphysical group to learn about the 1975 series of con-tacts was Ilse von Jacobi of Wiesbaden, Germany. Jacobi had first heard about Billy Meier's stories through her friend Mar-garet Rufer, one of the study group's members. Intrigued, Jacobi traveled to Switzerland with Rufer to meet with and interview Billy.[33]

Jacobi said she found Meier to be credible and a "conser-vative man of few words."[34] Jacobi, nonetheless, was able to obtain enough information and photographs from the Swiss farmer to write a seven-page article. It was published in the August 1976 issue of the widely read Italian magazine *Il Gior-nale dei Misteri* (The Journal of Mysteries).

The next prominent UFO researcher to investigate the Meier case firsthand was Lou Zinsstag, who lived in the city of Basel, a mere ninety miles away.[35] Zinsstag heard details of the Meier case through her friend and traveling companion, English UFO researcher Timothy Good.[36]

According to Zinsstag, she also found Meier to be sincere

and the case to be genuine. She stated as much a year later in a letter to Good: "If Meier turns out to be a fake, then I shall take my whole collection of photographs to the ferry boat and drown it in the old man river of Basel."[37]

In 1976 Zinsstag and Good visited the United States to gather research for a new UFO book they would later co-author. On September 1, 1976, the two arrived at the Greyhound bus station in Tucson, Arizona, to visit a mutual acquaintance, UFO researcher Lt. Colonel (retired) Wendelle C. Stevens.[38]

Wendelle Castyle Stevens was born in Little Sauk, Minnesota, on January 18, 1923. In the early 1940s he enlisted in what is now known as the United States Air Force and retired as a lieutenant colonel on October 31, 1963.[39]

Although we are told that "historic events always appeared to be an integral part of Stevens's life,"[40] his USAF Career Service Record does not bear this out. Indeed, accord-

Fig. 1. Since January 28, 1975, Eduard "Billy" Meier claims he has been visited more than 700 times by aliens from this star cluster known as the Pleiades. According to Meier, a Pleiadian "cosmonaut" named "Semjase" contacts him regularly. (Photo courtesy: Lick Observatory.)

ing to his own military file, the Colonel enjoyed a career as an ordinary pilot and an airplane mechanic.[41] Moreover, despite having spent nearly forty years studying UFO reports, Stevens was, until 1979, a relatively obscure figure, although an avid collector of material. His contributions to the UFO field at that time came primarily from authoring perhaps a dozen small photo essays, and to Stevens's credit, accumulating what is believed to be the single largest private collection of UFO photographs in the world.

As the three acquaintances sat around trading stories, Zinsstag told Stevens in detail about the Meier case. She then took out sixteen of Meier's photographs for Stevens to examine in detail. Colonel Stevens, always impressed by "good-looking" UFO photographs, was in awe and "just had to have some copies."[42] Zinsstag allowed Stevens to choose only four photos, which he in turn photographed with his 35mm camera.[43]

While Stevens was busy acquainting himself with the intricate details of Meier's numerous contact stories and UFO photographs, in Europe Meier's claims continued to receive widespread publicity.

Almost simultaneously, the German magazine *Quick* published a condensed version of Jacobi's *Il Giornale dei Misteri* piece. *Quick*'s story on Meier appeared in the July 1976 issue. The avalanche of publicity was just beginning.

On Sunday, September 5, 1976, the largest gossip tabloid in Switzerland, *Sonntag's Blick* (a paper similar to the U.S.-published *National Enquirer*), featured a front-page article on Meier and his extensive claims. Headlined: *"Zürcher verblüffte Erich von Däniken: Ich filmte Besucher aus dem All"* ("Zürich Man Amazes Erich von Däniken: 'I Filmed Visitors and All' "), the feature story rode the tidal wave of publicity on the Swiss farmer's tales of contact. Needless to say, the story lacked objective critical reporting of Meier's claims. Instead, millions of people were led to believe his stories were true.

As the year 1976 drew to a close, Billy Meier made plans to move his family. The Hinwill town government invoked the Swiss equivalent of U.S. eminent domain laws, telling Meier his farm was to be torn down and replaced by modern apartments.[44]

In April 1977[45] the Meier family moved into the mountains and settled on fifty acres of farmland in the small remote village of Hinterschmidrüti (pronounced HIN•ter•schmid •RUEH•tee), a thirty-to-thirty-five-minute drive from Hinwill.[46] They still reside there as of this writing.[47]

Since the Meier family was relatively poor and could not afford the property they were now in the process of acquiring, the approximately $240,000 needed to buy what was known then as the "Herzog farm" was raised by Meier's friends and those who believed in his stories of repeated UFO contact![48]

The old Herzog farm proved to be an excellent choice for Meier and his followers. The land was fairly fertile, its location remote, and the property was big enough to accommodate both guests and residents. It also provided a means of self-sufficiency, especially if available resources were used wisely. For Meier, whose farming skills were quite developed, this issue was not a problem.

Within the next two years Meier would transform both the farm and his informal metaphysical study group into his own private religious cult,[49] complete with visitor's parking![50] As of this writing, the situation remains unchanged, although the members of Billy Meier's Semjase Silver Star Center (as it is now called) prefer not to think of themselves as a "religious cult."[51]

Fig. 2. Two of the first press articles ever to appear on the Meier case were printed in the August 1976 issue of Italy's *Il Giornale dei Misteri* and in the September 5, 1976 issue of the Swiss tabloid *Sonntag's Blick*. (Photo courtesy: ICUFON, Inc.)

Where and How the Genesis III Productions Began

On October 21, 1977, Wendelle Stevens took the first of what were to be many trips to see Billy Meier in Switzerland.[52] With Ilse von Jacobi accompanying him, Stevens wanted to meet Meier face-to-face so that he could "look him in the eye and ask some of my hundreds of questions and try to get some answers."[53]

After spending four days at Meier's farm in Hinterschmidrüti, Stevens became convinced that the experiences of Meier had "actually happened, that the disc-shaped craft photographed is really a UFO and that the case is legitimate."[54]

Meier even claimed to have his eighty-ninth and ninetieth "contacts" while Stevens was there![55]

When Stevens finished "investigating" the Meier case, he returned home to Tucson with three hundred of Meier's UFO photographs and several hundred pages of written notes, including direct quotations and "messages" allegedly received by Meier from the "Pleiadians."[56]

Before Stevens originally left for Switzerland, he promised his friends from nearby Phoenix, Lee and Deborah or "Brit" Elders, to come back and tell the details of what he found. The Elders knew about the Meier case because they were present in Tucson on September 1, 1977, when Lou Zinsstag and Timothy Good originally visited Wendelle and told him about it.[57]

Stevens returned home convinced that the Meier case was genuine. So bold was his conviction of the case's legitimacy that he even declared the Billy Meier series of "contacts" as the "hands-down greatest UFO case of all time."[58]

Stevens returned for a second visit to Switzerland in April 1978. Accompanying him this time were Brit and Lee Elders.[59] Once again, during their stay at Meier's complex, the Swiss farmer claimed to have yet another contact—his 105th, which took place on April 4, 1978. Meier, of course, was the only "witness" to this event.[60]

When Stevens and the Elders returned to the United States, they pondered the results of their latest findings with the Elders. As the group was evaluating the evidence, the three friends discussed publishing the investigative material in the form of a book. In order to help bring the book project to completion, Stevens formed a partnership with Thomas K. Welch and Lee and Brit Elders. The new venture was called Genesis III Productions Limited and Lee Elders signed a personal rights agreement with Meier. Billy would supply the material and Genesis III would promote it, acting as his sole materials/information distributor.[61]

Although the agreement was signed with Meier, they lacked financial backing. To alleviate this dilemma, Genesis III received a loan for $39,923.57 from a skilled marketing agent named Michael Osborn. In exchange for the loan to be repaid with interest, Osborn promised to use his marketing skills to help promote the book.[62]

With money to back them, Genesis III contracted with Word Distributors in Phoenix, Arizona (in exchange for a good price and a percentage of the profits from the sale of the book), to privately print ten thousand copies of their elaborately illustrated 12 x 12-inch color photo-journal. They called it *UFO . . . Contact from the Pleiades, Volume I*.[63]

Pleiades was released to the general public in November 1979. Immediately the book generated controversy and, of course, healthy sales. By September 1980, less than one year later, a "revised edition" had been issued[64]—not a bad revenue stream considering that the suggested retail price for both versions was $24.95.[65]

In 1983 both Stevens and Genesis III released separate additional books on the alleged experiences of Billy Meier.

Stevens's release was titled *UFO . . . Contact from the Pleiades: A Preliminary Investigation Report*. Retailing for $17.95, the book was 542 pages—by far the "best buy" of all the pro-Meier publications at the time.[66] However, if a nice color companion volume similar in design to the original coffee-table style Pleiades photo-journal was wanted, then the Genesis III release, simply titled *UFO . . . Contact from the Pleiades, Volume II*, was also available. Volume II retailed for $34.95 and sold out.[67]

Other authors jumped on the Meier gravy train, too. In 1985 author Gary Kinder was commissioned by publisher Morgan Entrekin of the Atlantic Monthly Press to write a book about the Meier case.[68] On May 26, 1987, Kinder's work was released to the public under the title *Light Years: An Investigation into the Extraterrestrial Experiences of Eduard Meier*.[69] *Light Years* was well received, sold well and quickly, and in less than a year made the transition to the mass paperback market under the Pocket Books imprint by February 1988.[70] In 1988 Genesis III Publishing released the book *Message from the*

Pleiades—The Contact Notes of Eduard Billy Meier, which was edited and annotated by Stevens. The book was the first volume of what would prove to be a series, with this particular treatise detailing the verbatim contents of Meier's first thirty-five "contacts" with the alleged Pleiadians.[71]

In 1989 Wendelle Stevens released a sequel to his 1983 book on the Meier case. Titled *UFO . . . Contact from the Pleiades: A Supplementary Investigation Report,* the 553-page work presented the most updated information about the material contained in its predecessor. Then, in 1990, Stevens and Genesis III teamed up again and released *Message from the Pleiades—The Contact Notes of Eduard Billy Meier, Volume II,* a second volume of verbatim transcripts of Meier's "conversations" with the Pleiadians. In this book, the details of his reported contacts numbers thirty-six through fifty-five were presented.[72]

Fig. 3. The book that launched Billy Meier into worldwide stardom, *UFO . . . Contact from the Pleiades, Volume I.* Originally released in November 1979, the book has since gone into three printings and is considered a "collector's item," fetching as much as $300 in today's numerous markets for out-of-print, limited edition release books!

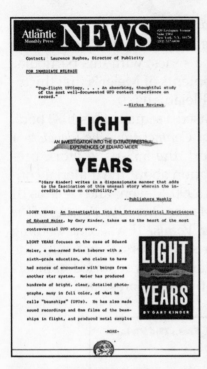

Fig. 4. *(Left)* A press release: two-sided flyer for the Atlantic Monthly Press book *Light Years* by Gary Kinder. *(Right)* The cover of the book *Message from the Pleiades, Volume I*, the first in an ongoing series of works detailing the verbatim "conversations" Billy Meier claims to have had with the Pleiadian aliens.

In August of 1991, German publisher Michael Hesemann and Meier devotee-follower Guido Moosbrugger copublished a book in German called . . . *und sie fliegen doch!*[73] (And They Still Fly!), "which is the most accurate book on Billy Meier."[74] Like its predecessors, Moosbrugger's book has since become popular and as recently as June 1994 had been serialized and translated into four languages, including Czechoslovakian, a rarity for a UFO-related title.[75]

Fig. 5. Guido Moosbrugger's book, copublished with the sponsorship of Meier-supporter and German publisher Michael Hesemann in Dusseldorf.

In 1991 two more Meier-related books were published: the original photo-journal of *UFO . . . Contact from the Pleiades, Volume I*,[76] and a third volume of translated "contact notes," *Message from the Pleiades, Volume III*, detailing the verbatim conversations Billy Meier claims allegedly took place during his contacts fifty-five through seventy-six.[77]

The series will continue to be published until all of the notes from Meier's hundreds of "contacts" are printed, promising many more volumes for years to come.[78]

From 1992 through 1994 three more major books on Meier

would be published, all of which were popular on the New Age circuit. There was *Celestial Teachings* by Dr. James Deardorff, a retired college professor in Oregon who has since become a believer and enthusiastic supporter of Billy Meier's messianic claims.[79] Deardorff's book focused on the religious and "spiritual" aspects of Meier's writings as they appear in a document called the Talmud Immanuel.[80]

Not to be outdone, Billy Meier himself wrote a book titled the *Talmud Immanuel* which was released in the United States by Wild Flower Press. Based in Newburg, Oregon, the company had previously published Deardorff's tome.[81]

In 1994 Eduard Meier's former official representative and spokesman, Randolph Winters, published a book called *The Pleiadian Mission—A Time of Awareness*. Other than the writings penned by Meier himself, Winters's book presents the most comprehensive overview of the supposedly religious aspects of the case, containing a wealth of information about Meier's messianic claims, which Genesis III, Gary Kinder, and Wendelle Stevens almost completely ignore.

The Eduard "Billy" Meier case is the subject of no less than twelve books and video documentaries, and dozens of audiocassettes. In addition to the global coverage the print media has given this case for some twenty years as of this writing, Meier's UFO photographs and stories of repeated extraterrestrial contact have also been featured on numerous television stations and in lectures and conventions throughout the world. Moreover, each year thousands of Meier's purportedly genuine "UFO" photographs are sold around the world in the form of direct prints, calendars, paintings, and posters. The Billy Meier "evidence" is now a money-making machine that shows no signs of slowing down.

What is it about the Eduard "Billy" Meier case that fascinates so many people? A short summary of the Meier "evidence" explains the widespread interest.

The Billy Meier "Evidence"—A Summary

According to Billy Meier and his proponents:

• Between January 27, 1975, and August 18, 1991, Meier has had more than *seven hundred* contacts with aliens, most of which have been with a "Pleiadian female cosmonaut" named Semjase (pronounced sem•YA•see).[82] These alleged extraterrestrial contacts are said to still continue as of this writing.[83]

• Meier has taken over *one thousand* photographs of the "Pleiadian" and various other spacecraft and ten 8mm films, plus many other pictures of other worlds, alien life forms, etc., the latter of which were obtained during his five-day "trip" into space/time while on board a Pleiadian saucer-shaped spacecraft.[84]

• Meier took his UFO photographs and 8mm films not only with the handicap of having *just one arm*, but did so by shooting most of them "from his right hip" (since the viewfinder on his camera was broken). In addition, the lens of the camera he used for most of the photos he took was set at a fixed focus; its lens was jammed just short of the "infinity" setting due to having been accidentally dropped.[85]

• There exist "dozens of witnesses" who can vouch for Meier's claims of alien contact, some of whom have even seen and independently photographed the Pleiadian craft.[86]

• The Pleiadians have left behind physical evidence to prove their existence in the form of "landing-tracks"[87] as well as rock, metal, and mineral[88] samples for scientists to study and evaluate. Objective testing of the various Meier evidence by numerous academics and scientists, including universities and professional and private institutions, have all verified the validity of the Meier case.[89]

• The Meier evidence, in particular the UFO photographs, are even more impressive when one considers that Billy Meier has only a sixth-grade education,[90] suffers the handicap of having only one arm, and is a poor, humble Swiss farmer who is barely able to feed his family![91]

• No one has ever managed to duplicate *even one* of Billy Meier's UFO photographs or films. Furthermore, no confederate has ever come forward nor has anyone ever witnessed or offered any firsthand evidence of Meier knowingly committing fraud.[92]

• Eduard "Billy" Meier was chosen by the Pleiadians to be a Prophet of Humanity and help lead humankind into the "New Age," as we head toward the year 2000 and beyond.[93]

• Billy Meier has traveled *backward and forward in time.* During one of these alleged time-travel adventures in the past, he met with Jesus Christ![94] Meier even saved Jesus from a beating one time.[95] Moreover, Jesus was so impressed with Billy Meier's "superior intellect" that after the two of them met, Jesus ended up being a servant and admirer of Meier![96]

• Eduard "Billy" Meier, in this "incarnation" at the present time (1995), is not only a prophet whose "wisdom" we should heed and live our lives by,[97] but he *is* Jesus Christ reincarnated![98]

• Meier is on a mission to "save" humanity, and is guided by the "Pleiadians," who are trying to help us Earthlings "evolve" to a higher spiritual existence.[99]

• The Billy Meier case is the most highly documented, thoroughly investigated incident in UFO history. It has been called "the hands-down greatest UFO case of all time."[100]

It is an understatement to say that if Billy Meier's startling claims are true, then they qualify as perhaps the single most important series of events ever to take place in human history. Let's take a hard, objective, and scientific look at the evidence that exists in this case and try to determine the facts without prejudice.

Is the Meier case *really* what both its widespread supporters and the numerous books written about it claim it is, the most thoroughly documented UFO case of all time?

Our analysis and quest for the truth starts with a trip to Switzerland for a firsthand look.

Notes

1. Simone, personal interview with Kal Korff and Tina Layton, Semjase Silver Star Center, Hinterschmidrüti, Switzerland, August 18, 1991.

2. Ibid.

3. Guido Moosbrugger, . . . *und sie fliegen doch! UFOs: Die größte Heraus-forderung des 20 Jahrhunderts* (München, Germany: Michael Hesemann Verlag, 1991), p. 104.

4. Gary Kinder, *Light Years: An Investigation into the Extraterrestrial Experiences of Eduard Meier* (New York: Atlantic Monthly Press, 1987), p. 79.

5. Ibid.

6. Jim Lorenzen, personal interview with Kal K. Korff, Tucson, Arizona, May 28, 1983.

7. Kinder, *Light Years*, p. 79.

8. Wendelle Stevens, *UFO . . . Contact from the Pleiades: A Supplementary Investigation Report—The Report of an Ongoing Contact* (Tucson, Ariz.: Wendelle Stevens, 1989), p. 27.

9. Ibid.

10. Ibid., pp. 27–28.

11. Ibid., p. 28.

12. Kinder, *Light Years*, p. 79.

13. Moosbrugger, . . . *und sie fliegen doch!* p. 105.

14. Kinder, *Light Years*, p. 81.

15. Moosbrugger, . . . *und sie fliegen doch!* p. 105.

16. Kinder, *Light Years*, p. 81. *See also* Stevens, *UFO . . . Contact from the Pleiades—A Supplementary Investigation Report*, p. 29.

17. Moosbrugger, . . . *und sie fliegen doch!* p. 106. *See also* Stevens, *UFO . . . Contact from the Pleiades—A Supplementary Investigation Report*, p. 29; *also* Kinder, *Light Years*, pp. 8, 81.

18. Kinder, *Light Years*, pp. 24, 82.

19. Moosbrugger, . . . *und sie fliegen doch!* p. 106.

20. Eduard "Billy" Meier, *Stimme der Wassermannzeit* (Hinterschmidrüti, Switzerland, 1976).

21. Ibid.

22. Kinder, *Light Years*, pp. 9, 63.

23. Author's travel times when driving from Zürich and the surrounding areas to Hinwill repeatedly.

24. Kinder, *Light Years*, p. 8.

25. Claudia Jacob, Margrit Jacob, personal interviews with Kal K. Korff and Tina Layton, Wetzikon, Switzerland, August 15, 1991.

26. Hans Jacob, private correspondence, February 15, 1978. *Betrage: Eduard Meier (Billy) der sich UFO-Kontaktler nennt (Schweiz)*, p. 1.

27. Kinder, *Light Years*, p. 11.

28. Hans Jacob, private correspondence, February 15, 1978. *Betrage*, p. 1.

29. Ibid.

30. Dr. J. Allen Hynek, UFOlogist, astronomer, personal correspondence with Kal K. Korff, 1976 to 1985.

31. Hans Jacob, private correspondence, February 15, 1978. *Betrage*, pp. 1–3.

32. Ibid.

33. Wendelle Stevens, *UFO . . . Contact from the Pleiades—A Preliminary Investigation Report—The Report of an Ongoing Contact* (Tucson, Ariz.: Wendelle Stevens, 1983), p. 19.

34. Ibid.

35. Ibid.

36. Kinder, *Light Years*, p. 50.

37. Ibid., p. 53.

38. Wendelle Stevens, original unpublished manuscript for *UFO . . . Contact from the Pleiades*, p. 20.

39. Wendelle C. Stevens, *USAF Career Service Record*, United States Air Force records, pp. 1–4.

40. *UFO . . . Contact from the Pleiades, Volume I*, 1st ed. (Phoenix, Ariz.: Genesis III Productions, Ltd., 1979), pp. 42–44, 71.

41. Wendelle C. Stevens, *USAF Career Service Record*, pp. 1–4.

42. Stevens, *UFO . . . Contact from the Pleiades—A Preliminary Investigation Report*, pp. 16, 19.

43. Ibid., p. 19.

44. Kinder, *Light Years*, pp. 57–58.

45. Ibid., p. 58.

46. Author's actual travel time by car when driving from Hinwill to Hinterschmidrüti repeatedly.

47. Kal K. Korff, personal phone call to Billy Meier's residence, October 10, 1994, just before sending manuscript off to publisher, Prometheus Books.

48. Elisabeth Gruber, personal interview with Kal K. Korff and Tina Layton, Semjase Silver Star Center, Hinterschmidrüti, Switzerland, August 18, 1991.

49. Konrad Schutzbach, letter of resignation from the Semjase Silver Star Center, Greifensee, Switzerland, June 1979.

50. Kal K. Korff's and Tina Layton's personal observations while at the Semjase Silver Star Center, Hinterschmidrüti, Switzerland, August 18, 1991, as seen on hidden camera videotapes recorded at the Meier compound.

51. Bernadette Brand, personal interview with Kal Korff and Tina Layton, Semjase Silver Star Center, Hinterschmidrüti, Switzerland, August 18, 1991.

52. Stevens, *UFO . . . Contact from the Pleiades—A Preliminary Investigation Report*, p. 12.

53. Ibid.

54. Ibid., pp. 27–28.

55. Ibid., p. 23.

56. Stevens, *UFO . . . Contact from the Pleiades—A Preliminary Investigation Report*, pp. 23–24.

57. Ibid., p. 16.

58. Ibid.

59. Stevens, original unpublished manuscript for *UFO . . . Contact from the Pleiades*, chapter 2, "First Contact," pp. 1, 17. *See also* Kinder, *Light Years*, pp. 98–100; *also Pleiades, Volume 1*, 1st ed., p. 60. *See also* Stevens, *UFO . . . Contact from the Pleiades—A Preliminary Investigation Report*, p. 27.

60. *Pleiades, Volume I*, 1st ed., p. 60.

61. Court Document Exhibit, Rights Agreement with Billy Meier, p. 2, Maricopa County Courthouse Records, Case Numbers: C417254 and C422380, 1980–1981.

62. Maricopa County Superior Court document File Number C422380, Counterclaim: *Michael R. Osborn and Susan Osborn, husband and wife, v. Thomas K. Welch, Lee Elders and Britt Nilsson-Elders, his wife; John and Jane Does 1–X; and XYZ Corporations 1–X*, November 13, 1980, pp. 2–6.

63. Maricopa County Superior Court document File Number C417254, *Word Distributors Incorporated v. Thomas K. Welch, Lee Elders and Britt Nilsson-Elders, dba Genesis III*, September 2, 1980, pp. 4–7.

64. *UFO . . . Contact from the Pleiades, Volume I*, rev. ed., p. 3.

65. Ibid., inside flap copy.

66. Wendelle Stevens, advertisement flyer for *UFO . . . Contact from the Pleiades—A Preliminary Investigation Report—The Report of an Ongoing Contact*, sent to Kal K. Korff, May 1983.

67. *UFO . . . Contact from the Pleiades, Volume II* (Phoenix, Ariz.: Genesis III Productions, Ltd., 1983), inside flap copy.

68. Gary Kinder, letter to Kal Korff, March 28, 1975.

69. Atlantic Monthly Press, press release, "Light Years: An Investigation Into the Extraterrestrial Experiences of Eduard Meier," April 1987, back page.

70. Kinder, *Light Years*, p. 4 and back cover.

71. Wendelle Stevens, *Message from the Pleiades: The Contact Notes of Eduard "Billy" Meier, Volume I* (Phoenix, Ariz.: Wendelle C. Stevens and Genesis III Publishing, 1988).

72. *Message from the Pleiades: The Contact Notes of Eduard "Billy" Meier Volume II* (Phoenix, Ariz.: Wendelle C. Stevens and Genesis III Publishing, 1990).

73. Elisabeth Gruber, personal interview with Kal Korff and Tina Layton, Hinterschmidrüti, Switzerland, August 18, 1991.

74. Kal K. Korff, personal conversation with Michael Hesemann, UFO Expo West '94 LA conference, Los Angeles, California, June 12, 1994.

75. Ibid.

76. *UFO . . . Contact from the Pleiades, Volume I*, rev. ed. (Phoenix, Ariz.: Genesis III Productions, Ltd., 1979), p. 3.

77. *Message from the Pleiades: The Contact Notes of Eduard "Billy" Meier, Volume III* (Phoenix, Ariz.: Wendelle C. Stevens and Genesis III Publishing, 1991).

78. Statements made to Kal K. Korff from three independent book vendors at the UFO Expo West '94 LA conference, Los Angeles, California, June 12, 1994.

79. Kal Korff, personal conversation with Dr. James Deardorff via telephone. Corvallis, Oregon, November 1994.

80. Bernadette Brand, personal interview with Kal Korff and Tina Layton, Hinterschmidrüti, Switzerland, August 18, 1991.

81. Ibid.

82. Simone, personal interview with Kal Korff and Tina Layton, Hinterschmidrüti, Switzerland, August 18, 1991.

83. Kal K. Korff, personal phone call to the Semjase Silver Star Center, answered by member Eva Bieri, Hinterschmidrüti, Switzerland, October 13, 1994, 3:55 A.M. (PST).

84. Elisabeth Gruber and Simone, personal interviews with Kal Korff and Tina Layton, Semjase Silver Star Center, Hinterschmidrüti, Switzerland, August 18, 1991.

85. Wendelle Stevens, "Ongoing Contact Cases," lecture at the UFO '80 convention, Oakland, California, August 23, 1980. *See also* Jim Dilettoso, tape-recorded personal interview for the record with Kal K. Korff, Al Reed, and Barbara Reed, at the offices of Publication Professionals, Sunnyvale, California, September 6, 1980.

86. Stevens, *UFO . . . Contact from the Pleiades—A Preliminary Investigation Report*, p. 126.

87. Ibid., p. 363.

88. Ibid., p. 412.

89. Jim Dilettoso, tape-recorded personal interview for the record with Kal K. Korff, Al Reed, and Barbara Reed, September 6, 1980.

90. Kinder, *Light Years*, pp. 8, 79.

91. Jim Dilettoso, tape-recorded personal interview for the record with Kal K. Korff, Al Reed, and Barbara Reed, September 6, 1980.

92. Wendelle Stevens, "Kal Korff and the Meier 'Hoax'—A Response, Part 2," *MUFON UFO Journal* (November 1991), p. 13. *See also* Stevens, *UFO . . . Contact from the Pleiades—A Preliminary Investigation Report*, p. 254.

93. Randolph Winters, *The Pleiadian Mission—A Time of Awareness* (Atwood, Calif.: The Pleiades Project, Inc., 1994), pp. 18–20. *Also* Bernadette Brand, personal interview with Kal K. Korff and Tina Layton, Hinterschmidrüti, Switzerland, August 18, 1991.

94. Bernadette Brand, personal interview with Kal K. Korff and Tina Layton, Hinterschmidrüti, Switzerland, August 18, 1991. *See also* Michael Arends, *Eduard Meier—Prophet Der Neuzeit?* (Rimsting, Germany: October 1976), pp. 2–5. *See also* Confidential letter dated June 23, 1980 from Ph.D. source in Switzerland who participated in the Meier documents/evidence study and requests anonymity due to the negative conclusions found. The unedited letter revealing the names of the people who conducted the Meier document studies, as well as their conclusions, analyses, and specific requests for anonymity are on file, along with their addresses, at MUFON and TotalResearch.

95. Randolph Winters, Lecture on Billy Meier at MUFON Meeting, November 17, 1994. *See also* Glen Hoyen and Kal K. Korff, personal conversation with Randolph Winters, MUFON Meeting, near Santa Barbara, California, November 13, 1994.

96. Letter from firsthand sources in Switzerland to Walt Andrus, June 23, 1980, pp. 1–3. Copy of letter was kindly forwarded by Mr. Andrus

to Kal Korff, and is on file at both TotalResearch and MUFON headquarters. The authors of this letter prefer to remain anonymous, but their names are in the document and their information is easily verifiable.

97. Billy Meier, *Stimme der Wassermannzeit*, December 1976, pp. 3–26. *See also* Billy Meier, *Stimme der Wassermannzeit*, February 1989, pp. 1–30.

98. Bernadette Brand, personal interview with Kal K. Korff and Tina Layton, Hinterschmidrüti, Switzerland, August 18, 1991. *See also* Konrad Schutzbach, Letter of Resignation from the Meier Cult, Greifensee, Switzerland, June 1979. *Also* Glen Hoyen, Lecture on Billy Meier by Randolph Winters at MUFON Meeting, near Santa Barbara, California, November 19, 1994. *See also* Guido Moosbrugger, Lecture on Billy Meier at UFO Expo West '94 in San Mateo, California, November 6, 1994, during question and answer sessions. *See also* Hans Jacob, private correspondence, February 15, 1978. *Betrage: Eduard Meier (Billy) der sich UFO-Kontaktler nennt (Schweiz)*, pp. 1–2.

99. Kal K. Korff's and Tina Layton's personal observations at the Meier compound, Hinterschmidrüti, Switzerland, August 18, 1991. *See also* Guido Moosbrugger, Lecture on Billy Meier at the UFO Expo West '94 in San Mateo, California, November 6, 1994, during "Q and A" sessions. *See also* Winters, *The Pleiadian Mission*, pp. iv, 8–35.

100. Stevens, *UFO . . . Contact from the Pleiades—A Preliminary Investigation Report*, p. 16.

2

The Undercover Trip to Switzerland

Well, what would you do if, say, Kal Korff or someone like *that* ever came here?

> Kal Korff, investigating undercover as "Steve Thomas," talking with Bernadette Brand of the Meier cult[1]

We were warned about him from Lee (Elders). We would not let him in, or we would never let him leave.

> Bernadette Brand

During August and September 1991, I traveled undercover to Switzerland to investigate the Meier case firsthand. Accompanying me was fellow paranormal researcher Tina Layton, an employee at Lawrence Berkeley Laboratory in Berkeley, California. Tina and I were in Europe for three weeks, and we visited the Meier compound six times, officially signing their guest register twice.

While a firsthand investigation of the Meier evidence might seem like a straightforward procedure, there were numerous considerations not ordinarily part of UFO research that required elaborate planning. For example, one of the first issues that had to be addressed was how to handle any poten-

45

tial problems concerning my name. In 1981, I wrote a small book on Billy Meier stating that the case was a hoax.[2] In addition, between 1981 and 1986 I had numerous articles published in various scientific and UFO-related magazines debating Wendelle Stevens regarding the authenticity of the Meier evidence.[3] I have also given many lectures on the subject, and on one occasion I directly challenged Stevens during one of my lectures at the 1983 National UFO Conference in his hometown of Tucson, Arizona.[4]

If I had traveled to Switzerland to visit Meier under my own name, it's possible there could have been hostile consequences. Would I be allowed on the Meier property to study the evidence freely or would I be viewed as the enemy? I pondered the situation and thought it prudent not to use my real name. To show up as Kal Korff meant risking not being allowed on the Meier property at all, unable to acquire at least some photographs or interview potential witnesses—the very minimum research I wanted to conduct. A second factor in my decision to use an alias was the issue of personal safety. I remembered that my encounters with pro-Meier factions over the past fourteen years (some of which are recounted throughout this book) have ranged from extremely pleasant to downright nasty. It was this "nastiness" which concerned me, and the increased potential for it due to the fact that I would be on Meier's home turf.

The idea of being on the cult leader's property—on foreign soil—stuck behind electric fences and lockable gates, where everyone *but me* knew the terrain, was not an attractive one. Thus, it seemed that the only way to study the Meier case firsthand, quietly, safely, and objectively, was to go undercover and use an alias. Therefore, as hokey as it sounds, I reveal here for the first time that while visiting the Meier compound and in parts of Europe, I traveled under the alias of Steve Thomas, a fictional character diametrically *opposite* in many ways to myself. I did my best to fit his contrived profile, presenting myself as a "true believer" in Meier's claims, hoping it would help increase my chances of gaining access to the Meier evidence.

To play the role of Steve Thomas convincingly, I had to devise both a cover story and alter my physical appearance. The cover story was a relatively simple one that I worked out over time with Tina Layton. She and I would pose as Meier believers, making the pilgrimage to Switzerland in order to pay homage to the Swiss contactee and find the spiritual truth behind his claims. Since we knew that hundreds of visitors flock to Meier's farm each year for similar reasons,* I figured that this would allow us to fit in with relative ease, as long as we were convincing in our roles.

There was, however, a slight problem. In my opinion, I had to find a way to raise some of the objections to Meier's claims that I had cited in my original exposé without offending members of his group or blowing my cover. I wanted total freedom to ask any questions, friendly or otherwise.

In science and scientific UFOlogy alike, such freedom of inquiry permits the opportunity for investigative classification or understanding and, if you are as fortunate as Tina and I were, definitive resolution.

To solve the "feel free to ask them any question, but don't anger them so they clam up" dilemma, I decided on the following, somewhat ironic approach: I would *pretend* not only to be Steve Thomas, but I also made sure everyone at Meier's

---

*During our many visits to Meier's farm, we met individuals from the USSR, San Diego, Austria, England, and New Zealand. Although the reasons these people decided to visit Meier's compound varied, interest in the case is truly global. Visitors to Meier's place can purchase copies of more than one thousand of his UFO and UFO-related photographs, videos of his films, documentaries, publications, membership pins, T-shirts, and bumper stickers. Meier's merchandise is also widely available both in the United States through mail order advertisements in various magazines, and at the major UFO and "New Age" conventions.

place knew that this Steve Thomas was sick and tired of hearing Kal Korff and the Intercontinental UFO Network (ICU-
FON) president Colman VonKeviczky "bad mouthing" the
Meier case in the United States. Thus, I told the members of
Meier's group and anyone else who would listen that Tina
and I had made the pilgrimage to Switzerland for the additional purpose of taking back conclusive "evidence" that we
could use to silence such "idiots" as Korff and VonKeviczky,
who obviously did not know what they were talking about!
With our cover story now basically set, the rest of the logistics
and the planning of the investigation could proceed.*

Members of the pro-Meier factions had seen me before, and
this time I did *not* want to be recognized. I had to disguise my
physical appearance. In addition, since I did not know just
whom I might accidentally meet while at the Meier compound,
this was yet another reason to disguise myself.

Remembering how I looked back in 1986, during my last

---

*After this author, Colman VonKeviczky and UFO researchers William
L. Moore (coauthor with Charles Berlitz of *The Roswell Incident*) and Underground Video are Billy Meier's chief critics. While Colman VonKeviczky
helped me during my initial investigation in 1979–1981, generously supplying the many photographs I used in my earlier exposé book, Bill Moore
arranged for the publishing contract for my original treatise and also
served as my editor on the project. Underground Video conducted their
own, independent investigation, working with the special effects house of
the UltraMatrix Corporation, and concluded that the Meier case was a
hoax. This is significant for two reasons: (1) Underground Video's investigation, although far more limited in scope than this author's, still concluded that the Meier case was a hoax. (2) When Underground Video
started its investigation, they were originally supporters of the Meier case!
Since Underground Video and myself were both working on our own
independent documentaries on the Meier case, in 1993 we agreed to coop-
erate rather than compete. Underground Video then ceased production of
its own Meier exposé video, and in exchange for doing so, I signed a deal
with them to produce and direct the video documentary *EXPOSED: The
Billy Meier UFO Hoax*, upon which this book is based.

public appearance where anyone connected with Meier could possibly have seen me, I decided that my new look would have to be just the *opposite*.

In 1990, as in 1986, I was clean-shaven except for a moustache and had short hair. To play the role of Steve Thomas, I would grow my hair very long and sport a beard. My reasoning was simple: The longer my hair and the wilder my beard, the more I would fit the stereotype of the "New Age dude" Steve Thomas was supposed to be.

Other than having to endure curious comments on occasion from my co-workers at Claris Corporation, who assumed "Kal is really letting himself go,"[5] the transformation looked credible and I was sure the hokey cover story would work to fool the Meier people. (It did.)

With the help of "Peggy," my travel agent, I booked two tickets to Switzerland. We also arranged for a rental car in Zürich. With Peggy's help, I was able to get the appropriate auto rental papers and other official paperwork for use in Switzerland in the name of Steve Thomas and Tina Layton. This extra level of protection meant that if the Meier people became suspicious and decided to check on us, my real name would not be found, only Tina's.

While the issues regarding my cover were being resolved, I continued to define additional objectives, deciding what strategies to use and how to implement them. Thus, the entire investigation in Switzerland was designed with the following criteria and/or objectives in mind:

1. Objectively reexamine all of the Meier evidence;

2. Visit specific photographic/landing locations for samples and measurements;

3. Interview authorities, locals, and any potential witnesses;

4. Uncover any previously unknown or "early" Meier evidence, if any existed;

5. Recreate Meier's photographs at the same locations, if possible;

6. Acquire the clearest, most pristine, and original evidence possible;

7. Make sure all results and conclusions can be independently verified.

The Seven Criteria Examined in Detail

An examination of the details behind each of these seven criteria helps explain their existence, function, and importance to our investigation.

1. Objectively reexamine all of the Meier evidence

Since I had already written an earlier treatise on the Meier case, it was tempting to take the "easy" way out and focus the investigation only on those areas which were sparsely covered in my original exposé. However, to be candid, the "UFOlogist" in me would not permit this. The only way I could ever be satisfied as a researcher was to disregard all *previous* ideas about the case and start all over. Hence, in order to help achieve this state of objectivity, Tina and I brought with us all of the Meier books (including my own) to Switzerland to research every claim possible while we were there. Both of us approached the Meier evidence with open minds, making sure we tested everyone's claims, charges, and counter-charges, including my own previous ones.

2. Visit photographic and landing locations for samples and measurements

In order to analyze Meier's UFO photographs properly, it was absolutely critical that I visit some of the locations where his pictures were taken. By doing this, I could obtain quantitative measurements which may prove invaluable in determining such factors as true object distance, perspective, or size of the alleged UFO.

Ironically, it was by visiting some of these photographic locations that we uncovered several "smoking guns," proving that Meier's photographs could not have been taken as claimed. The full results of our investigations are presented in chapter 4, "Conclusive Analyses of Billy Meier's 'UFO' Photographs."

The need for soil samples from the alleged UFO "landing sites" is science at its most fundamental level. Yet, I am amazed why supposedly "objective" and "competent" researchers and writers like Brit and Lee Elders, Gary Kinder, Guido Moosbrugger, Wendelle Stevens, Thomas Welch, and Randolph Winters *never bothered* getting any soil samples! Indeed, their collective *failure* to do so is scientifically inexcusable, and has never been adequately explained.

Suffice it to say, while visiting the physical locations of Meier's alleged UFO "contact" sites, we acquired both control *and* specimen soil samples for analysis back in the United States. The conclusions reached after analysis of these soil samples are presented in chapter 7.

3. Interview authorities, locals, and any potential witnesses

Interviewing as many people as possible who might have relevant information regarding Meier is another fundamental and scientifically critical step to the success of any serious UFO investigation.

In addition to "double-checking" alleged statements and claims obtained by other researchers, Tina and I sought out any potentially new or previously unknown witnesses who might exist. This was accomplished in part by asking people from the surrounding areas if they either heard, knew of, or had any information about Billy Meier. We also made it a point to pass his pictures around to show people in the hopes that this might bring forth additional witnesses.

Our results proved very successful. We encountered and successfully located several witnesses, all of whose names appear throughout this book. The individuals with whom we spoke ranged from local neighbors and close acquaintances of Meier to professional people and Swiss authorities.

4. Uncover any previously unknown or early Meier evidence, if any existed

While Tina and I did not know if it was possible to achieve this goal, it turned out that we were very successful in meeting this objective. Examples of such new, previously unknown Meier "evidence" that has never been published until now can be found in chapters 4 and 5.

5. Recreate or simulate Meier's photos at the same locations, if possible

One of the most persistent claims among Meier "believers" is that no one has been able to convincingly reproduce, using models or other hoax methodologies, any of Meier's UFO photographs.[6] This charge is simply untrue.

Before Tina and I made the successful reconstructions in Switzerland, Meier's photos were first effectively reproduced by both Bill Moore and me some *ten years before,* in 1981. This fact has been conveniently *ignored* by Meier proponents, in particular Wendelle Stevens.

Indeed, to illustrate just how *easy* simulating Meier's photographs was, UFO researcher Bill Moore and I wrote about what methods to use in a specific rebuttal to Wendelle Stevens when he first raised this same, unfounded argument. Our response appeared in the July 1982 issue of the *MUFON UFO Journal*, the official newsletter of the Mutual UFO Network, the world's largest civilian UFO organization in existence.

In spite of these facts, Stevens was still writing five years later, when he released his *Supplementary Investigation Report* book, that critics had failed to *"come up with just one good duplicate"* of Meier's UFO photographs.[7]

For this part of our investigation, Tina and I traveled to Switzerland with models, some assembled and ready to go, others in need of being finished, to duplicate Meier's photos at the exact locations Meier used. The results of our experiments are presented in chapter 4.

6. *Acquire the clearest, most pristine, and original evidence possible*

The acquisition of original or pristine evidence is yet another example of science at its most rudimentary level. Once again, without much difficulty, Tina and I acquired such materials as first- and second-generation copies of Meier's numerous UFO photographs, specimen and control soil samples, firsthand testimonies, and quantifiable measurements. Our acquisition of such material allowed us to later make definitive conclusions not previously possible until now.

7. *Make sure all results and conclusions can be independently verified*

This last criterion is the most important, for obvious reasons. Any investigation, whether it involves UFOs or not, is valid *only* if the results obtained can be *independently* verified by *anyone* wishing to do so.

A fact is a fact; anyone should be able to double-check it. This is the approach I have always advocated toward UFO investigative standards in the past, and continue to do so today. As stated in the preface, this book has been written so that anyone wishing to do so can independently verify the research.

To help insure the scientific and historical integrity of the investigative record regarding our Swiss study and analysis of the Meier UFO evidence, I videotaped or captured on color 35mm photographic prints every relevant activity.

The data from these recordings not only helped reconstruct the facts for this book, but was instrumental in proving conclusively that many of Meier's UFO photographs are hoaxes. Some of this footage is featured in Underground Video's documentary production of this book, and was the main feature story in an episode of the FOX TV Network's popular television series "Encounters," which aired nationwide on December 18, 1994.

In my original 1981 exposé of Billy Meier, several photographs taken in Switzerland are credited to Colman VonKeviczky and ICUFON. While VonKeviczky supplied these photographs and has always been generous in allowing me to use them free and unconditionally when telling people about Meier, he had received much of *his* material from Swiss UFO researcher Hans Jacob, who preferred to remain anonymous.[8]

Hans Jacob was one of the original witnesses and one of the first ten members of Meier's shortlived Metaphysical Study Group. He had known Billy from the beginning of his "contactee origins," having responded to the original *Esotera* magazine advertisement Meier placed. He was also present when Meier announced to the study group in February 1975 that he was in contact with "Pleiadians."[9]

Jacob, who studied UFOs and the occult, spent much time around Meier, accompanying him into the woods at night during several of his "contacts." Jacob even reported seeing the alleged spacecraft on a few occasions![10]

Jacob and Meier had a "falling out" nearly a year after he announced that he was in contact with Pleiadians. By 1977, their friendship for all practical purposes was over. Thus, when the Meier family moved away to Hinterschmidrüti, the Jacobs barely saw anything more of Billy Meier.[11]

I knew Jacob was probably our most important witness; our first priority would be to locate him, even before trying to meet directly with Billy Meier.

I telephoned Colman VonKeviczky approximately three weeks before I left for Switzerland, and told him my plan. We had not spoken in over six years. After quickly catching up on old times, I asked Colman for any information or advice he might have and for the names and telephone numbers of people I should interview. After this information was furnished to me, I asked Colman for a "credential" letter that would help introduce me to the Jacob family. Colman promised to help and, true to his word, sent me a letter which I took to Switzerland with us. Included was Hans Jacob's last known address and telephone number, which was in the town of Wetzikon[12] (pronounced VETZ•ee•con).

Tina and I departed San Francisco for Switzerland on August 13, 1991. We arrived in Zürich on August 14. The first stop in our investigation was in the small town of Wetzikon, located about a thirty-minute drive from Zürich.

Wetzikon is a town of 40,000, surrounded by a series of smaller villages such as Hinwil, Ilnau (pronounced EEL•now), Pfäffikon (pronounced PFEF•ee•con), and Bäretswil (pronounced BARE•ets•vil). Wetzikon was an ideal strategic location for our investigation.

August 15, 1991—Wetzikon, Switzerland

Our first task upon arriving in Wetzikon was to locate the whereabouts of UFO researcher Hans Jacob, preferably while it was still daylight. We easily located the Jacob residence, which was in the hills off of the main road coming from Zürich, but when we arrived no one was at home. Deciding to return a few hours later, we drove into the center of town to learn about how to get to Billy Meier's farm.

Because we could not locate the small town of Hinterschmidrüti on any of the maps we had brought with us, Tina and I decided to stop in a local bookstore to purchase a more detailed map and ask for some directions.

The bookstore was called Schnarwiler (pronounced SCHNAR•vy•ler), and within moments we found a clerk who was willing to help us out.

"Excuse me, we are looking for the small town of Hinterschmidrüti," I asked the clerk behind the desk.

"Ah, you are seeking Mr. Meier then?" the clerk said.

"How do you know we want to visit Mr. Meier?" I asked.

"Everyone who goes to Hinterschmidrüti seeks Mr. Meier," she replied.

Fortunately, the woman we happened to meet was Mrs. Karin Schröder, the bookstore manager. She was very familiar with Meier because he had a business account at their bookstore! It should be noted that most people, especially "poor Swiss farmers"[13] who are supposedly "illiterate"[14] and possess only a "sixth-grade education,"[15] do not usually have business accounts at bookstores.

"Can you tell us how to get to Billy Meier's?" I inquired.

I opened up the map and listened very carefully as she gave us directions and tried to follow along. The store clerk seemed to know where Meier lived, but wouldn't offer much more information than that. Clearly, she was curious about us, and we about her, and it was obvious that she knew more than she let on.

When I asked her for details about Meier, she volunteered that he visited their store often and reiterated that he had an account there which he used to buy books.

When I inquired about what kind of books Mr. Meier purchased, Karin Schröder replied, "He reads everything."[16]

"What kind of books does he read? What subjects?" I continued to press.

"Space, science, history, many things," she answered.

Another bookstore employee, Ruth Wieser, corroborated what Schröder stated. Wieser had personally processed several of Billy Meier's book orders in the past and usually saw him whenever he came into the store.[17]

"How often does he come around?" I asked her.

"About every six weeks. I am not sure. He usually comes with a group of them," she stated.

I then asked Wieser about what specific book titles she recalled Meier buying or showing any interest in. She stated the same thing Karin Schröder did, that "Meier reads everything," but she had a hard time naming specifics. She promised to think about it, however.

"It is so hard to name one thing because he reads everything," she repeatedly said while trying to remember.

We told both Schröder and Wieser, who were always professional and extremely polite to us, that we would be back sometime later and thanked them for their directions, the map, and the information.

When Tina and I left Schnarwiler, I stepped out to record on my video camera the front of the building for the Meier documentary we were also filming. We then proceeded up the street a few stores to the Hobbie Technik, a plastic model and miniature shop where we purchased glue, X-acto blades, and silver spray paint for the unassembled UFO models we brought with us.

Tina and I returned to the Jacob residence about two-and-one-half hours later. This time we noticed that someone was home. We didn't know it at the time, but it turned out to be Jacob's daughter, Claudia, an attractive woman in her early thirties.

"I am a friend of Colman VonKeviczky, from the United States of America. Can we speak with Mr. Hans Jacob, please?"

I handed her Colman's last letter to me, which listed the Jacob residence, as proof of my identity and to establish credibility.

Much to my sadness, we learned that Hans Jacob had died approximately eighteen months earlier.

"Did you know my father?" she asked.

"No, I never got to meet him. However, some of your father's material and photographs appeared in my book many years ago."

As she looked at me curiously, I retrieved a copy of my original Meier exposé, opened it to page 33, showing her a photograph of her father that I was sure she would recognize. She did, nodding yes while looking at the photo in the book and said, "So you travel from America all the way here to study Billy Meier?"

"Yes."

"But why waste your time on him? No one takes him seriously here, and there is all this faking of evidence, you know?"

"But he's very big in the United States. Millions of people believe that his case and photographs are real."

Claudia could hardly contain herself as she started laughing. She really did find it incredible that people could be fooled by Meier.

"Would it be possible to ask you some questions about what you know about him?" I asked, gently.

Claudia smiled, then excused herself and said she would be back in a few minutes.

While Claudia was inside the house, I remarked how lucky we were to still get help, especially after having arrived totally unaware that Hans Jacob had passed away.

When Claudia Jacob returned within a few minutes, she had with her two large navy blue binders, each about two inches thick. After quickly thumbing through the first, she shifted her attention to the other binder and held it out on the table in front of us. She then opened it to a page which contained Meier photographs.

"Is this what you want to see?" she asked.

I could hardly believe my eyes, for in spite of the unfortunate news about Hans Jacob, his investigative records and research had survived him and were now available for independent examination.

"I run my father's book service and library since he passed away," she said.

As Claudia turned the binder toward me, I thumbed through a few pages and then started at the very beginning as Tina drew closer. While I had seen some of these images before because they had been featured in my earlier book, here I was looking at the original masters from which my copies and those of VonKeviczky had come.

Starting at the beginning of the Jacob binder, the photos were laid out in chronological order. Included in the front of the binder was a combination "Index/Table of Contents," which Jacob himself typed up in German listing the specific times, dates, locations, numbers, and details of each picture.

Hans Jacob was a meticulous researcher and the organization of both his Meier photo-binder and the office/library where he once worked reflected this.

The three of us glanced through the binder page by page, finishing with it in about ten minutes.

"Are they helpful? Did you find what you were after?" Claudia asked.

"Yes, you have no idea. This is it," I said, while motioning to her father's photo-binder.

A short time later, Claudia's mother, Margrit Jacob, came home. Claudia immediately explained who Tina and I were and why we were there.

"So you want to talk about Billy?" Margrit asked.

"Yes."

While Claudia translated, I explained to Margrit Jacob exactly what it was Tina and I were doing. This, coupled with the fact that I could often speak in German myself, helped ensure that no translational errors would occur.

While the four of us sat at the table in the Jacobs' back yard, I asked Claudia and Margrit about some of the specific locations where Meier's photographs had been taken and if they could give us directions to them.

Both Claudia and Margrit replied that they were familiar with several of the locations and even offered to take us to visit them. This was an unexpected but welcome development.

The specific comments the Jacobs had concerning some of the locations visible in Billy Meier's photographs are presented in chapter 4. The Jacobs' testimonies are critically important since they personally accompanied Billy Meier on several occasions to many of his "contacts" with Semjase. Indeed, the Jacobs were around Billy Meier so often that they even appear in some of his UFO photographs!

As the subject of Billy Meier wound down in our discussion for the day, Claudia asked how long we would be visiting Switzerland. After learning that we would be staying for three weeks, Margrit offered her hospitality as our host. We were honored to accept.

On our first evening in Wetzikon, I telephoned Billy Meier's place to give them my cover story spiel. I wanted to arrive at the compound as a "known" entity, yet still stick to my cover story. So, I decided to try first what I called the "naive American" version of the Steve Thomas façade, pretending that I did not understand a single word of German except for maybe a few words.

When I dialed Billy Meier's Semjase Silver Star Center telephone number, which I found in Stevens's *Supplementary Investigation Report*, I was able to get through.

"Hello, Sprechen Sie English?" I asked the woman who answered the phone.

After hearing her reply that she did not, the phone was handed over to someone else. I then introduced myself by telling my cover story.

"I am an American named Steve Thomas and I am a big believer in Billy Meier. I would like to visit your Semjase Silver Star Center to donate some money."

"This is good. You come on Sunday. That is the day for visitors," she replied.

"What time can I be there?" I inquired.

"You come after 10:00."

I then thanked her profusely, deliberately hyping my emotions a bit. I wanted her to think that visiting Billy Meier's place was the most important thing to me in the universe. I also made a point to deliberately mention money and my intent to spend it freely.

With the trip to Billy Meier's farm now set to take place in a few days, Tina and I used this interim time to ask the Jacobs numerous questions, visit the Meier contact sites, and finish building our UFO models so that we could conduct experiments.

The information obtained during discussions with the Jacobs and visiting the Meier contact sites, and the data acquired through conducting the UFO model experiments are covered in chapters 4 and 5.

August 18, 1991—Hinterschmidrüti, Switzerland (Billy Meier 's Place)

Tina and I awoke early in the morning to arrive at Billy Meier's compound on time. The plan was to obtain as much evidence as possible by using whatever means were practical. This included spending the night at Billy Meier's if necessary, which meant that Tina and I would have to agree to work in the fields during the day if we were to be granted this "privilege." While we were willing to do this if necessary, it turned out that we didn't have to; the evidence we needed was gathered very easily.

After breakfast, we left the Jacob house and took the road through Bäretswil to Hinterschmidrüti to get to Billy Meier's place. Because we already had Meier's address and phone number in case we got lost, I figured locating Billy Meier's residence would not be that difficult.

After driving a scenic thirty minutes into the mountains above Wetzikon, we came to the town of Hinterschmidrüti and located Billy Meier's place via the help of a local Swiss guide who happened to live in the hills above him. Tina and I parked our car in what was a gravel-covered lot for visitors.

As we unpacked everything, I made sure my Hi-8mm video camera was running, and I would attempt to keep it recording as long as possible. With ten hours worth of fully charged batteries and plenty of Hi-8mm broadcast-quality videotapes with me, I wanted our trip to be documented as thoroughly as possible.

Around my neck hung my 35mm camera, loaded with ASA 200 color print film. Like the videotapes, I also had an ample supply of color 35mm print film for my still camera.

When Tina and I noticed there was no one stationed at the front entrance, we quickly posed for pictures separately in front of the huge stone at the front gate which has the words

Fig. 6. August 18, 1991, 10:12 A.M., Swiss time. The author, having grown his beard and hair as long as possible, poses as "Meier believer Steve Thomas," while standing at the front entrance of Billy Meier's Semjase Silver Star Center, preparing to go inside undercover. (Photo courtesy: Tina Layton/UFOComp Computer Archives.)

"Semjase Silver Star Center, 1978" engraved on a large metal plaque mounted on it.

I grabbed our gear and we promptly went inside, having no idea how long I would be able to videotape or take stills. We walked quickly and discreetly.

After making it past the front entrance, I noticed to my left that there were some cows and two large gardens further up ahead. It was obvious from the way the land was farmed and maintained that the compound was pretty much self-suffi- cient. I stopped to record with both my still and video cameras images of these areas for our documentary. So far, no one had noticed us.

As Tina and I walked down the long gravel road that snaked through the compound, we passed several side trails which shot off to our right side. Since this was our first visit, I decided not to venture off from the main road until I had familiarized myself with the area.

Although we had made it only a few hundred feet onto the property, it was already obvious that Meier was anything *but* "poor," contrary to what his proponents would have everyone believe.

In truth, the fifty acres of land Billy Meier lives on is not only well maintained, but it denotes a level of wealth and financial stature above that of the average middle-class family, whether they live in Switzerland or the United States. This was my first real surprise as we continued to explore the property.

After walking about ten minutes, Tina and I came across a large brown wooden building with an angled roof off to our left. As we would later discover, this was a "guest house" where people lived and where the center keeps the hundreds of UFO pictures it sells to the general public.[18] Slowing down to capture everything possible, with both video and still photographs, I noticed that a man was walking toward us in a nervous manner. He seemed unprepared for our arrival, trying to steer us away from where we were heading, which was now straight for Meier's house.

I recognized him from photographs in the various Meier books: it was Jacobus Bertschinger, who looks like he could be Billy Meier's younger brother. Tina and I ignored his utterances in Swiss-German, pretending we did not notice or understand him.

On the right side of the road, a little further up was a pond with running water flowing into it. The pond was obviously artificial and was decorated with all kinds of shiny colored

Figs. 7 and 8. One of several well-kept tree farms and small gardens at Billy Meier's fifty-acre, self-sufficient compound in Hinterschmidrüti. Meier's place has areas for prayer and meditation, and members must live according to the rules of the "Pleiadians" as they are communicated and written down by Billy Meier himself.

Fig. 9. A large guest house at Meier's compound where various members live. This is also the building where Meier's UFO photographs are archived and reproduced for sale to visiting tourists.

pieces of glass designed to look something like real crystals. In addition, toy elves and dwarfs of all sizes and colors adorned the pond and the small lush-green gardens surrounding it. Past the pond was a cement stairway that ascended up a hill.

As I looked closely at the cement steps, I noticed that many people had carved their initials and various signatures into it before the concrete had firmly set. If the information I observed was accurate, then many people from different countries had participated, including the Soviets. The initials "CCCP" were etched in large letters on one of the steps, and stood out in size compared to all the other markings that were visible.

On the right, just past this concrete stairway, was a patio area with numerous benches and tables painted bright red-orange. I recognized this area from pictures I had seen in Wendelle Stevens's *Preliminary Investigation Report* book and Volume II of the *Pleiades* photo-journal. This patio section was where Meier and his followers entertained scores of visitors and sold their merchandise to the faithful.

Jacobus Bertschinger gave up following us. My "I'm ignoring you because I'm a näive American who doesn't understand a word of Swiss-German" routine had managed to work. Tina and I continued walking past the visitor's area. Before allowing Meier's people to control our access to the Semjase Silver Star Center and what it was we were exposed to, I wanted to look around as much as possible.

On our left now was a "Privat" (private) area where guests were not allowed. I ignored the posted warning signs and walked up as close as I could to take pictures. From where I stood, at the railing which prevented me from straying off the main gravel roadway, I could see down at the bottom of the hillside what were the faint remnants of three "UFO landing rings" that had been there since at least June 1980. I recalled seeing pictures of this area in Stevens's *Preliminary Investigation Report*[19] and Gary Kinder's *Light Years*.[20] Even though the landing tracks were eleven years old by the time of my visit, and were barely visible to the naked eye, obtaining soil samples from them might still reveal something of interest. For the sake of scientific inquiry, I had to find a way to obtain some samples.

After finishing taking still photographs of the UFO landing-track area, I recorded them on video, pushing the zoom feature on my camera to its limit. Even though my video camera has a 10x zoom lens, the landing-tracks proved to be too far away to observe any meaningful details from the location where I was standing. This was unfortunate, because where I stood was a natural observation point which afforded a fairly wide panoramic view of the backside of Meier's place where the property sweeps downward into a steep hillside. Evidently the people at the Meier cult agree; they have "no trespassing" signs posted at this location in several languages. Thus, my recording and photographing of the landing-tracks proved only useful for the historical record. The tracks were simply too far away and too faded to make even an interesting photograph. I could not get any closer to them without disobeying the signs and trespassing, which I was not prepared to do just yet.

The video footage I obtained and the zoom shots, which are the only images that show anything of significance, are featured in Underground Video's documentary video release of this book, along with other undercover footage taken at Meier's place. I made a mental note to myself to try and devise a way to get to these landing-tracks, or others, in order to obtain soil and control samples from them.

While there was no guarantee that anything of importance would be found, especially after the passage of so much time since the marks were purportedly made, at least for the *first time ever* in the history of the Meier case *somebody* would have collected soil samples. Incredibly, *neither* Lee Elders, Brit Elders, Michael Hesemann, Gary Kinder, Guido Moosbrugger, Wendelle Stevens, nor Thomas K. Welch *have obtained even one* soil sample from Meier's numerous "Pleiadian landing-track" locations! This fact is inexcusable, especially since *all of these individuals* have personally visited these alleged landing-track sites numerous times.

Indeed, their collective failure to obtain just *one soil sample*, or blade of flattened or burnt grass, speaks volumes about both their *lack* of thoroughness and their basic scientific professionalism concerning "investigations."

This is especially true of Brit and Lee Elders, Gary Kinder, and Wendelle Stevens, who have spent *several consecutive weeks* living with Billy Meier at his residence, where a set of these "UFO landing-tracks" resides in Meier's very own back yard![21]

While the Elders and Stevens have never explained their failure to obtain any landing-track samples, incredibly Gary

Kinder says he *never saw* any landing-tracks[22] during the entire *five weeks*[23] he spent living at Meier's place! Instead, Kinder claims he only "talked to several people who had seen them and who had photographed them while still fresh."[24] It is doubtful that Gary Kinder's claim is true, since the three UFO landing-tracks on Billy Meier's property are *directly behind his house and down the hill in his own back yard!* Not only are they easily visible from numerous locations throughout the property, but are in fact *impossible to miss* most of the time when walking back and forth between the guest house and Billy Meier's residence. Figure 10 shows the approximate locations of the three alleged "Pleiadian landing-tracks." This drawing illustrates how Kinder's claims of not having seen any UFO tracks while living with Meier are hard to accept as factual. Even if Kinder is sincerely mistaken, there is no excuse for the fact that he never obtained samples.

After leaving the site overlooking the landing-tracks I noticed, on the other side of the gravel road, a small ceramic elf standing on top of what were more of Meier's "crystals." The elf was holding a lantern and stood on a sign which read in both German and English, "Visitor's Bell."

It was obvious that the powers that be who run the Meier compound wanted all strangers to ring the bell when walking past this point. Since I did not wish to have my presence known by anyone else yet (only Bertschinger knew we were there so far), I pretended the doorbell did not exist.

I wanted us to explore around on our own as long as possible. To announce our presence at Billy Meier's house this very moment would have guaranteed that from then on our options for exploration would be limited. Besides, we could always knock on Billy's door on our way *back* toward his house, which is what we opted to do. We quickly kept on walking, passing Meier's house and the visitor's area, and headed along the gravel roadway which now curved to the right and sloped downward.

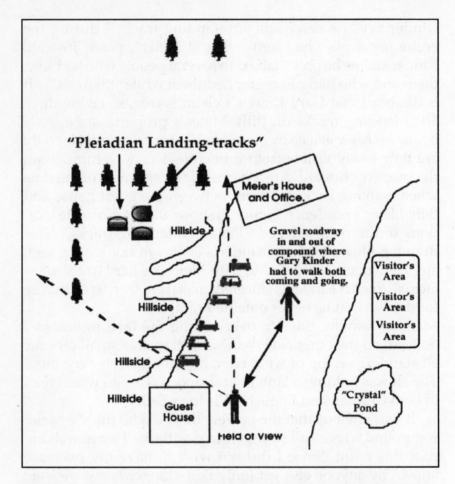

"Pleiadian Landing-tracks"

Meier's House and Office.

Hillside

Gravel roadway in and out of compound where Gary Kinder had to walk both coming and going.

Visitor's Area

Visitor's Area

Visitor's Area

Hillside

Hillside

"Crystal" Pond

Hillside   Guest House

Field of View

Fig. 10. Drawing of Meier's compound (not to scale) showing approximate locations of the three alleged "Pleiadian landing-tracks" made during a purported landing on June 14, 1980, by Semjase. Their close location to Billy Meier's house (literally in his backyard!) makes them impossible to miss when visiting the Semjase Silver Star Center. The three "UFO" marks were still visible when I traveled to Meier's place in 1991, some eleven years after they were first made, which is some six to seven years after Gary Kinder supposedly "never saw" them during the five weeks he lived with Billy Meier!

As we made our way down the grade, we noticed on our right side a metal art sculpture and two young girls playing on a pair of swings. They smiled at us as I continued to videotape everything and take pictures. I still had no idea how much longer Tina and I could continue to roam about freely without anyone asking us what we were doing there. We were lucky to have made it so far without being intercepted.

After following the road to its end, Tina and I turned around and walked straight back toward Billy Meier's house. The next step was simple: I would try to ingratiate myself with the Meier people and meet Billy Meier directly.

When I walked up to the front of his house, I became distracted when I saw through my viewfinder a large face suddenly in front of me.

Pulling my eye away from my camera, I was startled to see the very image of none other than Eduard "Billy" Meier himself! It wasn't the *real* Billy Meier I encountered, but rather his effigy. As figure 11 proves, Billy Meier has a metal etching of himself on the front of his house. The plaque makes him look like some sort of stereotypical guru, messiah, or prophet, a figure to be revered.

After recovering from the surprise of seeing Meier's "humble" effigy, I proceeded straight toward his front door, only to be stopped by an elderly, heavyset woman who came barreling out the entrance.

"Vat are you doing here?" she demanded.

"I am a great fan of Billy Meier's," I replied all excited. "We came all the way from America to visit Billy Meier."

Before I could finish, she motioned for us to leave the porch quickly and go plant ourselves in the visitor's area.

"Someone vill be there vith you in a few moments," she barked while walking back into Meier's house.

Tina and I quickly walked the short distance from the Meier house back to the visitor's area in order to get things ready. I wanted to secretly videotape all of my actions in

Fig. 11. A copper-colored effigy of Billy Meier etched in metal adorns the front of his house.

front of the Meier people, including asking them numerous questions, both supportive and challenging ones.

Acting quickly, we sat down at a table in the middle of the visitor's area. I then placed my black bag containing the hidden video camera in the far right corner of the visitor's area patio so that no one would see that it was recording. To be sure of this, I piled my things haphazardly in the corner where the bag was, deliberately making a mess of my stuff so that it would dissuade anyone from taking a close look at the bag and its contents. Next, I turned on the video recorder and quickly glanced through the viewfinder, locking the focus for the widest possible view. Such a setting would permit us to capture on video as many people as possible in the event that several showed up. I then returned to the table and sat down next to Tina.

By the time my video camera started recording, the woman who turned out to be our "host" for most of this first visit had already arrived and was seated opposite of us. Fortunately, she had just sat down, so we missed nothing of importance on tape.

As luck would have it, our host turned out to be Elisabeth Gruber, the wife of Guido Moosbrugger, one of Billy Meier's most senior members and devoted followers. Moosbrugger travels around the world lecturing audiences on Billy Meier's behalf, helping to spread the "messages" of the "Pleiadians."[25]

The fact that we were being hosted by Moosbrugger's wife meant that Moosbrugger himself was probably present somewhere on the property, since both are very active members of Meier's group and would have likely traveled together from their home in Germany.

What is meant by the term "host" as it pertains to Moosbrugger's wife concerns a duty each member of Billy Meier's group must perform one weekend each month, which is to donate their time and money to the Semjase Silver Star Center.[26] In the case of Guido's wife, it was her turn to play "host" to the public this day, which required her to sit patiently and answer any visitor's questions and try and sell them copies of Meier's UFO photographs and assorted literature. Each host works a total of ninety minutes before being relieved of duty by some other member.[27]

After Tina and I introduced ourselves, Gruber handed us the large guest register all visitors to the Meier compound are required to sign.

At first Elisabeth Gruber was all business, carefully watching us to make sure that we signed their register, which solicited our addresses and phone numbers.

While Tina signed her real name, I signed as "Steve Thomas" and then scrawled my real signature underneath it. Since I know that my real signature is illegible to most people (at least this is what everyone tells me!), I thought this would be an ironic souvenir for Billy Meier when he discovered later that I had successfully penetrated his private utopia.

Gruber handed me the first of what would be nearly a dozen photo-binders containing over one thousand of Billy Meier's UFO and UFO-related photographs which they offer for sale to the general public.

As the undercover video footage proves, Tina and I looked at every single photo in every picture album they allowed us to view, on camera. While doing this, I jotted down the individual number of each photograph I wished to purchase, for which we were charged the sum of five Swiss francs each per standard color copy print. While thumbing through the photos, I began asking questions.

As Elisabeth Gruber sat patiently and answered them, she confirmed key "facts" for me about the Meier case, Gruber assured both Tina and me that Billy Meier's claims of being in contact with Pleiadians, of having taken more than 1,000 UFO photos and 12 motion picture films, etc., were all true. Gruber also confirmed the additional, controversial claims about time-travel, of Meier being some sort of "prophet," of his being given the last testament of Jesus Christ to present to humanity, and so forth. Nearly all of what Gruber reported to Tina and me matched what Wendelle Stevens and others have written about this case.

Gruber's affirmations of both the evidence and the various peripheral aspects of Meier's claims were significant because they provided somewhat of a control standard against which we could test the various elements of the Meier evidence. Because we now knew firsthand what the various claims were, we could begin to test them, often with a surprising degree of absolute certainty.

After spending nearly an hour perusing the numerous photo-binders and questioning Gruber about specific pictures, I finished making my selections. I purchased 186 of Billy Meier's UFO photographs for analysis and study.

Since it was not practical nor possible to analyze conclusively all of Billy Meier's more than 1000 UFO photographs,* I made sure that when I chose the 186 specific pictures I purchased that I picked the very best of Meier's photos and that their selection was logical and in line with the objectives of the investigation. For example, for those UFO photographic sequences where twelve or fewer pictures were made, the entire set of photos was purchased.

By comparison, whenever more than twelve UFO photographs were allegedly taken, a cross sampling of the best pictures from the series which yielded the *greatest analytical potential* was chosen for examination.

Another criteria I used in my selection was to compare these photos to the exceptionally clear copies that existed in the Jacob photo-binder. Thus, some of the pictures purchased at the Meier compound were selected for visual comparison purposes and a study in contrast between the two collections and those versions published by Stevens. In most cases where the same photos existed among the various collections, the Jacob versions were almost always superior in color, quality, and resolution.

Whatever photo(s) made sense for us to acquire for the purposes of conducting the most thorough examination possible, we obtained. This was also true during our acquisition and study of other Meier-related material such as his direct and personal writings, and the literature and official publications of the Semjase Silver Star Center.

As I counted out the money, Elisabeth Gruber made out a handwritten receipt totaling 1,056 Swiss francs, the amount I

---

*The clarity and quality of *some* of Meier's UFO photos available for sale are very poor. Tina and I noticed that many of them were off-color, faded, or saturated, due to generational loss. Still others had dirt specs visible, indicative of poor handling. For this reason (in addition to the fact that there are no original negatives to study), it is not possible to definitively analyze *every one* of Meier's 1058 UFO and UFO-related photos.

spent to purchase the 186 UFO pictures. Gruber's receipt is on file at TotalResearch,[28] Underground Video, and has been posted electronically on computer bulletin boards around the world.[29]

Gruber was surprised yet pleased by the size of my order. However, she told Tina and me that she could not guarantee that all of the photos I requested would be in stock. She then asked me to chose alternative selections, in the event that some of them were not available.

Politely, I resisted, and told her that I needed the specific photos I had requested in order to go back to the United States and silence such critics as Kal Korff and Colman VonKeviczky!

Elisabeth Gruber agreed, then told Tina and me that she would try to do her best to fulfill our order.

Gruber asked us if we wanted to leave and come back later in the afternoon, since it would take her "some time" to gather all of the photos. She told us that our prints would be ready after 4:00 P.M.

Not wanting to take the chance of not being allowed back on the Meier property, and still wanting to spend as much time there gathering evidence and observing things, I politely refused.

In justifying my reaction, I told Gruber that I "loved" Billy's place so much, that I was willing to wait all day if necessary, until we received the UFO and UFO-related photographs we had paid for.

I kept telling her how happy I was to have made the pilgrimage to Meier's place. I stressed to her how important this trip was for me.

It was a lie, but it worked nonetheless. Gruber actually cracked a smile.

After Elisabeth Gruber left, a woman named Bernadette Brand came over to keep us company. Brand is one of the most senior members of Meier's group, and when Tina and I interviewed her, our acting skills were tested to the limit.

When Bernadette Brand saw how much money I was

throwing around, she became curious and tried to prompt and encourage us to purchase their religious material. Refusing to spend more money, I showed her the one issue of Billy Meier's *Wassermannzeit* magazine that Gruber had given me and told her that this sample was enough for now. Undeterred, Brand then gave me three more sample issues of *Wassermannzeit*, stressing their spiritual importance.

When I asked Bernadette Brand what she thought of Billy Meier's UFO photographs, she commented that they were "very pretty," but what mattered to her most was the "spiritual" messages of the "Pleiadians" and what Billy taught her. At this point Brand became rather animated and started letting us in on what obviously were to her important little "secrets" such as the "fact" that Billy Meier's full, true name is purportedly "Eduard Albert Meier-Zafiriou."* However, a subsequent check of the local Canton Police for Meier's region in the town of Hinwil revealed that there is no record of Billy Meier's "true" name containing the word "Zafiriou" in it.[30]

As Bernadette Brand continued to try and impress Meier's religious messages on us, she turned our attention to a thick binder she had with her. She handed it to Tina and me to examine in detail.

"This is one of our new publications. I am working (editing the book) to make sure the contents have no errors. This is the last testament of Immanuel."

"You mean Jesus Christ?" I asked.

"Yes, this is the last testament which was given to Billy Meier. This is written by Judas Iscariot," she said matter-of-factly.

Curious, I asked Bernadette Brand (and so did Tina) if this was the same Judas Iscariot who had betrayed Jesus Christ, according to the New Testament in the Bible.

---

*The name "Zafiriou" has been added by Meier in recent years as his "mission" has taken on more religious overtones. Zafiriou is supposed to be Meier's name as a prophet, reincarnated from a past life.

Brand replied, "No. This is another Judas Iscariot."

Although I am not expert on ancient Christian documents, I refrained from telling Brand that I knew her publication was a hoax!

The *Talmud Immanuel*

The *Talmud Immanuel* is the name of the book Brand held in her hands. Meier's Semjase Silver Star Center publishes it in various editions. It is available in a version written by Billy Meier,[31] or it can be obtained in the form of another book called *Celestial Teachings: The Talmud Immanuel* by Dr. James Deardorff, published by Wild Flower Press.

The *Talmud Immanuel* is literally the Meier followers' "Bible" and professes to be the last true testament of Jesus Christ written after his crucifixion. It also is supposed to be the most accurate version of the Bible yet handed down to humanity.[32]

Jesus, according to Meier and his followers, is *not* the Son of God, but is a *Pleiadian,* having been taught all he knows by "the celestial sons from the Pleiades."[33] According to Meier, Christ was born not as the Son of God sent here to die for our sins, but was conceived instead because his Pleiadian father, "Plejos," wanted to return home to the Pleiades to live out his last days![34] Plejos had been living on this planet for years, and not wishing to leave the Earth "void" of any "Pleiadians," used the angel Gabriel (who is also a Pleiadian) to impregnate the virgin Mary so that Jesus could be born and later become the prophet who would carry on the teachings of Plejos, "Creation," and the Pleiadians.[35]

Meier and his followers claim that Jesus Christ and Billy Meier have so much in common, they even share the same birthdays! Meier says that Jesus Christ was born not on December 25, but on February 3, the same day as himself.[36]

Incredibly, Meier's claim that his and Jesus' birthdays are on the same day is considered among his followers to be further evidence that Meier's mission from the Pleiadians is entirely genuine![37] Of course, there's no scientific test to determine when Jesus Christ was born, so Meier's claim that he shares the same birthday with Jesus is meaningless, since there's no way of proving it. It is a claim which science cannot address adequately, so it must be relegated to the category of interesting, but unprovable and unproven. Besides, even if their birthdays were on the same day, this in itself is not enough to prove anything.

Meier claims that he acquired the "last testament of Jesus Christ" from a Catholic Priest named "Rashid," who was led in 1963 by the Pleiadians to a location where the *Talmud Immanuel* scrolls lay buried for nearly two thousand years.[38]

Meier says that "Rashid" began translating these scrolls from their original Aramaic into German, and would then mail the transcripts to him in Switzerland from the priest's home in Baghdad.[39] Rashid sent these translations to Meier because he knew that Meier had been "chosen" by the Pleiadians to spread their "messages" to humanity to help with our spiritual evolution.[40] The *Talmud Immanuel* is intended to be part of this mass disclosure to the populace, as are Meier's *Wassermannzeit* publications.[41]

However, what Meier's followers and those people who espouse the *Talmud Immanuel* as being real ignore is the fact that there are *no original scrolls or text* one can use to independently verify its contents! No originals exist.

In other words, unlike the ancient texts and scrolls which exist of the Bible, the Koran, and the Torah, the only complete version of the *Talmud Immanuel* in existence is the German translation in Meier's possession, which he claims he received from "Rashid" in the early 1970s.[42] The "2,000-year-old scrolls" that this "Rashid" allegedly unearthed with the guidance of the Pleiadians have never been found, and were conveniently "lost" by "Rashid" while purportedly in Lebanon.[43]

In addition to the fact that there is no original text, there is absolutely no evidence (other than Billy Meier's assurance) that this "Rashid" ever existed! Meier supplies no details of Rashid's alleged life which allow for independent verification of his existence.[44]

The *Talmud Immanuel* is "hearsay" by all standards of credible evidence, and is therefore inadmissible. Its existence is evidence of nothing until, if, and when the original scrolls are ever found. Meier and his followers seem to forget that the Talmud's mere *existence* does not prove its claims.

Proof that the *Talmud Immanuel* Is a Hoax

What most people don't know is that the *Talmud Immanuel* is not unique as a document, nor is it original in its premise.[45] Indeed, the *Talmud Immanuel* is based on the school of thought that Jesus did not die on the cross, as is popularly believed by most Christians. Instead, the *Talmud Immanuel* claims Jesus *survived* the crucifixion.[46]

An unconscious Jesus was supposedly spirited away by his followers through a secret entrance after being entombed. According to the *Talmud Immanuel*, Jesus went to live in India where, in his newfound homeland and fully aware of the movement he had started, he remained in hiding. Jesus eventually settled down and raised a family.[47] The story states that Jesus eventually died of "natural causes" at the age of roughly 115.[48]

While this alternative version of Jesus' life and variations of it have been around for centuries,[49] it was widely popularized in Europe with the release of a book called *Jesus Lived in India* by German author and historian Holger Kersten. In truth, Meier had even read Kersten's book![50]

Another fact that most people don't know is that in the summer of 1976, the German typewritten translations allegedly made by "Rashid" and sent to Billy Meier in 1974[51] were analyzed by various scholars in Germany and Switzerland, three of whom had Ph.D.s.[52] Detailed reports were prepared on all of the evidence examined (which included other material such as Meier's Semjase "contact" notes, his UFO and time-travel photos, etc.), and because *none* of the evidence studied was deemed either impressive or credible, these scholars decided *not to publish their results!*[53]

Although their study had been done primarily in 1976, as the Meier case continued to receive widespread publicity (especially in Europe), some of these scientists maintained a passive interest in the case. This enabled them in June 1980 to give Dr. J. Allen Hynek, the founder and director of the Center for UFO Studies, an up-to-date briefing on their findings during his surprise visit to their private UFO study group in Zürich.[54]

It was through this group's briefing of Dr. Hynek, and their subsequent decision to share the details of their presentation in a series of confidential reports to Mr. Walt Andrus, international director of the Mutual UFO Network, that we even know about their work.[55]

The German and Swiss scientists and scholars had, in fact, identified a number of problems with a great deal of the Meier "evidence," labeling much of it an outright fraud.[56] The following are some remarks written by one of the Ph.D. scientists in Switzerland who was part of the group.[57] These comments are written by the scientist himself, whose native language is German and not English. The remarks are from a confidential summary report prepared specifically by the Swiss scientist for Andrus on June 23, 1980, a few days after Dr. Hynek had left Switzerland.

In 1976 Mr. Eduard Meier's "collected works" consisted of an album of color photographs, a 500-page manuscript typewritten in stages and distributed among his followers, and the "Talmud Immanuel."

The Talmud Immanuel (Immanuel=Jesus) is, according to Mr. Meier, the true version of the New Testament which lay buried since the day it was written, but was discovered in 1963 by a

Catholic priest in Iraq, who translated it and sent the translation to Mr. Meier together with a letter explaining the circumstances of discovery and subsequent loss of the original. This letter in facsimile is appended to the Talmud Immanuel. The Talmud turns out to be the *New Testament verbatim,* but with a large number of *additions* without much ethical value. It is hard to see how the New Testament can agree *word for word* with the original—apart from the added passages—if the latter lay buried all the time. More significant, however, is the fact that both the additions and the letter of the priest are written in Mr. Meier's characteristic style, containing all the errors in German also found in the Semjase manuscript. In addition, comparison shows the letter alleged to have been written by the priest in Iraq actually to have been typed on the *same typewriter* as the Semjase manuscript. (Emphasis added)

In commenting on other Meier evidence the group examined, such as Meier's contact notes with Semjase, the Swiss scientist stated:

Most of the 500-page manuscript is an account of numerous conversations between Mr. Meier and his extraterrestrial friend Semjase. Reading it one is struck by the lavish praise bestowed upon Mr. Meier by Semjase in response to his very commonplace remarks. She constantly admires Mr. Meier's "profound knowledge," of which the unbiased reader detects no trace whatsoever in over 500 manuscript pages. No one, incidentally, including his wife and children, has ever seen Semjase. The manuscript makes it abundantly clear that she wishes to confine her contacts strictly to Mr. Meier alone. Certainly a convenient wish.

No contactee can refrain for long from making some remarks about topics in astronomy, cosmology, and astrophysics, and few, if any, avoid the pitfalls inherent in the assumption that one can discuss these subjects without any familiarity with science. Mr. Meier is no exception, and his Semjase manuscript abounds with scientific nonsense. Here are some examples: Asteroids have resulted from the explosion of a planet a few thousand years ago; Venus is a latecomer to the solar system and originated in interstellar space; the moon originated "near the Milky Way"; a certain comet passed several stars in 575.5 years; matter in space disintegrates at velocities of a few miles per hour; there is a large hall under Cheops' pyramid; nuclear destruction of the earth would have a large effect on other stars and even galaxies; the age of the earth is 646 million years. Questioned about this latter point he (Meier) claimed a typographical error. Actually, he had meant to write 646 *billion* years!

Among other things the manuscript relates the account of a meeting between Jesus and Mr. Meier, who had had himself transported back in time to Jerusalem. The Lord listens patiently to a great deal of religious philosophy on the part of Mr. Meier and duly admires his high intelligence.

While Mr. Meier's German is fluent, he does make certain characteristic mistakes, in addition to making excessive use of certain expressions. The most frequent mistakes are use of the redundant term "yet however," use of the little word "so" in the sense of "so that," writing Mount of Oilives instead of Olives (in rough translation), plus several others too hard to render into English. "Logical" and "forms of life" are two favorite expressions of his.

In another analysis of the *Talmud Immanuel, Eduard Meier — Prophet Der Neuzeit?* written by German UFO researcher Michael Arends, similarities were noted between the typewriter used by Billy Meier to transcribe his "contact" notes with Semjase and the "Rashid" translations Meier claimed to have received from Baghdad.[58] Arends identified specific letter characters which he found indicative that the same typewriter had been used (meaning Meier was the real author), and also discovered that entire passages had been embellished on and lifted from a standard Lutheran version of the Bible.[59]

Finally, the most recent significant analysis of the *Talmud Immanuel*, as of this writing, has been conducted by Underground Video. Their analysis is important because it is independent of the earlier German and Swiss studies, and was made without any knowledge of them. Underground Video even discovered evidence proving that the *Talmud Immanuel* does not contain Aramaic![60]

Despite the fact that the *Talmud Immanuel* lacks any credible evidence of its legitimacy, the book has recently become

popular among New Age circles ever since its two major publication releases in 1992.

Although Billy Meier may deny it, *he* is the true author of
the *Talmud Immanuel*. The document is simply the New Testament with passages added by Meier.

Bernadette Brand's attempts to "woo" Tina and me with
the *Talmud Immanuel* went nowhere. While I could not share
with Brand everything I knew about the publication being a
hoax, I continued to listen to her politely.

Still pressing on with the spiritual aspect of the Meier case,
Bernadette Brand gave me yet another free issue of Billy Meier's
Wassermannzeit (the February 1989 issue) and said emphatically:
"You must not copy this publication. You must not copy it. You
cannot give it to anyone. They must buy their own copy if they
want to read. You may share the contents with them but do not
let them read your copy. They must buy their own."

Surprised, I replied that we wouldn't "pirate" Meier's
publications. I then asked her *why* she mentioned this point in
the first place. Tina also jumped in. Brand's reply was
astounding.

"These materials [Meier's printed literature] contain spir-
itually advanced material. When a person reads a book, their
aura penetrates the pages; if the material is understood, and a
spiritual bonding occurs, you will then understand.

"If you were to loan this book to someone else, or use a
copy machine, anyone else reading it after us would have our
auras contaminating theirs and it would interfere with both
their spiritual and intellectual understanding of the book,"
Bernadette Brand stated emphatically.

Keeping in mind that Brand's native language was not
English, I repeated back to her my understanding of what she
had just said.

"Yes," she replied, "you see this is spiritual material. It is
the messages of the Pleiadians and how to live a good life.

"The UFO photos are not important. People who come

here think they are. But it is the messages of the Pleiadians, the word of the Immanuel (Jesus) that is very important. Billy Meier. You will understand."

"Yes," I replied, since it was all I could think of to say.

"So you must read this material. And do not make photocopies of this material and give it to your friends. They must buy their own copies or they will not understand."

Ms. Brand reassured me that her request that people *buy* their own copies of Meier's literature had absolutely nothing to do with the fact that the Semjase Silver Star Center needs money. She said that she raised the issue out of concern only for people's auras, nothing more.

Whenever I asked either Ms. Brand or Mrs. Gruber to specifically refute any of either Kal Korff's or Colman Von-Keviczky's criticisms of the Meier case, they refused to do so. Gruber then left our table.

Realizing I had to press the issue, I said, "Well, I was wondering if you could give me some evidence that I could take back to America with me to use against Kal Korff. He is really destroying you back in the United States."

"Yes," Brand said.

"Well, what would you do if, say, Kal Korff or someone like *that* ever came here?" I asked her.

Bernadette Brand then looked at Tina and me and replied, "We were warned about him from Lee (Elders). We would not let him in, or we would never let him leave."*

Surprised, I decided to press Brand for any proof that I could be given to disprove the claims of Kal Korff regarding the Meier case.

---

*Bernadette Brand's comment about Kal Korff, as well as the remarks made by Elisabeth Gruber and Simone, were captured on the hidden videotape footage by this author. In addition, Tina Layton was also present when Brand's remarks were made regarding Korff and is a witness to this event.

At this point Elisabeth Gruber returned to our table, catching the tail end of the conversation Brand and I were having.

When I asked both of them once more for any evidence I could take back with me to the United States to destroy the arguments of Kal Korff, Brand and Gruber referred me to a new book written by Guido Moosbrugger titled . . . *und sie fliegen doch! UFOs: Die größte Herausforderung des 20. Jahrhunderts* (And They Do Indeed Fly! . . . UFOs: The Greatest Challenge of the 20th Century). Moosbrugger's book, Brand and Gruber assured me, answered every criticism of Kal Korff and Colman VonKeviczky![61]

Naturally, I was curious to see this book, and was promptly offered a copy that I could buy. Realizing it was available only in German, I inquired as to when, if ever, it might be translated into English.

Although it was not a problem at all for me to read Moosbrugger's book in its original German, I wanted to know if it was going to be made available in English so it would be easier for me to explain it to people if I ever needed to refer to it publicly.

By asking this question, it also helped insure that I would at least learn of any possible future publication plans that might in turn yield additional insights into Meier and his future plans.

Gruber replied that it would be published in the English language "next year" (1992). As of this writing, the English-language translation of Moosbrugger's book has yet to materialize, although it since has been published in four different languages.[62]

Guido Moosbrugger is one of Billy Meier's closest friends. He has been a member of Meier's Semjase Silver Star Center since its early beginnings, and was one of the members of Meier's original metaphysical study group mentioned in chapter 1. Moosbrugger is literally Billy Meier's ambassador to the outside world. He travels around the globe giving lectures about Meier and his "Pleiadian messages" and the various activities of the Semjase Silver Star Center.[63]

Fig. 12. Two issues of Meier's spiritual and religious literature, *Stimme der Wassermannzeit,* which sell for 4.50 Swiss francs each. These publications contain information on living life, raising children, diet, work, politics, Meier's "mission" here on Earth, and often entire transcripts of Meier's "conversations" with the Pleiadians. Meier followers use them for guidance.

Drawing large crowds at many of the places he gives his speeches, Guido Moosbrugger is the only individual, as of this writing, "empowered" by Billy Meier to roam the world spreading the "gospel of the Pleiadians" on Meier's behalf.[64]

For the credibility of the Eduard "Billy" Meier case, Guido Moosbrugger's book is an important publication, since it is written by the man who is Meier's official "ambassador" and it is the only book about Billy Meier which has his direct, hands-on involvement![65]

"How does this [Moosbrugger's book] compare to Wendelle Stevens's books?" I asked both Brand and Gruber.

"Stevens's books have some errors in them. He also water

down some of it. He do not write about the spiritual messages," Brand complained.

"We like Steve [Wendelle Stevens], but his books do not tell the full story," Brand reiterated.

"You mean the religious, spiritual stuff?" I asked.

"Yes," Brand replied.

Guido Moosbrugger's book was copublished by himself and pro-Meier supporter Michael Hesemann, the president of 2000 Verlag, one of the largest, if not the largest, publishers and distributors of UFO-related material in Germany.[66]

As I thumbed through Moosbrugger's tome, I noticed that it was lavishly illustrated, containing some eighty-five photos in color, several of which had never been published before. To be honest, I found his book to be a welcome relief from Wendelle Stevens's tired, self-published volumes, and was astonished to see the extent to which the book challenged "head-on" its critics—including me.

Listed as "Documentation K," Moosbrugger quoted from my original Meier exposé book no less than twelve times, excerpting entire paragraphs *verbatim* in attempts to refute what I had written. While Moosbrugger certainly has every right to do this, I wish he had bothered to check with me in advance to verify the accuracy of his so-called refutations.

If Moosbrugger had bothered to do this, he would have avoided making some of the many errors which plague his book. Moosbrugger's inaccuracies are addressed throughout the present volume, and most of the evidence presented in here *refutes* virtually the *entire contents* of Moosbrugger's much-vaunted work.

I could not resist the urge to purchase a copy of Moosbrugger's tome. The integrity of the investigation demanded it, if for no other reason. However, since I had already paid for my film order and was now out of Swiss francs, I made arrangements to stop by the next day to pick up my copy of Moosbrugger's book, for which I would pay twenty-five Swiss francs.

Shortly after this, Guido Moosbrugger himself came out-side, seemingly intrigued that people were talking about his new book. You could tell, like most new authors, that he was proud of his work.

When Moosbrugger walked over and sat down at the table next to us, I was already standing at the far corner of the patio in the visitor's area, discreetly changing the battery and video-tape on my hidden video camera in order to reload and take more footage.*

Realizing the irony of the situation, that Moosbrugger had no idea that I was really Kal Korff, I quietly took his picture with my 35mm camera while he was busy talking with a young woman named Simone.

Simone is another of Billy Meier's followers who devotes her free time to serving the cause of the "Pleiadians." Like all members of the Semjase Silver Star Center, Simone must engage in what one might call "Pleiadian tithing," that is, donate a minimum of ten percent of her monthly salary, if not more, to Billy Meier.[67]

Other conditions of her membership are that she must study and live her life according to the teachings of the Pleia-dians. Each member of Meier's cult must also follow a strict meditation and prayer calendar and schedule, which hangs on a wall inside their official prayer and meditation room at the center, built in honor of Semjase.[68]

Once a month, Simone volunteers at the visitor's center to patiently answer people's questions, sell them merchandise, and help preach the Pleiadian messages and way of life to all who stop by.

Such public duties are a standard set of functions all mem-

---

*When Moosbrugger lectures on the Meier case in various countries around the world, he repeatedly attacks my work during the course of his presentation. Despite this fact, Moosbrugger refuses to debate me, turning down the latest opportunities at the UFO West '93, '94, and '95 Expos held in San Mateo and Los Angeles, California.

bers of the Meier cult must perform, since it is by mingling
with the public and showing them the numerous pieces of
"evidence" that Billy Meier is able to sell his UFO photographs by the thousands.[69]

After we finished talking with Bernadette Brand, she and
Gruber left, and Simone came over and sat down at our table
directly across from us. Tina and I spoke with her for the
remainder of our first visit, while the photos we had ordered
through Gruber were being processed. Using the excuse of
needing to stretch my legs, Simone and I started walking
around the Meier compound, which provided me with a sub-
tle opportunity to observe. I remained in my Steve Thomas
persona, slamming Kal Korff a few more times while praising
the beauty of the Semjase Silver Star Center.

As Simone and I walked back toward the rock "crystal"
garden near the visitor's area, she told me that Billy Meier had
made the garden himself for the purpose of transchanneling
and focusing his messages from the Pleiadians.

"Billy made this with his one arm?" I asked her.

"Yes," Simone replied.

"Are these real crystals?" I inquired.

"No, they are colored glass. They are beautiful, no?"

The garden's existence was proof that Billy Meier is very
skilled with his single hand. If Meier could build an entire garden pond by *himself*, which involved at a *minimum* mixing
and laying cement and stone, shaping and polishing glass,
digging and setting up of irrigation and plumbing for the
water, coloring the glass, etc., he was certainly capable of making "UFO" models out of ordinary materials.

When I asked Simone how everyone "got by" financially at
the Semjase Silver Star Center, she replied that it was through
donations and sales, and that each member must work one
weekend a month, donating time, labor, and money. While she
admitted to having a full-time job elsewhere, she stated that she
spent as much of her free time as possible at Meier's place.

Figs. 13 and 14. Photographs of what Meier and his followers call the "Pleiadian Crystal Channeling Garden Water Pond." Designed and built personally by Billy Meier, the "crystals" in this "channeling garden" are said to help Meier receive his instructions from the Pleiadians because they are tuned to the right "vibrational frequencies"! When I asked Simone, one of the Meier cult members, if these were real crystals, she replied that they were simply "colored glass, to simulate crystals. They are beautiful, no?"

Fig. 15. My hidden 35mm camera snapped this photograph of Guido Moosbrugger and Simone (arrows), two members of Billy Meier's private religious UFO cult. The other people shown are various visitors who were present and children from the families of other group members.

Because Simone was clearly not of the mind to permit an objective examination of the facts, I made a point to say nothing but pro-Meier statements, keeping my criticisms to myself. Simone and I talked for about twenty-five minutes.

Around four in the afternoon our huge photo order was finally ready. Every picture that we had requested had either been located or freshly duplicated. As an additional bonus, Elisabeth Gruber diligently numbered the back side of each one of the photographs so that we could cross-reference them accurately.

Despite the fact that we had been at the compound for six hours, we never did get to see Billy Meier on this first visit. Trying to find a way to force such a meeting, I mentioned to Gruber that I had brought a gift from America for Billy which I wished to give to him.

Delighted, Gruber asked what it was and I showed it to her. It was a silver-colored quartz watch/pen with an LED display in it that flashed either the date or the time.

Since I knew from my past interactions with various Meier supporters that Billy Meier was into what I call the "quartz-meditation thing," I decided to try and use this to my advantage.

Keeping a straight face, I pointed out to Gruber that because this watch/pen had a quartz crystal in it, Meier could meditate on the crystal in the pen, and when he contacted Semjase, he'd have the time displayed right there for him and a pen handy to write down all his contact notes.

The gift was intended as a practical joke "gift" for Billy Meier. I knew from my previous ownership of this particular brand of pen that after only a few weeks of use it no longer kept the date and the time accurately! Therefore, if Meier decided to write more of his ongoing "Pleiadian contact notes" with this pen, using its built-in quartz crystal to "transchannel" with, he would not be able to count on the accuracy of the information it displayed, nor its supposed ability to "tune into" the Pleiadians! Although the pen always showed the correct information when first purchased, by the time we brought it with us to Switzerland it had already started acting up, changing the time at random whenever its display button was pressed.

"You know how important Billy's contact notes with Semjase are," I stressed to Gruber, hoping she would fall for the line. She did.

As I walked over to my black bag, I removed the pen and returned to Ms. Gruber's table to show it to her. She looked the item over carefully, and not wanting to lose control of this moment, I started explaining my rationalization for insisting that the pen be given directly to Billy Meier.

"The pen keeps the time and date," I explained to her as I pressed the little button at the end of the writing instrument that caused the two displays to toggle back and forth.

"Since Billy Meier is in contact with the space people, he

can use this pen to record the exact time and dates of his contacts, as well as meditate over the quartz crystal which is in it, to communicate with them," I stated.

Curious, Ms. Gruber looked at me for a moment and then nodded in the affirmative.

"Could I please meet Billy so I can give this to him?"

Elisabeth Gruber then took the pen and its decorative case and said, "I will see if this is OK."

With that comment, Gruber left us, walking directly into Meier's house, leaving just Simone, Tina, and me at the table.

When Ms. Gruber returned, she did not have the pen with her. Before I could ask her what she had done with it, she stated, "Billy thanks you for your gift. It is very nice."

Disappointed, I realized that there was no way I was going to be allowed to meet Billy Meier personally during this first visit, especially with the way his followers shielded him from all outsiders.

When I asked Gruber if Meier was going to use the pen for both his contacts and the writing of the transcripts from his meetings with aliens, she replied that he would and reiterated how nice the gift was.

"Billy thanks you very much for your gift," she said again.

After gathering up our newly purchased collection of evidence, Tina and I departed the compound, eventually returning to downtown Wetzikon where we stopped by Schnarwiler Books once more. It was our hope that we could learn additional facts about Billy Meier before calling it a day.

When Tina and I walked into Schnarwiler Books for what was now the second time, we were immediately recognized by Karin Schröder, the manager.

"So, did you find Billy Meier?" she asked us immediately, while smiling.

"Yes, he was very interesting," I replied.

"He is a very interesting man, no?" she commented.

Upon seeing Ruth Wieser for the second time, I walked up

to her and mentioned that we had just returned from Billy Meier's place and wanted to follow up on our earlier conversation as to what kind of books she remembered that Meier had read or purchased.

After stressing to us once again that "Meier reads lots of books," Wieser and I walked around the store looking at various titles. Now her memory was starting to come back. Wieser recalled that Meier had purchased a series of books called *Chronik,* an ongoing release of volumes covering the entire history of this century, one volume per year.

The *Chronik* titles are lavishly illustrated in color, printed in large format, and resemble the "Time-Life" series of books. The complete *Chronik* set will total ninety-nine volumes, covering the years 1900 to 1999.[70]

This information by Wieser was significant, for among the Meier faithful we encountered (as well as in the pro-Meier literature), we are told repeatedly that Billy Meier is a simple farmer who is illiterate and has only a sixth-grade education. Meier's supporters will emphasize such things as the rich historical and scientific details his "Pleiadian messages" allegedly contain, insisting that such information is beyond the educational level of Billy Meier.

While the contents of these "messages" may indeed be above the *official* level of education Meier possesses, the argument is irrelevant when one considers the fact that Billy Meier could always consult his ninety-two volume (as of 1991) historical and scientific set of books, plus all the other titles he buys.

As we walked around the store, Ruth Wieser identified additional books that Billy Meier had purchased on the subjects of photography, science, astronomy, and history. She ended her comments by stating that "Billy Meier reads all these books. He is interested in everything."

Tina and I left Schnarwiler Books a few minutes later and went to get dinner in downtown Wetzikon. We had had by now a full day's worth of Billy Meier-related activities and decided to take a break from it all.

Later that evening, when we returned to the Jacob residence, Tina and I recounted the details of our visit to Meier's place. The Jacobs were happy to learn that we were both safe and did not need to spend the night at Billy Meier's residence. So were we.

I knew that when Meier's people eventually found out that Kal Korff had been "on and off" their property without their knowing it, they would be upset. So far, our investigation and acquisition of Meier-related evidence had gone smoothly, and I looked forward to what lay ahead.

After mounting the hundreds of pictures chronologically into the two photo-binders I had purchased just for the occasion, Tina and I called it an evening. Tomorrow, "Steve Thomas" was to return to the Meier farm once again, to pick up my personal copy of Guido Moosbrugger's book. The other task was to take the two photo-binders and visit as many of Meier's photo locations as possible to try and reconstruct the details of his alleged contacts as accurately as science permits. It would be another full day, but worth it.

August 19, 1991—Hinterschumidrüti, Switzerland

When I returned to the Meier compound the following morning, Monday, August 19, there was no one stationed at the outside entrance so I just walked in. While I was taking a risk, I figured that since I had spent over 1,000 Swiss francs the previous day (which made the Meier people very happy), I figured I wouldn't get into too much trouble. Even if I did, I was prepared to use the cover excuse of having to pick up Moosbrugger's book, or that I was here to donate some more money, having been "profoundly moved" by my earlier visit to the Semjase Silver Star Center. Instead of bringing my video camera with me, I decided to take the 35mm camera into the compound, since being by myself and not having made any official arrangements to sit down and talk with people, it was not practical to try the hidden video camera routine a second time. Since no one knew that I was there, I decided to wander about as much as I could.

As I made my way toward Billy Meier's house, I noticed a young girl approaching from the opposite direction. We reached the front of Meier's house at the same time.

I could tell instinctively that she was an American. Since I was supposed to understand only English, I introduced myself accordingly and asked her where her mother was.

She startled me by replying, "She is back at home."

When I asked her what she was doing here, the girl replied matter-of-factly, "My mom could not afford to pay to send us both here. So she let me come by myself on the plane so that I could learn from the Pleiadians."

After quickly recovering from the shock of what she had said, I felt a sense of both anger and sadness. Once again, here was evidence right in front of me that the false messianic claims of Billy Meier had struck once more. This time, an "adult" had put her daughter on a plane by herself and sent her thousands of miles away to "learn from the Pleiadians." I wondered how much and what else the girl's mother had sacrificed for Billy Meier, especially financially.

When I asked the child where she was from, she replied "in Santa Barbara," California. She then told me her name and that her parents were divorced. It was obvious that "the Pleiadians" had become part of the girl's new post-divorce era "family," a sad state of affairs undoubtedly caused by her mother's gullibility.

As I continued talking to the girl, another cult member by the name of Eva Bieri came out and asked me what I was doing on the Meier compound.

I replied to her that I was here to purchase a copy of Moos-brugger's book and reminded her innocently of how much money I had spent during the previous visit. She then instructed me to wait where I was, and in a few minutes she returned with my copy of the book. The little girl, in the meantime, had run inside Meier's house, and I never saw her again.

After being sold a copy of Moosbrugger's book, Ms. Bieri stared at me for a moment, no doubt expecting me to leave.

I then turned around and walked back up the slope of the gravel road, and used this opportunity to look around the Meier compound some more after clearing the part of the road which snaked back toward the parking lot so that I was no longer visible from where Bieri stood. Once again, no one observed me, and I was able to take some more still pictures of Billy Meier's place, and explore several of the dirt side trails, or *wanderwegs*, throughout the property.

When I left the Meier farm, I decided to drive up the road which wound around the mountain and provided an overhead view of the property. My objective was to reconnoiter the Meier compound and figure out a way to sneak onto the premises, probably at night, to obtain some soil samples from any "UFO landing-tracks" I observed.

After parking and retrieving my video camera from the car, I peered at the property through the zoom lens, taking in all details. I figured out a route I could take that would allow me to bypass both the electrical fences and what appeared from a distance to be some video surveillance cameras. The perimeter of the Meier compound turned out to be fairly fortified; weaving my way through its defenses would prove to be a challenge. There was a high risk of being seen, due to the location of the tracks.

For this reason, I decided to return to the compound at night, dressed in U.S. Army camouflage clothing so that I would minimize my visibility.

As Tina and I drove back up the mountain past the Meier

property, we parked our car just on the other side of the hill and walked very carefully back down toward the upper parts of the compound. For safety reasons, I made sure that Tina stayed behind, close enough to our car so that she could drive away in the event I did not return or was caught.

When I approached one of the electric fences, I calmly slid underneath it, making sure that I did not touch any of its wires. After clearing the fence, I slipped on down the hill and around to where I saw the remains of one of the landing-tracks. Removing some plastic bottles from my pouch, I obtained both control and specimen soil samples. Now that I had my evidence, it was time to get out of there quickly before I got caught. With the existence of dogs at Meier's place,[71] a weapons depot for use by his people when the end of civilization nears,[72] security personnel,[73] and the fact that Meier himself often carries a pistol,[74] I am lucky I was not detected.

If I had even been seen, my ability to come back to Meier's compound freely during the day and operate according to plan would have been severely jeopardized. And how would I explain to the Meier people, if they recognized me, how I was dressed? This was Switzerland, after all, where all males are obligated to serve in the country's army. Awareness of military-related issues is much more common than in America, so coming up with an "explanation" for my clothing would never have worked.

Finally, if I were to be apprehended and the Meier group was to learn my real identity, the consequences would not be desirable. While I cannot say for certain what would have happened, I could only remember how Brand and Gruber reacted whenever the name of Kal Korff was mentioned. Brand and Gruber made it very clear that they, along with Billy Meier himself, wished me the worst of health.

When I returned a few minutes later to the electric fence, I quickly crawled back under it and escaped unharmed. I then ran to our car and Tina and I drove back to the Jacob residence where, once again, Claudia and Margrit were glad to see that we were safe.

While I would visit the Meier compound a total of six times, only three of these visits were "official" where I walked right in through the front entrance and spoke to several members of the Semjase Silver Star Center. The other trips I made to the Meier property were covert in nature, doing everything from observing the people there, to conducting reconnaissance and obtaining those all-important alleged UFO landing-track soil samples.

The remainder of the relevant information and material Tina and I obtained during our three-week investigation in Europe is recounted throughout the rest of this book. Since a good deal of this data pertains to the conclusive evidence we uncovered proving that several of Meier's "key" UFO pictures are frauds, this information is presented in chapters 4 and 5, along with the important testimonies of the relevant Jacob family members.

September 1, 1991—Hinterschmidrüti, Switzerland

For the third and final "official" visit to Billy Meier's place, Tina and I were there for several hours. Our purpose was to try once more to meet with Billy Meier and to reconfirm key aspects of the Meier evidence.

While walking near the very first garden on our way to the visitor's area, we suddenly saw none other than Billy Meier himself pass us by in a white van. Meier was seated in the passenger's side of the vehicle, and catching a glimpse of him out of the corner of my eye, I instinctively waved.

Billy Meier glanced at me noticeably; gave a wide, toothy grin; and raised his right arm to wave back. It was obvious at this point that we would not get to meet Billy Meier in person. Indeed, our quick sighting of him was as close as we would ever get during our stay in Switzerland.

At the visitor's center, our "host" for this trip turned out to be Bernadette Brand again, which was just fine since she was definitely in a position to answer every one of our questions. In other words, even though we never spoke *directly* with Billy Meier, it turned out to be unnecessary since we had interviewed every senior, key member of Meier's camp. This helped clarify the accuracy of the claims made in the numerous books written on this case.

When I told Brand that we had just seen Meier drive by, and inquired when and if I could meet him, she replied that Billy Meier was on his way to the train station, escorting a group of Russians so that they could return home.

The 1991 coup in the USSR which had toppled the Communist government had taken place just weeks earlier, and Brand said that Meier's Russian guests had been stranded at the compound since the Soviet Union's borders had been closed. The Russians were finally leaving Meier's place after they received word that it was safe to return to their homes.

I certainly understood this, since the popular uprising which put Boris Yeltsin in power had also affected the plans Tina and I had made as well. Many people in Europe during those tense days were unsure what the Russian troops stationed in *their* countries might do.

On this final official visit, I purchased one more publication, a small, green-colored book titled *Verzeichnis—Authentischer Farb–Photos* (Catalog: Authentic Color Photos). Written and published by Billy Meier and the Semjase Silver Star Center, this sixty-four-page book lists the dates, locations, times, cameras used, and photographers for all 1,058 UFO and UFO-related photographs Meier and others have taken. The publication would later prove invaluable because it would be used as a "control" to resolve any discrepancies among the Meier literature concerning the details of Billy Meier's many UFO photographs.

When Tina and I were leaving the compound, I encountered Kalliope Meier as we were passing the "crystal" garden pond. At first I did not recognize her, yet her face seemed familiar. Then it occurred to me who she was.

As Kalliope Meier, Tina, and I stood looking at each other, I raised my 35mm camera to take her picture. Mrs. Meier looked like an emotional wreck, her face like that of a walking zombie. When I went to take a photo of her, she stared at me with a look on her face that seemed to be saying to me, "I beg you, *please* don't take my picture." We stood facing each other for what seemed like an eternity. After about a minute, I lowered my camera, nodded in the affirmative, and never got the photograph of Meier's wife that I wanted.

Tina also expressed surprise in seeing how Meier's wife appeared, and made comments to this effect as we walked up the gravel path back toward the parking lot to our car.

On the last day of our stay with the Jacob family, Claudia Jacob came up to me and made me an offer I could not refuse. She said I could have her father's photo-binder containing Billy Meier's UFO photographs to take back with me to the United States for analysis and study! I could not believe my luck, and the extent of Claudia's generosity. She put no restrictions or conditions on its use, and neither did Margrit, as long as I agreed to publish the facts as best as they could be determined. Their request was more than reasonable; there was to be no sensationalizing of this material.

With all of the evidence we had now acquired during our investigation in Switzerland, the addition of the Jacob material (the most valuable source of information which existed) was a blessing beyond belief.

As Tina and I were loading our things into the rental car to leave, I noticed that Claudia had some scratch paper with her that she was using to write things on. This "scratch paper" turned out to be a copy of Meier's *Wassermannzeit*.

Surprised, I asked her why she was using this particular material for scratch paper. Claudia laughed and said, "We

Fig. 16. The *Verzeichnis* the author purchased directly from Elisabeth Gruber while visiting undercover at the Meier cult. The *Verzeichnis* is the official catalog of the Semjase Silver Star Center, listing all 1058 "UFO" and UFO-related photographs that Meier and his disciples sell to the thousands of visitors who have made the "pilgrimage" to Billy Meier's compound over the years.

have a lot of this paper down in the basement. I use it for my dog to go to the bathroom on."

I found it ironic that the very material Claudia regarded as worthy of her dog's feces and nothing more is considered by the Meier faithful to be holy words of wisdom from Billy.

While the UFOlogist in me wanted to preserve and mark as evidence this material for study and analysis, in this specific instance I made an exception, deciding to pass up the opportunity to do so, for obvious reasons.

Since Tina and I had acquired five issues of *Wassermannzeit* volumes, including a copy of the very first issue, we decided to content ourselves with this material. If needed, I could always order more issues of *Wassermannzeit* after returning home, since the members of the Semjase Silver Star Center would not know until October 31, 1993, that my real name was not Steve Thomas.[75]

When they found out, boy, were they upset.

Fig. 17. "The Terrific Trio" (left to right): Margrit Jacob, Tina Layton, and Claudia Jacob. The entire Jacob family (including Thomas and Cornelia) extended generous hospitality and valuable assistance to our successful undercover investigation of the Meier case.

With the bounty of firsthand, original evidence from Switzerland, plus using all known available information that has been published in the United States and elsewhere, we are now ready to begin our full analysis and examination of the Billy Meier evidence.

Notes

1. Bernadette Brand, personal interviews with Kal Korff and Tina Layton, August 18, 1991, Semjase Silver Star Center, Hinterschmidrüti, Switzerland.

2. Kal K. Korff, *The Meier Incident—The Most Infamous Hoax in UFOlogy* (Prescott, Ariz.: Townescribe Press, 1981).

3. Kal K. Korff, "The Billy Meier Hoax," *Frontiers of Science* 3, no. 3 (March–April 1981): 31–33, 44. *See also* Kal K. Korff, "The Meier Photographs—Hoax from the Pleiades," *UFO Report* 8, no. 6 (December 1980): 14–21, 44.

4. Kal Korff, "The UFO Phenomenon," illustrated lecture at the National UFO Conference, Tucson, Arizona, May 25, 1983.

5. Donna Ferrozzo, personal conversation with Kal Korff, UFO Expo West '93, San Mateo, California, October 31, 1993.

6. Wendelle Stevens, "Kal Korff and the Meier 'Hoax': A Response Part 2," *MUFON Journal* (November 1981). *See also* Wendelle Stevens, *UFO . . . Contact from the Pleiades: A Supplementary Investigation Report—The Report of an Ongoing Contact* (Tucson, Ariz.: Wendelle Stevens, 1989), p. 515.

7. Stevens, *UFO . . . Contact from the Pleiades: A Supplementary Investigation Report*, p. 515.

8. Colman VonKeviczky, telephone conversation with Kal K. Korff, September 1980.

9. Hans Jacob, private correspondence, February 15, 1978. *Betrage: Eduard Meier (Billy) der sich UFO-kontaktler nennt (Schwiez)*, p.1.

10. Claudia and Margrit Jacob, personal interviews with Kal K. Korff and Tina Layton, Wetzikon, Switzerland, August 18–19, 1991.

11. Ibid.

12. Colman VonKeviczky, letter to Kal K. Korff, July 11, 1991.

13. Jim Dilettoso, personal interviews with Kal K. Korff, Al and Barbara Reed, Sunnyvale, California, September 6, 1980.

14. Wendelle Stevens, remarks made at the UFO '80 Conference, Oakland, California, August 23–24, 1980.

15. Gary Kinder, *Light Years: An Investigation into the Extraterrestrial Experiences of Eduard Meier* (New York: Atlantic Monthly Press, 1987), pp. 8, 79.

16. Karin Schröder, personal interviews with Kal K. Korff and Tina Layton, Wetzikon, Switzerland, August 15, 1991.

17. Ruth Wieser, personal interviews with Kal K. Korff and Tina Layton, Wetzikon, Switzerland, August 15, 1991.

18. Elisabeth Gruber, personal interviews with Kal Korff and Tina Layton, August 18, 1991, Semjase Silver Star Center, Hinterschmidrüti, Switzerland.

19. Wendelle Stevens, *UFO . . . Contact from the Pleiades—A Preliminary Investigation Report—The Report of an Ongoing Contact* (Tucson, Ariz.: Wendelle Stevens, 1983), pp. 144, 156–57.

20. Kinder, *Light Years,* 11th color illustration facing p. 155.

21. Ibid., p. 263. *See also, UFO . . . Contact from the Pleiades, Volume II*

(Phoenix, Ariz.: Genesis III Productions, Ltd., 1983), p. 71. *See also* Stevens, *UFO . . . Contact from the Pleiades: A Supplementary Investigation Report*, p. 5.

22. Gary Kinder, *An Open Letter to the UFO Community*, letter sent directly to Kal Korff by Gary Kinder, dated March 6, 1987, p. 4.

23. Kinder, *Light Years*, p. 263.

24. Kinder, *An Open Letter to the UFO Community*, p. 4.

25. Author's personal observations of Guido Moosbrugger at the UFO Expo West conferences, San Mateo, California: October 30–31, 1993 and November 5–6, 1994.

26. Simone, personal interviews with Kal Korff and Tina Layton, August 18, 1991, Semjase Silver Star Center, Hinterschmidrüti, Switzerland.

27. Ibid.

28. UFOComp File Number UFO422.

29. Posted by TotalResearch on InterNet, *America On-Line*, and in *Omni* magazine's electronic *Antimatter* UFO forums.

30. Sergeant on duty, Suisse Canton Zürich Polizei office, Hinwil, Switzerland, August 20, 1991.

31. Author's personal observation while at the Semjase Silver Star Center, Hinterschmidrüti, Switzerland, August 18, 1991.

32. Bernadette Brand and Elisabeth Gruber, personal interviews with Kal Korff and Tina Layton, August 18, 1991, Semjase Silver Star Center, Hinterschmidrüti, Switzerland.

33. Randolph Winters, *The Pleiadian Mission: A Time of Awareness* (Atwood, Calif.: The Pleiades Project, Inc., 1994), p. 182.

34. Ibid.

35. Ibid.

36. Bernadette Brand and Elisabeth Gruber, personal interviews with Kal Korff and Tina Layton, August 18, 1991, Semjase Silver Star Center, Hinterschmidrüti, Switzerland. *See also* Winters, *The Pleiadian Mission*, p. 186.

37. Bernadette Brand and Elisabeth Gruber, personal interviews with Kal Korff and Tina Layton, August 18, 1991, Semjase Silver Star Center, Hinterschmidrüti, Switzerland. *Also* Randolph Winters, lecture on Billy Meier at MUFON meeting, near Ventura, California, November 19, 1994.

38. Winters, *The Pleiadian Mission*, pp. 188–89.

39. Ibid.

40. Randolph Winters, lecture on Billy Meier at MUFON meeting, near Ventura, California, November 19, 1994. *See also* Winters, *The Pleiadian Mission*, p. 189.

41. Bernadette Brand and Elisabeth Gruber, personal interviews with Kal Korff and Tina Layton, August 18, 1991.

42. Michael Arends, *Eduard Meier—Prophet der Neuzeit?* (Rimsting, Germany: October 1976), p. 2.

43. Winters, *The Pleiadian Mission*, p. 189.

44. Ibid., pp. 179–89.

45. Brad Sparks, renowned biblical scholar, phone conversation with Kal K. Korff, September 1991.

46. Winters, *The Pleiadian Mission*, pp. 185–88.

47. Ibid.

48. Ibid., p. 188.

49. Brad Sparks, renowned biblical scholar, phone conversation with Kal K. Korff, September 1991.

50. Randolph Winters, lecture on Billy Meier at MUFON meeting, near Ventura, California, November 19, 1994.

51. Confidential letter dated June 23, 1980, from Ph.D. source in Switzerland who participated in the Meier documents/evidence study and requests anonymity due to the negative conclusions found. The unedited letter revealing the names of the people who conducted the Meier document studies, as well as their conclusions, analyses, and specific requests for anonymity, are on file at MUFON and TotalResearch, along with their addresses.

52. Ibid.

53. Confidential letter dated May 24, 1980, from Ph.D. source in Switzerland who participated in the Meier documents/evidence study and requests anonymity due to the negative conclusions found. The unedited letter revealing the names of the people who conducted the Meier document studies, as well as their conclusions, analyses, and specific requests for anonymity, are on file at MUFON and TotalResearch, along with their addresses.

54. Confidential letter dated June 23, 1980, from Ph.D. source in Switzerland who participated in the Meier documents/evidence study and requests anonymity due to the negative conclusions found. The unedited letter revealing the names of the people who conducted the Meier document studies, as well as their conclusions, analyses, and specific requests for anonymity, are on file at MUFON and TotalResearch, along with their addresses.

55. Walter H. Andrus, personal correspondence with Kal K. Korff, September 21, 1982.

56. Ibid.

57. Ibid.

58. Michael Arends, *Eduard Meier—Prophet Der Neuzeit?* pp. 2–5.

59. Ibid.

60. Glen Hoyen, president of Underground Video, personal conversation with Kal K. Korff, Hollywood, California, November 19, 1994.

61. Bernadette Brand and Elisabeth Gruber, personal interviews with Kal Korff and Tina Layton, August 18, 1991.

62. Author's personal conversation with Michael Hesemann, Guido Moosbrugger's editor and publisher, at the UFO West '94 Expo, Los Angeles, California, June 12, 1994.

63. The author has personally seen Guido Moosbrugger acting in this capacity at the last two UFO West Expositions in San Mateo, California (1993 and 1994). For two years in a row at this conference, where this author has even spoken with Moosbrugger briefly, Guido has appeared with an English translator presenting his lectures to near-capacity crowds, with decent attendance at his one-on-one workshops. *Also* Bernadette Brand, personal interviews with Kal Korff and Tina Layton, August 18, 1991.

64. Author's personal observations of Guido Moosbrugger at the UFO Expo West conference, San Mateo, California, October 30–31, 1993 and November 5–6, 1994.

65. Bernadette Brand and Elisabeth Gruber, personal interviews with Kal Korff and Tina Layton, August 18, 1991.

66. Author's personal conversations with Michael Hesemann, June 11–12, 1994, Los Angeles, California, UFO West '94 Expo, and during author's lecture and workshop on the Meier case at the same conference.

67. Simone, personal interviews with Kal Korff and Tina Layton, August 18, 1991.

68. Winters, *The Pleiadian Mission*, p. 224.

69. Ibid.

70. Ruth Wieser, personal interviews with Kal K. Korff and Tina Layton, Wetzikon, Switzerland, August 15, 1991.

71. Kal K. Korff, "The Billy Meier UFO Hoax," illustrated lecture, UFO Expo West '93, San Mateo, California, October 31, 1993.

72. Konrad Schutzbach, letter of resignation from the Semjase Silver Star Center, Greifensee, Switzerland, June 1979.

73. Ibid.

74. Stevens, *UFO . . . Contact from the Pleiades—A Preliminary Investigation Report*, p. 18. See also Winters, *The Pleiadian Mission*, p. 24.

75. Kal K. Korff, "The Billy Meier UFO Hoax," illustrated lecture, UFO Expo West '93, San Mateo, California, October 31, 1993.

3

Genesis III's "Analyses" of Meier's UFO Photographs

We did not say, nor does the (Pleiades) book imply, that De Anza Systems "did some of the analysis." They aren't even mentioned anywhere in the (Pleiades) book.

Wendelle C. Stevens[1]

Our thanks go to De Anza Systems, Inc., manufacturers of the remarkable state-of-the-art computer graphics systems utilized to better illustrate some of the test procedures.

UFO . . . Contact from the Pleiades,Vol. I[2]

UFO photographs are extremely difficult to analyze. While they represent a challenge to the serious researcher, the fact that they can be so easily faked is enough to give any would-be analyst nightmares. After all, no one knows just *what* a "real" UFO looks like.

However, in any valid, scientific analysis of photographs, especially when they purport to show UFOs or other extraordinary phenomena, one must have the *original negatives* available for study and testing. Additionally, the camera that was used to make the pictures must also be available for examination. Finally, in cases where the "UFO" supposedly flew near objects of known size and distance (as is claimed in many of Meier's photographs), taking measurements at the location where the incident purportedly took place is also critical.

Of these three factors, having the original negative(s) for testing and analysis is by far the most important. *Without an original negative to study, any photograph of a "UFO" (regardless of what it purports to show) is worthless and cannot be accepted by science as evidence.* This is also true where any photograph is concerned, no matter what its content.

What most people don't realize about the Billy Meier case is that there are *no original photographic negatives or source materials of any of Meier's UFO pictures in existence.* Indeed, according to Meier proponents, the original negatives and other photographic source material have all either been "lost" in the mail or "stolen" by everyone from souvenir hunters to nebulous and nefarious intelligence operatives. Still other photographs have been "recalled" by the Pleiadians, meaning that Meier was ordered to turn them over to the aliens.[3] Thus, according to Wendelle Stevens, the best copies Genesis III could obtain from Meier for the purpose of photographic analysis and computer testing were internegatives which yielded anywhere from second- through sixth-generation copy prints.[4]

Nonetheless, in all of the pro-Meier books, the claim is made that several of Meier's UFO photographs have been analyzed by computers and various scientific experts who have been unable to find any evidence of a hoax. The implication in these books is that Meier's UFO photographs have been shown to be authentic.[5] Added to this longstanding claim are the statements of Stevens and Jim Dilettoso (another Meier supporter), the two individuals primarily responsible for the logistics and supposed integrity of these alleged scientific tests.[6]

According to Wendelle Stevens, Meier's photographs underwent "photogrammetric inspection by photo experts" and that these experts "still find no evidence of fraud or trickery in any of these photographs so enhanced. On the other hand, we find details revealed that tend more to establish the validity of the story told by the witness. The object appears quite large, like 20 feet or more, and hundreds of feet from the camera."[7]

Moreover, Dilettoso maintains that the computer testing was so complete on Meier's pictures that "in all the photographs we got the same thing. Twenty-two feet, three inches. No matter how big it was in the picture, and we did that on about 40 photographs."[8]

Just what scientific tests did Stevens and Genesis III conduct on Meier's photographs? How many pictures were analyzed and where are the laboratory reports that support these claims? Unfortunately, only Genesis III and Stevens know the full answers to these questions, since *none* of the data from these supposedly all-important scientific studies has ever been released.

While the Stevens and Genesis III Meier books present *some* information concerning the tests, most of it is vague, while other parts are deliberate fabrications. For example, in Volumes I, II, and in all of the reprints of the original *Pleiades* photo-journal book, the implication is made that a computing firm by the name of De Anza Systems in San Jose, California, analyzed some of Meier's UFO photographs and found no evidence of a hoax.[9]

When I checked with Mr. Wayne Heppler, the manager for De Anza Systems, I received a categorical *denial* that an analysis was ever conducted. This is what Heppler told me when I interviewed him for my original Meier exposé book in May 1980: "There was no analysis performed. What we did was some enhancing to make certain parts of the picture stand out."

"So your firm did not do an analysis?" I asked.

An adamant "No" was Heppler's reply.

"But the book implies that you did, and furthermore it states that via computer analysis the Meier photographs were shown to be authentic," I informed him.

"That is garbage!" the manager quipped.

"Look, what these guys did [some of the members of Genesis III] was come on down to De Anza Systems claiming that they wanted to *buy* a computer from us. So we took one of their pictures, one showing the UFO, and enhanced it to make certain parts of the pictures stand out. Then they took pictures of it, left, and stated that they would get back in touch with us. And we haven't heard from them since!"[10]

I then asked Heppler if his company possessed the technical capabilities to perform the kind of analyses the Genesis III photo-journals claim was conducted. Heppler replied: "No. We are in no position to do an analysis."[11]

I asked Heppler for the names of the individuals who had visited De Anza. Heppler replied that it was Jim Dilettoso and Thomas K. Welch. He also claimed to have recognized the name of Wendelle Stevens.[12]

A month later I telephoned De Anza Systems a second time in order to ask some more questions. Since Heppler was out of the office at the time, I was referred to another gentleman, Ken Dinwiddie, who possesses a Master's degree in Mechanical Engineering from Stanford University. As the product manager for image processing and display products for De Anza, Dinwiddie was the scientist who had actually *entered* the Meier photos into the firm's computers at Genesis III's and, specifically, Jim Dilettoso's requests. The following remarks were taken from two interviews conducted in June 1980 and on June 14, 1981, at his home. Present with me at the interview were UFO researchers William L. Moore; his associate, Nick; and Roma Donovan.

Bill Moore and I began our interview by showing Dinwiddie the Genesis III book, *UFO . . . Contact from the Pleiades, Volume I,* the original edition. It was the first time he had seen the book. Volume II of *Pleiades* had not yet been released.[13] We let Dinwiddie look through the book as long as he wanted. After thumbing through it for about five minutes, we then turned to the "Computer and Laser Photo Examination" section of the book and asked Ken Dinwiddie to comment on each "computer analyzed" photo.

Since it was Dinwiddie's own computer enhancements that Genesis III published in their book without either his knowledge or consent,[14] we asked him about the accuracy of the captions and analytical conclusions as stated by Genesis III which appear under each of his photos in the book *UFO . . . Contact from the Pleiades, Volume I.*

Dinwiddie started off the interview by stating that he had received most of his computer-image manipulation instructions from Jim Dilettoso. His next two comments were that "the captions below the photos are not our conclusions, but strictly theirs," and that the Genesis III "photo captions displayed here no longer bear any relationship to the data he's [Jim Dilettoso] seeking."

As Dinwiddie continued to read the captions under his computer images as they appear in the Genesis III book, clearly he was surprised. Having created these very images, he could not understand how the conclusions stated in the captions below them could possibly be correct.[15]

We then began our formal interview. The initials "BM" stand for Bill Moore, "KD" for Ken Dinwiddie, and "KK" for Kal Korff.

KK: Did you in fact conduct an analysis of the Meier photographs?

KD: No.

BM: How did you first meet the Genesis group?

KD: They came to De Anza under the pretext of wanting to buy our equipment. We demonstrated it and they snapped many pictures and left. We made no data interpretations whatsoever. *In fact, our encounter with Genesis has caused us a considerable hassle here at De Anza.*

BM: What is your company's equipment primarily used for?

KD: Nondestructive testing, especially medical, but also for aerial surveys by satellites, especially for interpretations.

KK: What about the captions which appear in the Genesis book under each photo? Are they correct?

KD: Those are *their* interpretations, not ours. Nothing we did would have defined what these results meant. We simply performed the operations (enhancements) that they asked for. They took pictures off of the monitor and provided their *own* interpretations.

They didn't even notify us that they were going to put them in there! As far as us being behind them, no way baby!

KK: Could Genesis possibly be correct in their conclusions if, say, they just *visually* interpreted the photos off your display screen?

KD: No.

KK: Do you think they did just that anyway?

KD: Obviously.

BM: Is it possible for the photos they took off your monitor to be used by another scientist to produce meaningful results?

KD: No, not likely because some significant data may well have been suppressed by the processes we used.

BM: Can I ask you about some of the photo captions which appear in the Meier book?

KD: Yes.

BM: What about this comment they make on page 52: "Film grain analysis by laser scanning micro-densitometer—shows consistent homogeneous patterns, no overlapping film grains; eliminates overlays, multiple exposures, multiple printings, and darkroom techniques"?

KD: There's no way to separate multiple exposures by this technique, if they were well done, since the negative would show a single exposure of two previous negatives or paste-ups.

The white lines here (the ones supposedly showing density contour plots) are overlaid on the screen. *These are not photos of the actual readouts!*

KK: What about: "Density Average—object is 3-dimensional due to variable colors"?

KD: *As far as I'm concerned it's absurd!**

BM: What about the remark: "Z-scale contour of infrared copy print with band pass filtering—topographical view

---

*To elaborate on Dinwiddie's point, in the digital enhancement process known as false color contouring, the computer assigns a specific color to each item in a picture that has a separate density or light value. This means that the Genesis III photo caption is incorrect. Just because an object shows "variable colors" under false color contouring does not *prove* that it is a three-dimensional or physically real object. Since it is the properties of *visible light* the computer uses to determine which colors to assign, what the "object" is actually made of is irrelevant!

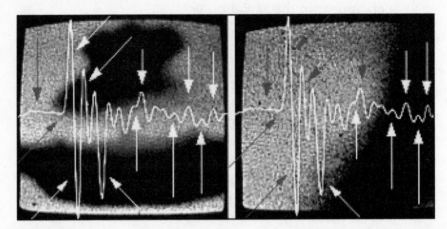

Fig. 18. The "film grain analysis" images as they appear in *UFO... Contact from the Pleiades, Volume I.* The white lines on these photos were over-laid by a *graphic artist* and are *not* actual density readings, nor are they a portion of any scientific analysis, contrary to what is claimed in the book. As the arrows indicate, a careful study of these two white lines reveals that they are *identical* pieces of art and haphazardly extend *beyond* the actual borders of the display monitor they are juxtapositioned on—a physical *impossibility* if this were a real analysis or scan display from a microdensitometer as claimed by Genesis III and Dilettoso. (Photo courtesy: UFO-Comp Computer Archives.)

based upon illumination . . . jet exhaust visible, amplified by infrared"?

KD: This conclusion is not substantiated by the data presented. Infrared cannot be determined by Kodacolor or regular film. *Anyone who would make such a statement is either grossly misinterpreting the data or grossly ignorant of the processes involved, or both.**

---

*Dinwiddie is referring to the fact that the infrared spectrum of light does not register on normal daylight color 35mm film. This is why infrared

KK: What about this remark: "Thermogram—Color density separations—low frequencies properties of light/time of day are correct; light values on ground are reflected in craft bottom; eliminates double exposure and paste-ups"?

KD: No, *we* put those colors in the photo! Jim [Dilettoso] said, "Can you make the bottom of the object appear to reflect the ground below?" I said yes, and we performed the operations that they asked for.

KK: Are *any* of the photo interpretations Genesis used in their book accurate?

KD: *No.*

BM: Were the prints or negatives you enhanced first generation?

KD: No. The largest picture was a print. The negatives we had were virtually useless until the SPIE [Society of Photo Instrument Engineers] conference. That's when Jim Dilettoso "borrowed" some equipment which enabled them [he and Genesis III] to get better images.

---

film exists so that light from the infrared spectrum can be photographed. Since Meier used ordinary color 35mm Agfa, Kodak, and Peruz daylight film (Stevens, *Preliminary Investigation Report*, p. 400; Meier's *Verzeichnis*, p. iv), any "infrared" reading(s) allegedly detected by Jim Dilettoso and Genesis III are meaningless, since Meier's film was not sensitive to this portion of the light spectrum in the first place! Jim Dilettoso's references to "infrared" detecting *anything* in Meier's photos is a typical example of pseudoscience at its best.

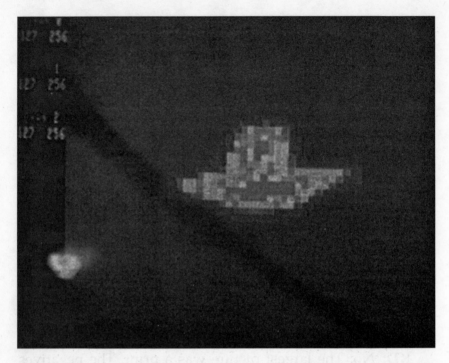

Fig. 19. One of the computer-enhancement illustrations as it appears in *UFO...Contact from the Pleiades, Volume I.* When Ken Dinwiddie was asked to comment on this specific caption which appears underneath this photo in the Genesis III book and reads *"Density Average—object is 3-dimensional due to variable colors,"* his reply was, "As far as I'm concerned, it's absurd." Ken Dinwiddie is the best authority to render an opinion on this image and to identify for the record its true nature since he is the computer technician who created it for Genesis III at their request! (Photo courtesy: UFOComp Computer Archives.)

KK: In your opinion, would this "better equipment" have enabled them to perform a more accurate analysis?

KD: No. You can use the most sophisticated equipment in the world, but that's not going to do you any good.

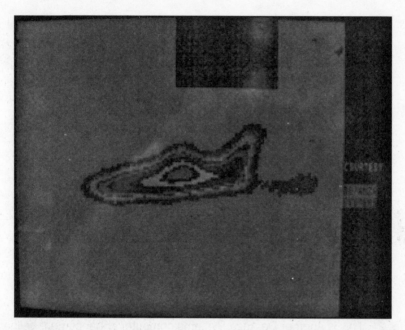

Fig. 20. This is a photo of one of the original De Anza Systems computer enhancements supplied by Wendelle Stevens to UFO researcher Jim Lorenzen. Lorenzen later gave the entire print set he received from Stevens to me in Tucson, Arizona, in May 1983. This is the very same image that appears on page 53 of *UFO . . . Contact from the Pleiades, Volume I,* and has the following caption underneath it: "Z-scale contour of infra-(sic)red copy print with band pass filtering—topographical view based upon illumination...jet exhaust visible, amplified by infrared." Since light from the infrared part of the spectrum cannot be detected by the ordinary daylight 35mm color film that Meier used to take his UFO pictures, the infrared "discovery" claims of Jim Dilettoso and Genesis III are meaningless. (Photo courtesy: Jim and Coral Lorenzen/APRO.)

KK: In other words, if you put garbage into a computer, regardless of how sophisticated it may be, you're still going to get garbage right back out.

KD: Yes.

Fig. 21. This is another De Anza Systems computer enhancement deliberately misrepresented by Genesis III. This photo appears on page 53 of *UFO . . . Contact from the Pleiades, Volume I,* and appears with the caption: "Thermogram—Color density separations—low frequencies properties of light/time of day are correct; light values on ground are reflected in craft bottom; eliminates double exposure and paste-ups" underneath it. According to Dinwiddie, the technician who made this actual enhancement, the caption is a total fabrication and the "reflection" was digitally inserted at Jim Dilettoso's request! Such remarks are fine examples of the pseudoscientific puffery and deception used to promote the Meier case by its numerous proponents around the world. (Photo courtesy: Jim and Coral Lorenzen/APRO.)

BM: What do you know of Wendelle Stevens?

KD: Not much. He was supposed to have been involved in the original Air Force UFO project.* I met him at the SPIE in San Diego.

---

*Dinwiddie stated during our interview that Stevens had told him that he was a former member of the original U.S. Air Force Project Blue Book investigation team, which studied UFO reports. While it is true that Stevens was indeed a career officer in the USAF, he was *never* a member of Project Blue Book.

BM: What is your opinion of Jim Dilettoso?

KD: *My impression of Jim Dilettoso is that he freely chooses to use whatever descriptive text he enjoys to describe things. He is not particularly versed in computer technology.* He's a pretty good piano player though.

Dinwiddie ended our interview by emphasizing once again that "De Anza does not typically offer analysis services to anyone, what we do is sell equipment. We were doing a *demo* for them (Genesis III)."

A final irony concerning the distortions found in Genesis III's "computer analysis" sections in the *Pleiades* photo-journals is the fact that Jim Dilettoso's *own* "Confidential Transcript of Communication Log, 1978–1982" *confirms* that only a *demo* and no analysis was ever conducted at De Anza Systems. Dilettoso's log reads August 24, 1979 [the exact date he and Stevens visited De Anza systems and met with Dinwiddie]: "De Anza Computer Company (ip) demo of IP/PGA system; no string."[16] The "(ip)" notation is shorthand for "in person," according to the legend which exists in Dilettoso's confidential log.[17] This means that Dilettoso was present at De Anza Systems when the enhancements were done, just as Dinwiddie and Heppler have stated. The "IP/PGA system" abbreviation is more of Dilettoso's shorthand, which stands for "Image Processing/PhotoGrammetric Analysis system."[18]

The key word in Dilettoso's log entry is "demo." The notation that "no string" was found by Dilettoso is meaningless, since no tests were ever conducted to try and find one. De Anza Systems was only performing a demo. The captions that appear under their computer images in all three editions of Genesis III's *UFO...Contact from the Pleiades, Volume I,* and *UFO...Contact from the Pleiades, Volume II,* are void of any meaningful or real data.

What about claims concerning other purported scientific

testing or analysis of Meier's UFO photographs? Are any of these other examinations credible?

Physicist Neil Davis's Analysis

Gary Kinder in *Light Years* cites an analysis by Design Technology's physicist, Neil Davis, as one of several scientists who could find no evidence of a hoax in Meier's photographs.[19] In Kinder's treatment of Neil Davis's analysis, we see one of many problems with the professed accuracy of *Light Years*. As chapter 10 explains in more detail, Kinder tells the reader only *one side* of the story. For example, Kinder quotes from Davis's report, correctly noting that it stated: "Nothing was found in the examination of the print which would cause me to believe that the object in the photo is anything other than a large object photographed a distance from the camera."[20]

While the report does say this, what Kinder *fails* to mention is that this *one sentence* he chooses to quote from is the *only sentence* in Davis's *entire four-page report* that is a positive comment about the Meier UFO photograph he examined! For example, these are the comments Davis makes in the very *next two paragraphs* of his report:

1. These results are *preliminary* and *qualitative* in nature because of the unknown processing history of the print, and its presumed inferior quality to the original negative. A more detailed, quantitative analysis of this photo can *only properly be made on the original film.* It is most desirable that all 6 original photos be examined. It is possible to optically or digitally superimpose the several images of the object resulting in an image with increased resolution. (Emphasis added)

2. With the original photo available it should be possible to compute the distance from the camera to the object using the decrease in contrast due to haze at greater distance. To perform this calcu-

lation it is necessary to know the distances from the camera to features in the scene such as the near trees and the increasingly distant hills. If it is not possible to obtain these measurements at the site then an aerial photograph or topographic map with those features identified would be needed.

Had Kinder bothered to include the *full* details of Davis's report, it would have changed significantly this portion of *Light Years,* informing the reader of the simple fact that Davis's analysis was inconclusive. Davis was limited by the fact he had *no original negative* or first-generation photograph to study, even noting this fact in the paragraph *above* the one Kinder cited: "Many small black specks, apparently caused by dirt on the previous positive, were found on the print. Their presence indicates that this print is either a second-generation print from a color negative original or that the original is a positive transparency (and) not a negative as was stated in the supporting data."[21]

Because of Kinder's selective omissions, the reader is *misled* to believe that the Meier picture Davis examined might be genuine. In truth, such a determination was not possible, due to the poor quality of the image that Stevens gave Neil Davis to work with.

Eric Eliason's Analysis

On February 26, 1981, Jim Dilettoso telephoned computer image processing expert Eric Eliason at his office at the United States Geological Survey (USGS) in Flagstaff, Arizona. After briefing him on the Meier UFO photographs, Eliason agreed to meet with Dilettoso to study the images.[22]

Dilettoso arrived at Eliason's office on March 9, 1981,[23] with only *two* of the four Meier photographs he had digitized on November 21, 1980, while visiting the Image Processing

Center at the University of Southern California.[24] Why Dilettoso brought only two images, instead of the four he digitized, has never been explained.

For two days Eliason examined the Meier UFO images.
After careful study, he concluded that the "UFOs" in the photographs "certainly hadn't been dubbed in. There was just a
natural transition. If you had a sharp contrast boundary, you
might think, well, that looks pretty hokey. But right along
these boundaries there were no sharp breaks where you could
see it had been somehow artificially dubbed. And if that dubbing was registered in the film, the computer would have seen
it. We didn't see anything."[25] Eliason went on to qualify his
statement, however, by adding: "You need to start with the
original if you're going to play games like this. So in a sense
this is not really a scientifically valid statement."[26]

While Eliason's image enhancements did not detect any
evidence that the two Meier photographs were montages
("dubbed in" as he called it), there is an easy way Eliason's (or
anyone else's) computers could have been easily fooled. That
method would be to photograph the master montage print
with another camera whose lens is set just slightly out-of-
focus. This technique would blur the edges of the paste-up
"UFO" wherever it meets the background sky.

It is critical to any scientific examination to have the original negative(s). Without the negative(s), even a simple issue
such as whether or not a photo was fabricated using montage
or paste-up techniques cannot be resolved.

When Eliason was asked about Dilettoso's objectivity, he
said that Dilettoso "wanted so badly to believe that this was
the real thing, he went ahead and believed it anyway."[27]

He added that Dilettoso "struck me as [a man who would
take] whatever I said about a particular issue [as] the all-
encompassing truth. I don't like that because the world just
isn't that way. There are too many uncertainties."[28]

Analyses of Meier's Photos by Wally Gentleman

Another "analysis" of Meier's UFO pictures widely touted by Jim Dilettoso, Gary Kinder, Guido Moosbrugger, and Wendelle Stevens was allegedly conducted by special effects expert Wally Gentleman, who at the time worked for the Film Effects corporation in Hollywood.[29] Gentleman was introduced to the Meier case by Bill Jenkins, a former radio talk-show host for KABC in Los Angeles.[30]

Through his association with Jenkins, Gentleman was introduced to Lee Elders, who showed various copies of Meier's photographs, 8mm movie films, and other evidence to him. Gentleman was impressed by what he saw.[31]

After finishing his examination, Gentleman would go on record as saying that there was no way Meier could have faked his pictures alone.[32] He then declared that "Meier really had to have a fleet of clever assistants, at least fifteen people" in order to fake his photographs.[33] Gentleman finally added that he would need $80,000 worth of equipment and resources if he were to try to equal the quality of Meier's UFO photographs and motion picture films.[34]

Suffice it to say, the statements by Wally Gentleman are welcome news to Meier's supporters and others who want very badly to believe in the case.

The relevant question, however, is just how accurate are Wally Gentleman's comments?

Do his remarks improve on what has been an unimpressive track record regarding Genesis III's handling of Meier's photographic evidence?

Did Wally Gentleman succeed in authenticating in any credible way Billy Meier's UFO photographic evidence, whether it be his still pictures or his movie footage?

A close examination of Gentleman's "analysis" reveals that he did *not* authenticate Meier's UFO photographic evidence.

Some of his conclusions contain fundamental errors in basic analytical logic, while his other mistakes are quite understandable, considering the fact that he is a Hollywood *special effects artist and not a trained photo analyst!* Here are some examples:

1. Although it is true that Gentleman found no evidence of a hoax when he examined the Meier photographs and films, Gentleman had *no negatives to examine,* a limitation everyone else has suffered when they have attempted to legitimately study Meier's pictorial evidence. Meier supporters such as Jim Dilettoso, Guido Moosbrugger, and Wendelle Stevens fail to mention the fact that Gentleman prefaced his own comments by stating, "My big problem area with the Meier pictures is that I have never seen an original negative. And without that I could never really be sure that it had not been doctored in any way at all."[35]

2. Gary Kinder describes an analytical technique Gentleman purportedly used called "perspective interlocking."

> In addition to examining the films, Gentleman subjected several of the Meier photos to "perspective interlock," a drawing board geometric analysis which he had applied in the independent frame process at Pinewood Studios. If Meier maintained that the beamships he had photographed measured approximately twenty-one feet in diameter, Gentleman could take the size of a known object in the scene, a measured tree trunk for instance, and locate where in the scene a beamship of that size would have to be. The photograph could appear to be authentic, but perspective interlock would expose subtle inconsistencies. Placing the photos on his drawing board and then tracing perspective lines, Gentleman calculated that the beamships were exactly as Meier had said they were, in size and location.[36]

This example by Gary Kinder, which sounds impressive upon casual examination, is most revealing for the following reasons: (a) it shows an uncritical acceptance and ignorance by Kinder of Gentleman's "facts"; and (b) it shows a simple, but severe lapse in logic on the part of Wally Gentleman when he studied Meier's photographs, the kind of basic mistake a trained photo analyst would not make.

The flaw in Gentleman's analysis can be found among Kinder's own words when he writes: "Gentleman could take the size of a known object in the scene, a measured tree trunk for instance, and locate where in the scene a beamship of that size would have to be."[37] While Gentleman's "perspective interlock" method is quite valid (the technique is also known as "dimensioning" to technical illustrators[38]), the point is totally irrelevant since he *never once visited any of the locations depicted in Billy Meier's UFO photographs!* Gentleman had no way of knowing the accuracy of the dimensions he was given to work with.

The failure to obtain independent measurements, relying only on numerical values supplied by Genesis III and Billy Meier, relegates any so-called analysis of this kind to the realm of pseudoscience and not science.

Without the original photographic negative or other pristine source material to study, including the camera, independent verification and/or quantification of measurements is impossible to achieve, no matter who the expert is.

3. Gentleman's comment that it would take Billy Meier and a crew of "at least fifteen people" to stage his photographs has been thoroughly *disproven* in a series of experiments that I have conducted both in the United States and at the actual locations Billy Meier used in Switzerland. The results of these tests are included in chapters 4 and 5. Billy Meier's "UFO" and even his "time-travel" photographs can be duplicated easily for anywhere from twenty to one hundred dollars depending on which methods are used. My experiments also proved that they can be faked with very little effort, using

one or more people, depending on the complexity of the desired shots.[39]

4. To lay a credible foundation for the alleged scientific legitimacy of Wally Gentleman's studies of Meier's UFO photos, Jim Dilettoso, Genesis III, Guido Moosbrugger, and Wendelle Stevens cite his work on Stanley Kubrick's famous movie *2001: A Space Odyssey*. Gary Kinder also claims that: "While in Canada in 1961, Gentleman made a short film of mostly visual effects titled *Universe*, which was later discovered by Stanley Kubrick, who contacted Gentleman. He wanted to utilize the techniques Gentleman had created for *Universe* in his new film *2001*. For the next year and a half, Gentleman had served as director of special photographic effects for the Kubrick film."[40]

While it is true that Kubrick spoke with Gentleman concerning special effects for *2001*, it should be noted that Wally Gentleman *left the film project after only a few weeks*.[41] Indeed, Gentleman's contribution to the making of *2001* was not significant enough to warrant even a mention of him in the film's credits![42]

Dr. Michael Malin's Analysis

Michael Malin has a Ph.D. in Planetary Sciences from Cal Tech and is also an expert on computer image processing. He was teaching Planetary Geology and Geomorphology at Arizona State University in Tempe, Arizona, when Dilettoso contacted him in May 1981.[43]

Although Malin could not find any evidence of tampering visible in the Meier photographs, he had no negatives at his disposal to study, making his analysis inconclusive at best. Dr. Malin even commented on this, stating, "The important thing would have been the original film. Without the very detailed information about the originals, there's almost nothing you can say."[44] Malin had also requested the actual camera used to take the photographs and "the stuff that actually went through the camera,"[45] which is what any prudent, professional photographic scientist would do.

Curiously, neither Jim Dilettoso, Genesis III, nor Billy Meier ever complied with Malin's request, a task which should not have been difficult to do.

Dr. Robert Nathan's Analysis

Jim Dilettoso telephoned Dr. Robert Nathan on May 8, 1979, at the Jet Propulsion Laboratory (JPL) in Pasadena, California, to inquire about computer enhancement issues and to arrange to have the Meier photographs analyzed by their equipment.[46]

Dr. Robert Nathan is one of the pioneers in computer image processing and is considered a top expert in this field. Arguably, the Jet Propulsion Laboratory's computer photographic enhancement facilities are among the finest in the world, with many of them distinctly unique. JPL is known for having image-enhancement capabilities no one else has.

According to Dilettoso's Confidential Transcript and Communication Log, he and Wendelle Stevens delivered "ten 4x5 negatives" on August 9, 1979, to Dr. Nathan and his associate, Mr. Bob Post.[47] Dilettoso has subsequently gone on record as stating that Dr. Nathan analyzed some of Meier's UFO photographs and could find no evidence of a hoax.[48] Here are some of Dilettoso's remarks:

> We worked with a lot of people there (at the Jet Propulsion Laboratory) in doing this, [including] Bob Nathan.
>
> And (Nathan) made available a lot of people to us. In fact, he sent everybody home except for two lab technicians who worked with them, and we were there from two in the afternoon to near midnight; doing stuff after he gave everyone the day off.

So we took the first-generation photographs, he (Nathan) sent his lab home, about 15 people, one o'clock in the afternoon.

Nathan said that he couldn't find anything that was too out-of-character with the photographs.

Dr. Nathan has *denied* that the incident as Dilettoso describes it ever took place, further stating that while he *did* examine some of Meier's UFO photographs, he did *not* send any of his people home.[49] Nathan also said that when he looked at the Meier photographs they were "extremely poor in quality and of no analytical value."[50] In his expert opinion, however, they were "obvious hoaxes."

In addition to what Nathan told me, supporters of the Meier case often overlook other statements Nathan made seven years later, when he reflected back on the subject of Meier's UFO photographs:

All I know is the negatives he (Wendelle Stevens) gave us to work with were already out-of-focus and that's all he would let us have. They had to be a different, later generation, or a generation specifically made that was intentionally out-of-focus. They couldn't have been used to make the very high-resolution prints he flashed by me. He was not going to give me his best data, he wasn't showing me anything I could work with.

I was never impressed with the pictures. I was very unhappy with them. At no time was I ever of the feeling that they were anything but a hoax. But don't forget, all of my examination on this was extremely cursory. These things have not really been given a good examination because it isn't worth the time, from the quality of the images given us, to do anything. I have no proof that this is a fraud. But I have no proof that it is real. That's the second statement that should always accompany the first."[51]

For reasons unknown, Wendelle Stevens refused to give Dr. Nathan the clear photographic prints with which he had peaked the JPL photo expert's curiosity. *In truth, Nathan felt used by Stevens,* and even told author Gary Kinder this when they spoke seven years after Nathan's interview with me.[52] Gary Kinder has tried to rationalize Stevens's odd behavior by quoting Lee Elders, who blames *Meier* for not knowing what generation of negatives he really possesses.

The explanation offered by Kinder via Elders is that due to "so much theft of the original material,"[53] they had the negatives but did not know what generation they were.

Such "explanations," while convenient, hardly account for all of the facts as they are known.

Now that we have presented the different "analyses" Meier's proponents cite, let us conduct a genuine and objective study of Meier's "UFO" photographs and see what there is to discover.

Unlike the conclusions presented by the pro-Meier groups, the facts covered in these next two chapters can be *independently verified by anyone.* If you have access to a personal computer, you can perform the very same computer enhancements mentioned in this book.

Notes

1. Wendelle C. Stevens, "Kal Korff and the Billy Meier 'Hoax'—A Response, Part 2," *MUFON UFO Journal* (November 1981): 14.

2. *UFO . . . Contact from the Pleiades, Volume I,* 1st ed. (Phoenix, Ariz.: Genesis III Productions, Ltd., 1979), p. 71.

3. Stevens, "Kal Korff and the Billy Meier 'Hoax,'" p. 11. *See also* Jim Dilettoso, tape-recorded personal interview for the record with Kal K. Korff, Al Reed, and Barbara Reed at the offices of Publication Professionals, Sunnyvale, California, September 6, 1980. *Also* Elisabeth Gruber, personal interview with Kal Korff and Tina Layton, August 18, 1991, at the Semjase Silver Star Center, Hinterschmidrüti, Switzerland. *Also* Simone, personal interview with Kal Korff and Tina Layton, August 18, 1991, at the Semjase Silver Star Center, Hinterschmidrüti, Switzerland. *Also* Bernadette Brand, personal interview with Kal Korff and Tina Layton, August 18, 1991, at the Semjase Silver Star Center, Hinterschmidrüti, Switzerland. *Also* Glen Hoyen, personal interview with Kal K. Korff, San Mateo, California, October 31, 1993.

4. Stevens, "Kal Korff and the Billy Meier 'Hoax,'" p. 11.

5. *UFO . . . Contact from the Pleiades, Volume I*, 1st ed., pp. 52–54, 71. *See also UFO . . . Contact from the Pleiades, Volume II* (Phoenix, Ariz.: Genesis III Productions, Ltd., 1983), pp. 60–63. *See also* Guido Moosbrugger, *. . . und sie fliegen doch! UFOs: Die größte Herausforderung des 20 Jahrhunderts* (München, Germany: Michael Hesemann Verlag, 1991), pp. 276–77. *See also* Gary Kinder, *Light Years: An Investigation into the Extraterrestrial Experiences of Eduard Meier* (New York: Atlantic Monthly Press, 1987), back cover, hard-cover edition. Also Jim Dilettoso, tape-recorded personal interview for the record with Kal K. Korff, Al Reed, and Barbara Reed.

6. Jim Dilettoso, tape-recorded personal interview for the record with Kal K. Korff, Al Reed, and Barbara Reed. *See also* Wendelle Stevens, *UFO . . . Contact from the Pleiades: A Supplementary Investigation Report—The Report of an Ongoing Contact* (Tucson, Ariz.: Wendelle Stevens, 1989), pp. 546–47.

7. Wendelle Stevens, "Memorandum—Northern Europe UFO Case" (Tucson, Ariz.: Wendelle Stevens, 1987), pp. 1–6.

8. Jim Dilettoso, tape-recorded personal interview for the record with Kal K. Korff, Al Reed, and Barbara Reed, September 6, 1980.

9. *UFO . . . Contact from the Pleiades, Volume I*, 1st ed., pp. 52–54, 71. *See also, UFO . . . Contact from the Pleiades, Volume I*, rev. ed., pp. 52–54. *See also, UFO . . . Contact from the Pleiades, Volume II*, pp. 60–63.

10. Kal K. Korff, *The Meier Incident—The Most Infamous Hoax in UFOlogy* (Prescott, Ariz.: Townescribe Press, 1981), pp. 2–3.

11. Ibid.

12. Ibid.

13. *UFO . . . Contact from the Pleiades, Volume II*, p. 1.

14. Ken Dinwiddie, personal interview with Roma Donovan, "Nick," Bill Moore, and Kal Korff, Palo Alto, California, June 14, 1981.

15. Ibid.

16. Jim Dilettoso, *Confidential Transcript of Communication Log, 1978–1982*, p. 3. UFOComp Computer Archives, File Number UFO1212.

17. Ibid.

18. Ibid.

19. Kinder, *Light Years*, pp. 149–50.

20. Neil Davis, *Preliminary Photo Analysis*, Design Technology, Poway, California: March 13, 1978, p. 2.

21. Ibid.

22. Jim Dilettoso, *Confidential Transcript of Communication Log*, p. 4.

23. Ibid., p. 5.

24. Ibid., p. 6.

25. Kinder, *Light Years*, p. 235.

26. Ibid., p. 236.

27. Ibid.

28. Ibid.

29. Ibid., p. 242.

30. Ibid., pp. 243–44.

31. Ibid., pp. 244–46.

32. Ibid., p. 245.

33. Ibid.

34. Ibid.

35. Ibid., p. 244.

36. Ibid.

37. Ibid.

38. Kal Korff, personal conversation with Mr. Al Reed, technical illustrator and president of Publication Professionals, Sunnyvale, California, September 7, 1980.

39. Analysis of Meier's UFO photographs by the UltraMatrix special effects corporation and Underground Video, Los Angeles, California, 1993. *See also* Duplication of Meier's UFO photographs and motion picture films in a series of experiments conducted by TotalResearch: July 1991 through September 1994 in Switzerland and the United States. Featured in the documentary *EXPOSED: The Billy Meier UFO Hoax* by Underground Video.

40. Kinder, *Light Years*, p. 243.

41. Analysis of Meier's UFO photographs by the UltraMatrix special effects corporation and Underground Video, Los Angeles, California, 1993.

42. Author's observation after watching the film credits on a rental video version of Stanley Kubrick's *2001: A Space Odyssey.*

43. Kinder, *Light Years*, pp. 236–37.

44. Ibid., p. 238.

45. Ibid., pp. 237–38.

46. Jim Dilettoso, *Confidential Transcript of Communication Log*, p. 3.

47. Ibid.

48. Jim Dilettoso, tape-recorded personal interview for the record with Kal K. Korff, Al Reed, and Barbara Reed, September 6, 1980.

49. Dr. Bob Nathan, personal interview with Kal K. Korff via telephone, Pasadena, California, September 7, 1980.

50. Ibid.

51. Kinder, *Light Years*, pp. 220–21.

52. Ibid., p. 221.

53. Ibid.

4

Conclusive Analyses of Billy Meier's "UFO" Photographs

Korff's statement on camera optics (in regards to Billy Meier's camera) fails to conform to the facts, as anyone with a basic knowledge of photography will show.

Wendelle Stevens[1]

The statement (regarding the optics of Meier's camera) which you (Kal) have called to my attention is essentially correct.

Dr. Bruce Maccabee[2]

Since most of the Meier case rests on the purported authenticity of his hundreds of UFO photographs, the next step in our investigation calls for an independent analysis of these pictures. It became evident that analyzing Meier's photos wasn't going to be easy. Wendelle Stevens and Jim Dilettoso long ago refused to agree to a neutral, impartial evaluation,[3] and my efforts to solicit replies directly from Billy Meier proved unsuccessful. Thus, if a *real* analysis were to be conducted it would have to be done without the assistance of the two main principles involved. While this proved to be inconvenient, the task was not impossible to accomplish.

As noted previously, while it is unfortunate that no original negatives are available for study, it is still possible to analyze Meier's UFO photographs and determine some specifics about their alleged authenticity, up to a certain point. This is due to three very important reasons:

1. Unlike most UFO cases, in the Meier contacts we are told the *precise measurements of the craft!* The luxury of *knowing* this information *in advance* is an *exception* in UFO cases. We can therefore use this data, and factor into our equations for analysis, the figure of "seven meters" (22.75 feet) as stated by Jim Dilettoso, the Elders, Elisabeth Gruber, Billy Meier, Wendelle Stevens, and others, since this is the alleged diameter of Semjase's spaceship in most of Meier's pictures.[4]

2. Since both Meier's camera lens and its aperture were jammed at a fixed focal length, just "$1/32$ of an inch" short of the "infinity" setting,[5] this is another numerical constant that can be included in our equations and analyses of Meier's UFO photographs.

3. At many of the contact sites where pictures were taken, the dimensions have either been stated by Meier, who often says he took his own measurements, or have been independently checked by various investigators (including this author) over the years. Thus, these "control" measurement figures can also be factored in.

Photo Analysis Limitations and Study Parameters

As stated previously, I was given for study and analysis the original photo-binder that contains the actual UFO pictures Billy Meier gave to Hans Jacob when the two men were still friends. Since the photographs Billy Meier supplied to Jacob were first- and second-generation prints made from the *original negatives by Meier himself,* the quality and clarity of the

UFO images which appear in the Jacob versions are unsurpassed by any other copies known to exist.[6] This is significant, since the Jacob versions are at least one generation *closer* to Meier's original negatives than anything either Wendelle Stevens or Genesis III claim to possess.[7]

In our study of the Billy Meier UFO photographic evidence, in addition to the firsthand material brought back from Switzerland, all of the Meier literature was consulted.

For purposes of double-checking the photographic dates, times, and locations, the *Verzeichnis Authentischer Farb-Photos* (Catalog: Authentic Color Photos) book I purchased directly from the Semjase Silver Star Center has been used as the "definitive" source, since it is authored by Billy Meier himself.[8] Thus, whenever there were contradictions in the accounts between the dates, locations, and times listed in Genesis III's, Kinder's, Moosbrugger's, Stevens's, and other pro-Meier books (which happened often as will be shown), Billy Meier's *Verzeichnis* was used to resolve them.

Although there are a few constant numerical factors such as object size, camera focal length, and aperture setting that we can test for in our analysis of Meier's UFO photographs, our study is hampered scientifically by the fact that there are *no original negatives* available for examination. Using the *best generation copies available,* the approach to analyzing each Meier UFO photograph was to take the account of the experience as reported by Billy Meier himself, and compare the claims to whatever details can be quantified in the pictures.

The analyses of the Meier UFO photographs presented throughout this book are excerpted from various studies I have conducted since 1979. During this sixteen-year period, a wide variety of equipment was utilized, which included everything from Apple Macintosh® personal computers and Apple Macintosh PowerPCs®, to expensive NASA photo digitizing equipment manufactured by such industry heavyweights as IBM, Itek, Perceptics, Quantex, and Spatial Data Systems.

For the purpose of allowing readers to independently verify all aspects of my analyses, both industry-standard commercial software and consumer-standard personal computers have been used whenever possible.

The Meier photographic evidence examined in this book has been divided into two primary groups, Meier's "UFO" pictures and Meier's "time-travel" photos allegedly taken in outer space and on other planets. The analyses presented represent the most comprehensive and objective study of Billy Meier's pictorial evidence to date, and is published here for the first time ever.

We begin our examination of Billy Meier's core UFO photographs in chronological order, starting with the pictures he claims he took on his very first "contact" with Semjase in January 1975.

Billy Meier's Camera and the Laws of Optics

According to both the *Verzeichnis*[9] and Stevens's *Preliminary Investigation Report*,[10] Meier used an Olympus model 35mm ECR camera with a 42mm length lens that was jammed "maybe $\frac{1}{32}$ of an inch" short of the "infinity" setting.[11]

In camera optical physics, because of the depth-of-field characteristics inherent in *all* camera optics, a photograph of any object located between *five and six feet* from the camera and "infinity" (which in camera terminology means anything *over 50 feet* away) will be in *perfect focus* in any normal daylight exposure. Only objects *closer* than the five- or six-foot depth-of-field limit will appear fuzzy and out-of-focus, with the "fuzziness" *increasing* the *closer* the object is to the camera.[12] In simple terms, this means (with the exception of the five- to six-foot "focus window" already mentioned) that the *further* the object was from Billy Meier's camera, the *sharper* in focus it would be. Conversely, the *closer* the object to Meier's camera, the more *out-of-focus* it would appear.

A final consideration when analyzing Billy Meier's UFO pictures is the fact that the aperture of his camera was set for F2.8, which is the *narrowest* depth-of-field setting his lens had.[13] This means that the issues of relative focus, and whether or not objects in his photographs appear to be blurred or sharp, are especially important.

When one accounts for *all* of the optical limitations and unique properties of Meier's camera, which are literally a constant in each picture taken, and also factor in the circumstances under which Meier claims he took his photos, analysis of his UFO pictures becomes a relatively easy task. Indeed, much can be learned about the true nature of Billy Meier's UFO photographs by applying the use of simple mathematics and basic computer enhancement algorithms and formulas, as will be shown.

Let's begin our analyses of Billy Meier's UFO photographs and see what we can learn about them.

UFO Photos from Billy Meier's First Contact

Date(s):   January 28, 1975[14]

Time(s):   1400 hrs. according to Billy Meier[15]
                    1415 hrs. according to Stevens[16]

Location(s):   Frecht Nature Preserve, Switzerland[17]

Meier Photo
Number(s):   1, 3, 28, 29, 30, 37[18]

Photographer(s): Eduard "Billy" Meier[19]

Background Details

On January 28, 1975, Billy Meier claims that he was "tele-pathically led" by Semjase to a remote spot just inside the Frecht Nature Preserve, a few miles from the outskirts of his hometown of Hinwill.[20]

While stopping for a moment to view a large moving truck, Meier heard a "humming-whining" sound. He started looking around to ascertain the source of the noise when suddenly he saw a strange object descend from the sky. As the craft came shooting downward, it flew along the tops of the trees until it stopped to hover some 1,137 feet away, or roughly 379 yards.[21]

Quickly aiming his camera, Meier claims he snapped his first picture when the UFO was "150 meters" or 162.5 feet above the ground, and also 162.5 feet away.[22] Immediately after shooting his first picture, the UFO purportedly took off at a high rate of speed toward the west.

Within two minutes the UFO returned a second time, stopping to hover some 44 meters or 143 feet away, according to Billy Meier's own measurements. The object also hovered 100 meters or 325 feet above the truck.[23] It was when the UFO was stationed in this position, hovering 325 feet above the truck and 143 feet in the distance, that Billy Meier claims he took his second photograph of the Pleiadian ship, at 1418 hours.[24]

Although Billy Meier would take a total of seven UFO pictures on the day of his first alleged "contact" with Semjase,[25] a simple examination of just three of these photographs reveals that they pose a problem.

Analysis of the Frecht Nature Photographs

• Billy Meier claims that Semjase's spacecraft is 7 meters or 22.75 feet in diameter.[26] Since this is a constant dimension for many of his pictures, it is this claim of "7 meters" that establishes conclusively that the Frecht Nature photos are a hoax. For example, in Meier's first two pictures taken at the Frecht Nature Preserve, the "UFO" is *in focus*, yet the objects in the *background*, which are *several hundred feet further in the distance, are out-of-focus!* This obvious fact destroys Meier's claim that the "UFO" visible in his Frecht Nature series of pictures is a large object "22.75 feet" in diameter. It also proves that the focus of Meier's camera was set for *close range*, and not jammed just short of the "infinity" setting as claimed, otherwise the distant trees and the truck in the background would be in better focus than they are, since their distance is more than fifty feet away.

• The second photo in Meier's Frecht Nature series is especially damaging because Meier and his proponents claim that *both* the UFO and the large truck are supposed to be "44 meters away" (143 feet) in the distance, and that Semjase's ship is hovering 325 feet above the truck.[27]

Billy Meier swears that he later measured the distance from where he stood to this truck, so his "44 meters" figure is not merely speculation.[28] If this is true, then why is the "UFO" visible in Meier's second Frecht Nature Preserve photo in *perfect focus*, yet the large truck in the *same picture* which is supposedly the *same distance away,* is *blurred* and *out-of-focus!?*

This does not make any sense if *both* the UFO and the truck are 143 feet from Meier as claimed. Indeed, if the UFO and the truck were both the same distance away, they would be in *equal focus.*

The only logical explanation for this focus discrepancy visible in Billy Meier's Frecht Nature photos is that the "UFO" shown in these pictures is a *small* object positioned *close* to the camera.

• If the lens on Billy Meier's camera were truly "jammed just short of infinity" as claimed, and the aperture setting was F2.8, both the UFO and the large truck would be in *perfect focus*, which is *not* the case when one examines Meier's second Frecht Nature picture.

To test these facts yourself, find a large truck, mobile home, moving van, or anything that is 22.75 feet in length (the reported size of Semjase's spacecraft).

Park this vehicle next to a house, or any other large object, and walk 143 feet away from both objects in any direction.

After you adjust your lens and aperture settings on your 35mm camera so that they match those of Billy Meier's, take a picture of both objects and pay close attention to how their focus appears.

Their focus will be *identical,* no matter which angle you take your picture from. The reason is simple, the two objects are the *same* distance away from the camera.

• Similar problems also exist with the focus of the background trees and imagery visible in all of Meier's Frecht Nature photos: these objects are out-of-focus, yet the "UFO" is always in focus.

Conclusion

Meier's photographs taken at the Frecht Nature Preserve are of a small model positioned close to the camera.

Fig. 22. Of the seven "UFO" photos Meier took at the Frecht Nature Preserve on January 28, 1975, six have been published by Billy Meier, Guido Moosbrugger, and Wendelle Stevens. Curiously, the only photo *not* to be published of the series (until now) is this one! Officially listed in the *Verzeichnis* as Meier photo number 30 (p. 5), the author obtained this rare photo on August 18, 1991, while traveling undercover at the Semjase Silver Star Center in Hinterschmidrüti. Guido Moosbrugger's wife, Elisabeth Gruber, gave me this photograph. According to both Gruber and the *Verzeichnis,* this photo purportedly shows Semjase's "spaceship" as it "Wegflug," or is flying away from Meier. The fact that the "UFO" is *below* the treeline allows one to calculate true object size and distance for this image. As can be easily proven, the object is a *small model* positioned close to the camera. If the "UFO" were not below the treeline, there would be no definitive point of reference usable to prove its true size and distance. (Photo courtesy: Elisabeth Gruber.)

Fig. 23. This is the second photograph Billy Meier took of Semjase's "spacecraft." In truth, the "UFO" shown in this picture is a small object close to the camera and is not a large "flying saucer" 22.75 feet in diameter, contrary to what Meier and his supporters claim. The fact that the large truck in the background is out-of-focus, and the "UFO" is in perfect focus, proves this. (Photo courtesy: Claudia and Margrit Jacob.)

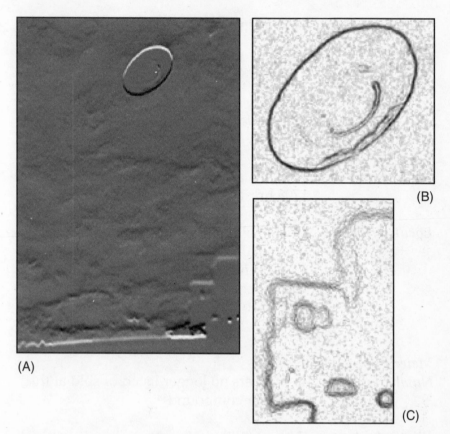

(A)

(B)

(C)

Fig. 24. (*A*) Computer edge enhancement shows how much the truck is out-of-focus compared to the "UFO." This is conclusive evidence that the disc-shaped image shown here is a *small object positioned close to the camera.* If the "UFO" really was hovering above the truck, as Meier and his supporters claim, then *both* the truck and object would be in *equal focus!* The fact that *only* the "UFO" is in focus suggests it's a small model positioned near the camera. (*B* and *C*) Enlargements showing the edges of both the "UFO" and the truck, using a Find Edges computer algorithm. The *farther* the object is from the camera, the *less defined* its edges are, as in the case of the truck. Conversely, the *closer* the object is to the camera, the *sharper* its edges are, as is the case with the "UFO." The discrepancies in the sharpness of the edges of these two objects prove conclusively that they are not the same distance away, and that the "UFO" is not hovering above the truck, contrary to what Billy Meier and his supporters would have everyone believe.

"Smoking Guns"—The Unter-Balm Photographs

Date(s):   February 27, 1975, according to
                   Guido Moosbrugger[29]
                   February 28, 1975, according to the
                   Verzeichnis[30]
                   February 29, 1975, according to Stevens[31]

Time(s):   1608 hrs. according to Billy Meier[32]
                   1708 hrs. according to Wendelle Stevens[33]

Location(s):   Unter-Balm, in the hills above Wetzikon[34]
                   Unter-Balm, according to Wendelle
                   Stevens[35]
                   Jakobsberg-Allenberg, according to
                   Guido Moosbrugger[36]

Meier Photo
Number(s):   41[37] Others no longer listed or sold at the
                   Meier compound[38]

Photographer(s): Eduard "Billy" Meier[39]

Background Details

Billy Meier claims that he was invited for a ride on board the
Pleiadian spacecraft on February 28, 1975,[40] and that he took
his Unter-Balm photograph number 41 while on board Semjase's spaceship.[41] Moreover, the "UFO" shown in his photograph is supposed to be another Pleiadian craft piloted by an
alien named "Quetzal," who is allegedly flying *alongside* Semjase's craft on the right side.[42]

    Is there credible evidence that Billy Meier actually flew

inside a Pleiadian spacecraft and photographed another one flying alongside him?

An objective study of these pictures reveals some intriguing issues, especially when visiting the actual location in Switzerland where they were taken.

Analysis of the Unter-Balm "UFO" Photographs

• Billy Meier claims that he took his photo of "Quetzal's" ship (see fig. 25) while aboard Semjase's spacecraft and aiming his camera through the ship's *porthole*.[43] This is the first obvious problem regarding the alleged authenticity of both Billy Meier's account and this particular picture. The "problem" rests with the simple fact that the orientation of the "portholes" on Semjase's spaceship (in all of Meier's other UFO photographs) are *vertical*, whereas the orientation of Billy Meier's Unter-Balm photograph number 41 is *horizontal*. This fact makes it highly unlikely, if not impossible, for Meier to have shot his picture through "Semjase's porthole" as he claims, since the orientation of the photograph is incorrect.

• Billy Meier claims that he was flying at "1,000 feet above the ground"[44] in Semjase's ship when he took his Unter-Balm photograph number 41. Hence, the "UFO" (Quetzal's craft in this case) is supposed to be flying alongside him at the same altitude.

On September 2, 1991, while Tina Layton and I were in Switzerland, we found the *exact location* where Meier took his famous picture at Unter-Balm.

When we stood in the *exact same spot* Billy Meier did when he made his photo, we discovered that the location is on top of a *small hill* that overlooks the roofs of several houses! The elevation of this hill is some *20 feet in the air* and not "1,000 feet" as claimed by Meier and his proponents.

• Figures 26–29 show pictures I took at the *exact spot* Billy Meier snapped his Unter-Balm photo number 41. In addition to *disproving* Meier's exaggerated "1,000 feet" altitude claim, figures 28 and 29 show Tina Layton illustrating how Meier staged and framed this photo for his camera.*

• The method Meier used to create his Unter-Balm photo was simple: a model was held out in *front* of his camera and the shot was taken in the *direction of the lake.* Because of the hill's *height* at the location where Meier stood, by shooting toward Lake Pfäffikon Meier was able to create the *false illusion* of "height" that is visible in his photograph.†

• A curious side note about this photo can be found in Moosbrugger's book. Although he includes this Unter-Balm picture in his book and touts it as genuine, Moosbrugger lists the *wrong location* where the picture was made, claiming that it was taken at *Jakobsberg-Allenberg.*[45]

Moosbrugger's *mislabeling* of the location of the Unter-Balm picture is inexcusable, since he is *quite familiar with the area.*[46] Those individuals who read his book and visit Switzerland hoping to independently research Meier's claims will be unable to do so.

Conclusion

Billy Meier's Unter-Balm photograph number 41 can only be a small model held in front of the camera and shot in the direction of Lake Pfäffikon, toward the west (see figure 28).

---

*Both Moosbrugger and Stevens claim in their books that Meier was "1,000 feet" in the air when he took his Unter-Balm photo number 41.

†The video footage Tina and I recorded of our visit to the Unter-Balm site and how we successfully recreated Billy Meier's photo number 41 are featured in the video documentary *EXPOSED: The Billy Meier UFO Hoax!*, available from Underground Video or this author in care of Prometheus Books.

Fig. 25. Billy Meier's Unter-Balm "UFO" photo number 41. Meier claims he was flying in Semjase's ship about "1,000 feet in the air" when he took this picture, allegedly shooting through the ship's porthole. (Photo courtesy: Margrit and Claudia Jacob.)

Fig. 26. Photo by the author showing *exact* Unter-Balm location where Meier stood when creating his picture, disproving Meier's claim that he was "1,000 feet in the air." In truth, this location is a small, 20-foot-high hill overlooking the roof of a house!

Fig. 27. Author's picture of the slope and edge of the small hill where Billy Meier stood and held his small "UFO" model aloft so that he could photograph it.

Fig. 28. Tina Layton holding one of the small "UFO" models we took with us to Switzerland. Here Tina demonstrates how Meier produced his Unter-Balm photo number 41.

Author's Photo

Meier's Photo

Author's Photo

Fig. 29. By standing on the hill and shooting his "UFO" model up close, deliberately cutting off the *bottom* of the object with his camera, Meier created the *illusion* that "Quetzal's spaceship" was flying above the lake! These recreations taken at the same location by the author illustrate the methods Billy Meier used to create his Unter-Balm "UFO" photographs. (Middle photo courtesy: Margrit and Claudia Jacob.

Billy Meier's Other "Unter-Balm UFO" Pictures

Background Details

Before Billy Meier allegedly "hopped on board" Semjase's spaceship for his ride, he claims that as he walked toward the craft he took several photographs.[47]

Analysis of Billy Meier's "Landed UFO"
Unter-Balm Photographs

- The size of the "UFO" pictured in all four known photos from Billy Meier's Unter-Balm "landed" sequence is supposed to be seven meters or 22.75 feet in diameter.[48] If this is true, and Meier's camera is jammed just short of the infinity setting, then *why* are the large tree forests and mountains in the background *out-of-focus*? It is obvious that Meier had to be more than thirty or even fifty feet from the "UFO" in order to get it framed in his pictures. In reality, Billy Meier's pictures are of small models instead, which he shot by focusing his camera on them. This caused the real distant trees and mountains in the background of his photos to be out-of-focus due to their distance!

- A careful examination of the different surface structures visible on this alleged "spaceship" reveals that its hull is *bent and warped,* and is literally coming apart at its seams! Such observable characteristics are conducive to a small model rather than a bonafide extraterrestrial craft.

- A visit to the location at Unter-Balm reveals that there are no terrain features or trees which match those visible in the background of Meier's "landed UFO" photos. This is conclusive proof that some of these pictures were *not* taken at Unter-Balm, contrary to what has been claimed.

- In addition to the background scenery discrepancies

Tina and I noticed, our visit to the Unter-Balm location also established that the site was surrounded by too many trees, is far too narrow, and is oriented in such a way that there is not enough open space there to land a large, "seven meter" spaceship as claimed.

Conclusion

Billy Meier's "landed UFO" pictures are hoaxes. They were fabricated by photographing small models positioned close to the camera. They are good examples of what is known as "table-top" photography.

Fig. 30. One of Billy Meier's photos which he claims shows Semjase's spaceship "landed" on the ground before he boarded it. The fact that the trees in the background are out-of-focus, whereas the "UFO" is in focus, proves once again that it is a small model close to the camera. (Photo courtesy: Margrit and Claudia Jacob.)

How to Fake "Landed UFO" Photos

If Billy Meier's "landed UFO" photos are so easy to duplicate as I am claiming, then how does one go about doing it successfully? Simply follow these seven easy steps:

1. Take two dinner plates and invert them one on top of the other.

2. Next, take a cereal bowl and place it upside down on top of the inverted upper plate. The cereal or soup bowl on top represents the "dome" of the ship for our experiment.

3. Take the stacked dinnerware "UFO" and place it on top of a table or other flat surface where there are trees or other objects visible in the background that are at least fifty or more feet away. This is the minimum distance necessary for any background object(s), in order for our experiment to work properly. The forests in Meier's four "landed UFO" photos, for example, are more than fifty feet away, so any distance this far or greater will suffice.

4. With a normal 35mm camera, adjust the lens so that it is set just short of the "infinity" setting by $\frac{1}{32}$ of an inch.

5. Make sure the aperture on the lens* is set for F2.8, the *narrowest* depth-of-field setting possible, just as on Billy Meier's camera.

---

*The aperture setting determines how much light is allowed to travel through the lens. The ability to control this factor can greatly influence the various planes of focus that affect the clarity of the picture.

6. After focusing in on the small plate/cereal bowl model, back up as far as you can so that the "UFO" takes up about *one-half* of the *horizontal* width of the picture, then center the image in your viewfinder.

7. Finally, if needed, kneel down so that your line of sight is *even* with the dinnerware model and that of any background trees or mountains. Notice that as you keep your distance from the UFO model so that it stays in focus, the background objects remain out-of-focus!

Figures 35–36 show the different results one can get by placing a small model on top of a fence or table-top and taking photographs using various "F stop" settings on your camera. By changing the aperture, background objects can be brought in and out of focus to achieve virtually any desired result.

If Meier had been a little more clever when he snapped his Unter-Balm pictures, he would have adjusted the aperture setting accordingly so that the blurry trees and mountains in the background would not be out-of-focus. Instead, Meier's ignorance of basic photography comes back to discredit him and his proponents.

Figs. 31 and 32. (*Above*) This "landed UFO" photo of Meier's has never been published before. It appears in the Jacob photo-binder. Although purportedly taken at Unter-Balm, analysis of the background scenery reveals that the picture was taken at a different location. (*Below*) Another of Billy Meier's many "landed UFO" photos and this author's recreation of them using a dinnerplate-sized model sitting on top of a table and some newspapers. (Top photo courtesy: Margrit and Claudia Jacob.)

Meier's Photo

Author's Photo

Fig. 33. Enlargement of Billy Meier's "landed UFO." Notice how the *left* side of this "spaceship's" hull is *warped and bent!* Also, the bottom of the craft's dome is not centered, as the arrows indicate. (Photos courtesy: Claudia and Margrit Jacob.)

Fig. 34. (*Below*) Illustration by the author showing what Billy Meier's "landed UFO" is likely made from, contrary to what his supporters claim.

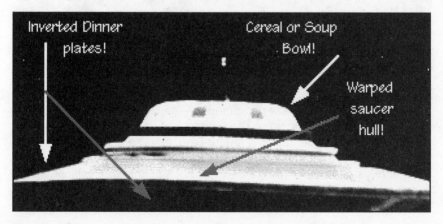

Figs. 35 and 36. (*Top*) I put a transparent "UFO" model on the Jacobs' fence in order to make these photographs. Notice how similar they look to Meier's "landed UFO" pictures. The background in the top photo is out-of-focus because the aperture was set for F2.8, just like on Meier's camera. (*Bottom*) By changing the aperture setting to achieve a greater depth-of-field, background objects in the distance such as this tree will come into focus, just as if this "spaceship" were a real, large object.

Fuchsbüel am Hofhalden

Date(s):   February 27, 1975[49]

Time(s):   1652 hrs.[50]

Location(s):   Fuchsbüel am Hofhalden[51]

Meier Photo   27[52] (Not published in any Meier book
Number(s):   until now)

Photographer(s):   Eduard "Billy" Meier[53]

Background Details

According to Billy Meier, Semjase flew her spaceship during this particular contact for the specific purpose of allowing him to take clear UFO photographs.[54] And true to his word, the Fuchsbüel photos are among the clearest he has ever produced.

I use the word "produced" because it can be easily proven once again that Meier's Fuchsbüel photo number 27 also has problems.

Analysis of Fuchsbüel Photo Number 27

• The hill and trees in the background of Meier's Fuchsbüel picture are *out-of-focus*, whereas the UFO visible in the photo is *sharp* and *perfectly clear*. This is impossible (for reasons already discussed) if the "Pleiadian spaceship" really were a large object 22.75 feet in diameter as Meier and his supporters claim. Given the lens settings on Billy Meier's camera, objects *greater than fifty feet away* should be in *perfect focus*. In Meier's Fuchsbüel photo number 27, however, only the "UFO" is in perfect focus while the background mountains that are *several hundred feet in the distance* are out-of-focus! This discrepancy proves that the "UFO" object in Meier's photo is a *small* one, and *not* a large "Pleiadian spacecraft."

• Tina Layton and I visited the *exact spot* where Meier took this particular picture, no less than six separate times. As our on-site investigation proves (see fig. 39), the "UFO" had to be a small model in order to fit within the frame of Meier's photograph, especially when considering the focus inconsistencies.

• Enlargements of the "spaceship's" surface detail reveal cosmetic and structural flaws consistent with the object being a small, hand-made model, not an advanced alien "spacecraft."

Conclusion

Billy Meier's Fuchsbüel photo number 27 shows a *small model* held aloft on top of a hill, with the camera *focused* on the object. This caused the background trees to be out-of-focus, proving conclusively that the "UFO" is a small model. If Meier's picture really showed a large spaceship, both the craft and background scenery would be *in focus.*

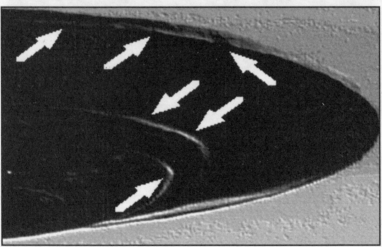

Figs. 37 and 38. (*Top*) Billy Meier's Fuchsbüel photo number 27, which supposedly shows "Semjase's seven meters (22.75 feet) spaceship." In truth, this picture shows a *small model close to the camera,* as is evident since the background foothills are out-of-focus! (*Bottom*) Computer enhancement by the author shows some of the surface flaws of Meier's UFO model. (Top photo courtesy: Margrit and Claudia Jacob.)

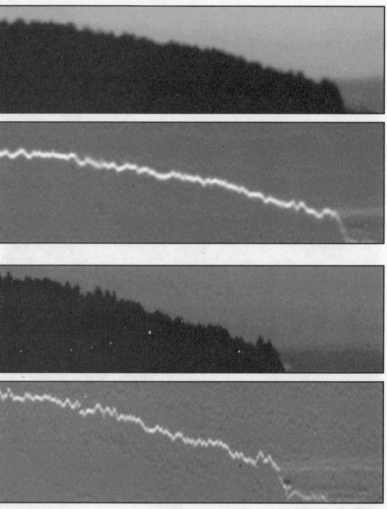

Fig. 39. The top two photos show an enlargement and a computer edge enhancement of the background trees in Meier's Fuchsbüel photo number 27, revealing their level of focus. The two bottom photos show an enlargement and a computer edge enhancement of my *own* picture taken in Switzerland at the *same* Fuchsbüel site, using the *same* camera settings Meier claims he used. Notice how much *sharper* my picture is, proof that if Meier's photos really did show a large spaceship, his background scenery would have been in better focus! (Top photos courtesy: Margrit and Claudia Jacob.)

Billy Meier's Jakobsberg-Allenberg Double Exposures

Date(s):   April 20, 1975[55]

Time(s):   1000 hrs.[56]

Location(s):   Jakobsberg-Allenberg, according to the
                        Verzeichnis[57]
                    Ravensbuhl, according to Stevens[58]
                    Jakobsberg-Allenberg, according to
                        Guido Moosbrugger[59]

Meier Photo   100, 101, 139, 140–47[60]
Number(s):

Photographer(s): Eduard "Billy" Meier[61]

Background Details

According to Wendelle Stevens, Billy Meier received a telepathic message from Semjase, telling him that he was going to
have another "contact." Meier then invited a group of his
friends to come along and witness the event for themselves,
and see that Semjase existed.[62]

   One of these invited "friends" was Hans Jacob,[63] who also
brought with him two of his daughters, Claudia and Cornelia,[64] to observe Billy Meier's "12th contact"[65] with Semjase.[66]

   On page 84 of Stevens's *Supplementary Investigation Report*
is the following account of how Billy Meier obtained what
Wendelle Stevens mistakenly calls the "Ravensbuhl" photos:

> The twelfth contact occurred at 3:11 in the afternoon of 20 April
> 1975, only a half hour after a photo demonstration. Meier had
> taken pictures of some friends at this site a little earlier in the day,

and now in the excitement of another flight demonstration and trying to get as many photos as possible, it appears that he had inadvertently reloaded the film with the pictures of spacecraft on top of the others in what appears to be a series of double exposures. When Meier got the developed slides back and had them printed, he was sure that the Pleiadians had posed their ship over the heads of the people, but in a computer we [Stevens and his associates] were able to separate the two pictures into their separate parts and they look to be double exposures. If they were double exposures, the film frames then matched together quite closely, which seems to be something very difficult to do, if not purely by accident. Semjase asked for the slides for study and did not bring them back. She criticized Meier for trying to get people and the spacecraft in the same picture though, saying that such photos may not be good for certain of those concerned.

Now that we have Wendelle Stevens's version of how Meier allegedly obtained his "Ravensbuhl" photos, let's compare his account to that of Claudia Jacob, who was present at the time of Meier's supposed contact, and remembered the incident.

This is the firsthand account Claudia Jacob told Tina and me on August 19, 1991, at her mother's home in Wetzikon:

CJ: I remember that Billy invited us to meet Semjase one day. So I went with my father. There was a group of us, and we stood for hours waiting and standing around. We never saw a ship. Nothing happened. And then Billy comes by days later with his film and shows us the pictures and says that Semjase was there above us all the time and that we just did not see her! (Laughing) So when this happened, my father was doubting about Billy Meier and what he was telling us. We were standing there. I remember there was no ship. And what does Meier say?

KK: Guido [Moosbrugger's] wife told us that the UFO was there the whole time and that you just didn't see it.

They're passing off the pictures as if they're photos of a real UFO, that's why I bought some of them as evidence so that you can see what they are saying.

CJ: (Shocked) No!

KK: Yes.

CJ: (Laughing) Why do people believe these things?

KK: I don't know.

CJ: But how can they sell these when they are so obvious fakes?

When I interviewed Cornelia Jacob about the incident, she *confirmed* her sister's story, stating that she stood for nearly an hour with her father and sister waiting for "Semjase's ship" to appear, but it never did.[67] Moreover, Margrit Jacob recalled how her husband and two daughters had returned from the supposed "contact," reporting how nothing had happened. They felt they had wasted their time.[68]

Analysis of the Jakobsberg–Allenberg Photographs

• A simple *visual examination* of Billy Meier's entire Jakobsberg-Allenberg sequence reveals that they are *deliberate, methodical double exposures.* The evidence for this exists in how all of the ten frames *line up with one another* in each of the double-exposed images. Such precision by pure coincidence is highly unlikely.

In other words, if Meier had *innocently* threaded the *same* roll of film *twice* through his camera (thereby *accidentally* double-exposing each frame, as Stevens would have us believe), then we should expect the *alignment* of the two resulting image frames to be slightly askew, since the odds of starting a re-loaded roll of film twice in the same exact spot are very small.

Yet when we study Meier's ten double-exposed Jakobs-berg-Allenberg images, we see ten perfectly aligned frames, indicating a precision matching of both the "UFO" and the people standing in the foreground that is not likely the result of pure coincidence.

• Another factor that argues against the authenticity of both Billy Meier's account and these particular photos is the curious fact that *only* in those pictures Billy Meier personally took at the Jakobsberg-Allenberg site do we see the double-exposed background scenery and "UFO" images. Conversely, in all other pictures on the roll of film not taken by Billy Meier (those made by Hans Jacob in this instance), neither the "UFO" nor the double-exposed background scenery images are visible!

Since Jacob and Meier were the *only two photographers* tak-ing pictures that day,[69] it is very suspicious that *only* in those photos taken *by Meier* do we see the supposed UFO.

Conclusion

The ten photos Wendelle Stevens mislabels as having been taken at "Ravensbuhl" were really made at Jakobsberg-Allen-berg. The ten images in the series which purport to show "Semjase's spaceship" are *deliberate double exposures*. Meier's "account" and Stevens's "explanation" concerning these pho-tos contradicts all available evidence both by witnesses who were actually present at the time of filming as well as the images visible in the pictures themselves.

A valid question to ask Billy Meier's supporters is: If Sem-jase's "spaceship" was *really* present that day, then *why* did Billy Meier feel the need to make deliberate double exposures and fake photographs of the alleged event?

Fig. 40. One of the ten deliberately double-exposed photos made by Billy Meier. The man in the trenchcoat is Hans Jacob, shown with two of his daughters, Cornelia and Claudia. The people are standing in this field at Meier's instructions, and are waiting for "Semjase's spaceship" to appear so that they may observe it. Meier promised this group, most of whom were his friends at the time, that Semjase would fly her "beamship" into view for all of them to witness. In reality, *not a single person* reported observing "Semjase's beamship" that day or anything else unusual. In truth, only Billy Meier claims to have seen Semjase's spaceship while the group was present, stating that her craft was hovering *above* everyone and that no one except him had noticed it! (Photo courtesy: Margrit and Claudia Jacob.)

Fig. 41. Another of the Jakobsberg-Allenberg series of photos. Hans Jacob snapped this specific picture. Billy Meier can be seen standing on the far left, and is shown in more detail in the digital enlargement at the top of the page. Notice in this photo by Hans Jacob that no "Pleiadian beamship" is visible! In the Jakobsberg-Allenberg series of photos the double-exposed images of "Semjase's beamship" only appears in those pictures specifically taken that day by Billy Meier himself. It was brazen attempts at fakery such as this (where Meier tried unsuccessfully to fool people with poorly made double-exposures) that caused Hans Jacob to eventually end his association and friendship with Billy Meier. (Photo courtesy: Margrit and Claudia Jacob.)

"Disappearing Tree" Photos at Fuchsbüel

Date(s):	July 9, 1975, according to Meier's *Verzeichnis*[70]
Time(s):	1507 hrs.–1514 hrs., according to Wendelle Stevens[71]
	1507 hrs.–1714 hrs., according to Billy Meier's *Verzeichnis*[72]
Location(s):	Fuchsbüel am Hofhalden, Switzerland[73]
Meier Photo Number(s):	55–57,[74] 64–66,[75] 69–71,[76] 76[77]
Photographer(s):	Eduard "Billy" Meier[78]

Background Details

While Billy Meier continued making his UFO photos, the people around him began to lose interest because none of his pictures ever showed any of the "spaceships" either hovering or flying in front of large, known, quantifiable objects, which would then rule out all possibility of a hoax. To alleviate this "problem," Meier claims that Semjase made a specific arrangement with him to stage a photo-demonstration "flyover" in front of a large tree, which would allow Meier to then produce the most credible UFO pictures ever taken.[79]

Wendelle Stevens describes on pages 332–33 in his *Preliminary Investigation Report* how the alleged photo opportunity flyover at Fuchsbüel purportedly took place:

> On a recent contact, Semjase had asked Meier how his photographs were coming out. He responded, "Very good, but anybody could obtain similar pictures by suspending a model on a

line and carefully shooting it." He thought they would be better with more subject matter in the frame for comparative reference. She then offered to fly the ship around a tree for him so as to provide such references. And upon departure this time she flew slowly around an old twenty-odd meters tall Wettertanne (Weather Pine). She flew it around slowly more than once and then flew off, and then returned and flew around it once again. She kept the ship in so close to the tree that the flange of the rim spread the branches in passing. The branches are easily seen reflected in the smooth shiny surface of the 7-meter craft. The Pfaffikersee [Lake Pfäffikon] is seen in the background.

One of the strange effects observed–the top of the tree glowed in the dark for some time after the photo was made. No radiation measurements were ever made for lack of equipment. One of Meier's friends who examined the tree estimated it as 28 meters tall by 33 centimeters through the trunk as high as he could reach. It (the tree) is a hermit species and does not grow in clumps. It is also less conical in shape than most pines. On a subsequent trip to the site the tree was found to have disappeared, leaving no trace of its former existence. When Meier asked about this, he was told that it still carried some harmful radiation and was removed. He was later given a demonstration of how the tree was removed. He photographed two small trees side-by-side. Then the Pleiadians removed one and he photographed the site and the remaining tree again. In the second photo there is no sign of the first tree ever having been there. Many of Meier's friends witnessed this demonstration.

Here Semjase's spaceship is seen going around the tree. One critic voiced the opinion that the craft was a model held in position by wires. It would have to be a big model and there's not much to fasten it to, or a very small potted tree to be able to transport it on a Mo-Ped alone. Neither is very likely.

When Tina Layton and I visited the Meier farm for the first time on August 18, 1991, I made a point to discuss the Fuchsbüel photographs with Elisabeth Gruber, Guido Moosbrugger's wife. In my conversations with Gruber, I asked specific questions about how the craft allegedly flew around the tree; what had happened to the tree; and most importantly, how and why Billy Meier was allowed to take these particular photos in the first place.[80] Gruber confirmed Wendelle Stevens's account of the Fuchsbüel "contact,"[81] and reiterated Meier's and the Semjase Silver Star Center's position that out of *all* of the hundreds of "UFO" pictures Billy Meier has taken, the ten photos of the craft circling the tree at Fuchsbüel are supposed to be *"the most authentic and greatest UFO pictures."*[82]

Just what do Billy Meier's Fuchsbüel/Tree photos *really* show? Are they truly "the most authentic and greatest UFO pictures" of all time?

Analysis of "Tree Sequence" Fuchsbüel UFO Photographs

• The total duration of observation for the ten photos Billy Meier took at Fuchsbüel is, according to Wendelle Stevens, "seven minutes."[83] However, when checking Billy Meier's *Verzeichnis*, it lists the duration of the photographic "encounter" at two hours![84] This discrepancy is illogical, since it contradicts Meier's claim that the flyover lasted only several minutes.[85] Therefore, the time listed in the *Verzeichnis* regarding the last photo Meier took at Fuchsbüel that day is a *typographical error*—it should read *1507 hours* and not 1707 hours.[86]

• According to Billy Meier, his first two Fuchsbüel pictures were taken at 1507 hours.[87] His next two pictures were shot at 1508 hours,[88] with photos five and six taken at 1509 hours.[89] Photos seven and eight, he claims, were taken at 1510 hours.[90] This makes a total of *eight pictures in four minutes,* with an *average time* between each picture of just *30 seconds.* Meier further claims that he took Fuchsbüel photo number nine at 1511 hours[91] and that the tenth and final picture was snapped at 1514 hours.[92] This means that *one whole minute* had elapsed between the taking of the *eighth and ninth* Fuchsbüel photos, and that *three minutes passed* between this *ninth* picture and Meier's final *tenth* one. Thus, there was the *most amount of time* between when the two very last pictures were taken.[93]

Since *eighty percent* or eight of Meier's ten Fuchsbüel photos were taken within the *same minute* of each other (i.e., the first two pictures were taken at 1507 hours, the second and third photos at 1508 hours, etc., as already noted), this means that the cloud formations visible in Meier's pictures should be almost *identical* from photo to photo, in at least eight out of the ten Fuchsbüel pictures. For the last photo, which was supposedly taken just seven minutes after the very first one, we should see cloud formation changes reflecting an elapsed time of about seven minutes. A careful examination of the *cloud formations visible in all ten Fuchsbüel photos disproves* Meier's "account" of not only how the pictures were purportedly taken, but the *time frames* as well.

Figures 42–46 show the first five Fuchsbüel photos that Billy Meier claims he took with his camera. Compare the visible cloud formations in each photo and remember that the elapsed time for these first five pictures is supposed to be just 2.5 minutes.[94]

However, since the weather records for the day Meier took his photos reveal that the wind was blowing at just 10–15 miles per hour,[95] the cloud formation changes visible in the Fuchsbüel photos are too drastic to support Meier's account of how he supposedly obtained these pictures. It is simply impossible that only "30 seconds" elapsed between the taking of each of them. If the reported duration of time for these pictures had really been just "four minutes" as claimed,[96] then the cloud formation changes would *not* be as drastic as they are.

• Wendelle Stevens has tried to rationalize these obvious cloud formation discrepancies for *fifteen years* now, by claiming that "the clouds do, in fact, move faster in the higher valleys"[97] in Switzerland. While this is certainly true, this specific argument made by Stevens is *irrelevant*, since the *altitude of the location* where Billy Meier took his Fuchsbüel photos is only *277 yards higher* than the normal elevation for the area, including Lake Pfäffikon, which is visible some two miles away in the background of most of Meier's Fuchsbüel photographs.[98]

Figs. 42 and 43. The first two photos at Fuchsbüel am Hofhalden that Billy Meier took of "Semjase's spaceship." Although Meier claims these two pictures were made only thirty seconds apart, the cloud formations visible in these photos disprove this claim. (Photos courtesy: Margrit and Claudia Jacob.)

Figs. 44 and 45. Meier's third and fourth Fuchsbüel photos, supposedly taken only thirty seconds apart. The cloud formation changes visible in these pictures indicate that the photos were taken longer than the "thirty seconds apart" claimed by Meier and his proponents. (Photos courtesy: Margrit and Claudia Jacob.)

How Stevens can make this claim in all seriousness is a mystery in itself since relief and elevation maps of the Fuchsbüel location (and others) appear throughout his own *Preliminary Investigation Report* book establishing this fact![99]

Stevens has gone one step further by proclaiming in his *Supplementary Investigation Report* that the spot where Meier made his Fuchsbüel photos is "located in a natural venturii* [sic] area near the Pfaffikersee."[100] This is also not true.[101] According to the Swiss Meteorological Service, the elevation of the location where Meier took his Fuchsbüel photos is not high enough for it to be a venturi area.[102]

Furthermore, the Fuchsbüel site is within a *two-minute drive* from the main road leading into Wetzikon from Zürich, further evidence of the location's low altitude, a fact confirmed by Tina Layton and me during six visits to the Fuchsbüel site.[103]

• The second obvious problem with Meier's Fuchsbüel photos being authentic is the fact that the *directions* they were taken from are *impossible*. According to Wendelle Stevens, Billy Meier was standing *in front of the tree facing west* toward Lake Pfäffikon when he took his ten Fuchsbüel photos.[104] This is also what Billy Meier himself has claimed,[105] and what Elisabeth Gruber also confirmed.[106] Guido Moosbrugger's book also states this.[107] Gruber, Meier, Moosbrugger, Stevens, et al., are correct: Lake Pfäffikon does indeed lay to the *west*, or in the direction of "straight ahead" when standing at the location where Billy Meier made his Fuchsbüel pictures.[108]

However, a careful examination of photos *six and seven* proves conclusively that the direction they were taken was to

---

*Venturi areas, not "venturii" as Stevens incorrectly spells the term, are locations of high altitude where clouds and winds change rapidly. Venturi areas are common among the higher Swiss and Bavarian Alps, and in many other areas of the world where high mountain ranges exist. The phenomenon was named after Italian physicist G. B. Venturi (1746–1822).

Fig. 46. Billy Meier's fifth Fuchsbüel photo taken 2.5 minutes after his first picture. Although this photograph was supposedly taken thirty seconds after his fourth shot, the cloud formation changes visible in the background prove once again that Billy Meier's "account" of his alleged experience cannot possibly be accurate. (Photo courtesy: Margrit and Claudia Jacob.)

the *south,* and *not* the west. This discovery, which can be easily verified by on-site investigation,[109] is significant because it indicates that if Meier's Fuchsbüel photos are genuine, then both *Billy Meier and the tree moved!*[110]

Meier shot his first five photos starting from a direction facing *west,* which is why Lake Pfäffikon appears in the background of his pictures.[111] Then Meier *moved 90° to the left* or what would be facing *south,* to take photos six and seven, which is why the lake is no longer visible, and why the Hofhalden hills appear in the background instead.[112] Finally, Meier moved *90° to the right,* facing back toward the *west,* to snap pictures eight through ten, which is why we see Lake Pfäffikon once again in the background.[113] If Meier's Fuchs-büel photos are genuine, then how is it that the *tree* managed to *move 90° twice across the horizon?*

As the ten Fuchsbüel photos clearly show, *the tree moved with Billy Meier* as he changed directions twice, since the *same side of the tree is always visible* in all ten of the pictures! Suffice it to say, trees do not move, especially *90° across the horizon twice;* from right to left and back to the right again.

• Wendelle Stevens published in his *Supplementary Investigation Report* book an illustration detailing how Billy Meier supposedly walked around the tree at Fuchsbüel from *right to left* while taking his ten pictures. Stevens's drawing shows the tree facing *west,* with Lake Pfäffikon in the background, and indicates that Meier took *all* of his pictures while facing west, with no other direction involved.[114] This *ignores entirely* Meier's sixth and seventh Fuchsbüel photos, which clearly show the *Hofhalden foothills in the background;* proving that they were taken while Meier was pointing his camera to the south![115]

Not only does Stevens *fail* to address the existence of Meier's sixth and seventh photos, but the illustration he includes on page 380 of his *Supplementary Investigation Report* book does not even show the Hofhalden foothills!

In his books, Stevens carefully crafts a scenario which lends credibility to these photos, yet he deliberately *ignores and omits* those details which prove these pictures are hoaxes. By omitting this information, Wendelle Stevens denies his reader the ability to study all ten of Meier's Fuchsbüel UFO photos objectively.

Indeed, until they were revealed in this writing, no one has ever known about the directional discrepancies which plague these photos unless they had visited the location at Fuchs-büel themselves.

• Another incriminating fact in *all ten* of Billy Meier's

Fuchsbüel UFO photographs is that the "tree" visible in his pictures *always faces the same side!* This is an *impossibility* if Meier's Fuchsbüel pictures are authentic and really do show a large craft circling a large tree. It is obvious that Meier moved around a lot while taking his ten pictures, covering *a minimum of 180° from horizon to horizon* as we've already established.

Yet the "tree" visible in Meier's photos always shows the *same one side, as if no significant change of angle or movement ever takes place!* The tree is the *only* object in Meier's Fuchsbüel photos which does *not* reflect accurately the changes in the movement of the photographer accordingly.

Figure 52 shows enlargements of *only the tree* from Meier's various Fuchsbüel photos, including those taken toward the west and south. Figure 54 also torpedos Stevens's version and drawing of how Meier snapped his Fuchsbüel photos, as he presents it in his *Supplementary Investigation Report* book. If Stevens's account were correct, then the *same side* of the tree would still *not* be visible in all of Billy Meier's pictures, since according to Stevens, Meier moved from right to left.[116]

Since the background of Meier's Fuchsbüel "UFO" photos changes, how is it then that the same side of the tree is always visible in all ten of his photographs?

Figs. 47 and 48. Billy Meier's sixth (*above*) and seventh (*below*) Fuchs-büel photos, taken at 1509 and 1510 hours, some "thirty seconds" to "one minute" after his fifth photo. Notice that the background scenery has changed entirely, and that the cloud formations do not resemble those in his first five pictures! (Photos courtesy: Margrit and Claudia Jacob.)

Figs. 49 and 50. Billy Meier's eighth (*above*) and ninth (*below*) Fuchsbüel photos, purportedly taken at 1510 and 1511 hours. Once again the cloud formations differ entirely from those in his sixth and seventh photos, and the background scenery has changed as well. The mountains that were visible in photos six and seven are suddenly gone, a discrepancy ignored by Meier's proponents. (Photos courtesy: Margrit and Claudia Jacob.)

Fig. 51. Billy Meier's tenth Fuchsbüel photo, allegedly taken at 1514 hours. This picture, like all the others from this series which show Lake Pfäffikon in the background, was taken with the camera pointing west. However, Meier's sixth and seventh (see page 179) Fuchsbüel photos were made with his camera pointing toward the *south*. (Photo courtesy: Margrit and Claudia Jacob.)

Fig. 52. Enlargements from four of the Fuchsbüel "UFO" photographs showing the tree in detail. Notice that the *same side of the tree* appears in *all* of Meier's photos, an *impossibility* in the real world, since different sides of the tree would have been visible as Meier walked around and shifted positions 180° while taking his ten photographs as previously demonstrated. Because the tree shows no signs of such obvious movements, this casts doubt on the authenticity of Meier's Fuchsbüel UFO photographs. (Photos courtesy: Margrit and Claudia Jacob.)

Fig. 53. A panoramic view of the Fuchsbüel site which I developed from pictures taken during one of six visits. This photo montage covers 180° across the horizon, taking in *both* the south and west views, the *two directions Billy Meier used* when he created his "UFO" pictures at Fuchsbüel. The two Meier images above the photo montage show the two directions from which they were taken, south (*top left*) and west (*top right*). The bottom two photos show me at the Fuchsbüel site pointing in the directions south (*bottom left*) and west (*bottom right*), illustrating the movement of Meier's camera. (Top photos courtesy: Margrit and Claudia Jacob/Bottom photos courtesy: Tina Layton.)

Fig. 54. The top left photo shows one of Billy Meier's Fuchsbüel photos taken with his camera pointing to the *west*. The top right photo is one of Meier's Fuchsbüel shots taken with his camera pointing *south*. The middle left and right, and bottom left and right pictures were taken by Tina Layton of me at the Fuchsbüel site, standing at the precise location where Meier stood when he made one of his ten "UFO" photographs. I illustrate by pointing, the two directions Meier aimed his camera when creating his Fuchsbüel sequence of pictures. (Top photos courtesy: Margrit and Claudia Jacob/Middle and bottom photos courtesy: Tina Layton.)

Billy Meier and the "Disappearing" Tree

In my 1981 exposé of the Meier case, I mentioned that the tree which is so prominently featured in the ten Fuchsbüel photos does not exist.[117] If one travels to the Fuchsbüel location today, the tree is *nowhere* to be found. The information I had to work with regarding the tree at the time of my original exposé had been furnished to me by Colman VonKeviczky.

VonKeviczky had been to Switzerland visiting his friend Hans Jacob, where the two of them traveled to the Fuchsbüel site as part of Jacob's briefing for VonKeviczky on the Meier case.[118] The fact that several of Meier's most important photographic/contact sites were within a few minutes drive from Jacob's house made the task of briefing Colman VonKeviczky on the complexities of the Meier case that much easier for both men.

Jacob had determined that the Meier case was a hoax, and started working out arrangements with VonKeviczky to get the information he had acquired during his investigations out to the general public.[119] Hans Jacob, however, desired no publicity, so as a result of a mutual arrangement between the two men, Jacob's information was released in very limited form through VonKeviczky's organization, ICUFON, Inc., in New York.[120] This is significant, because Wendelle Stevens has repeatedly criticized Colman VonKeviczky for spending just "one day" in Switzerland investigating the Meier case.[121]

Aside from the fact that VonKeviczky was in Switzerland for *four* days, not just one,[122] Stevens misses an important point. VonKeviczky had as his personal guide to introduce him to the Meier case Hans Jacob, the best person other than Meier himself to do so. Thus, the four days VonKeviczky spent in Switzerland was enough time to become thoroughly familiar with the case and its complex evidence. If Jacob and Meier had not ended their friendship by the time VonKe-

viczky had visited him in Wetzikon, Jacob would have introduced Colman personally to Meier.

Hans Jacob had already been to the site at Fuchsbüel much
earlier than when he took his trip with VonKeviczky. In fact,
Jacob went there shortly after Billy Meier took his Fuchsbüel
photos, taking with him a set of the prints that Meier had made
for Jacob from his original negatives.[123] Jacob noticed not only
the west and south directional problems mentioned earlier,
but was also surprised to find that no tree existed.[124] When
Hans Jacob asked Billy Meier about this, Meier "explained"
that because Semjase's spaceship had flown so close, the tree
had become *radioactive*. Therefore, the Pleiadians, out of alleged
concern for the health and safety of us poor Earthlings, sent the
tree *back in time*, thus making it disappear![125]

Now that we have heard what Jacob and VonKeviczky
claim Meier said, what does Billy Meier *himself* say about the
matter? In his own *Verzeichnis*, Meier does indeed make the
claim that Semjase "eliminated" the tree,[126] and so does Moosbrugger in his book about Meier.[127] Additionally, Wendelle
Stevens says the same thing in his *Preliminary* and *Supplementary Investigation* books,[128] and the claim is also made in the
Genesis III picture book, *UFO . . . Contact from the Pleiades, Volume II*.[129] Finally, when Tina Layton and I interviewed Elisabeth Gruber at the Meier farm, she also verified these various
accounts as to what had happened to the alleged tree.[130]

Now that we have established what Meier and his supporters would have us believe, what is the truth here? Was
there *really* a tree present at the Fuchsbüel location where Billy
Meier's "UFO" photographs show one?

The answer is no!

The land on which Billy Meier took his Fuchsbüel photographs is owned by Herrmann Wyss (pronounced Weece)
and his wife, who have farmed the land for *several decades*,
including many years *prior* to the date that Billy Meier's
Fuchsbüel UFO pictures were taken.[131]

The Wyss family has been good friends with the Jacobs for more than twenty-four years.[132] The Wyss-owned farm is just a few houses *above* the Jacobs' residence, literally a ninety-second drive by car up the hill and the main road from the Jacobs' house, as mentioned earlier.[133] Indeed, Tina and I learned during our ten-day stay with the Jacob family that it was not unusual for Margrit to visit with the Wyss family a *minimum* of once a week.[134]

Margrit Jacob introduced Tina and me to the Wysses and explained why we had accompanied her. I showed them Billy Meier's Fuchsbüel "UFO" photographs that I had purchased at the Meier compound.

Hermann Wyss and his wife listened patiently as Margrit and I questioned them in German about Billy Meier's Fuchsbüel "UFO" photographs. When the Wysses were asked if there had *ever* been a tree at the *location* where Billy Meier's Fuchsbüel photos show one, Hermann Wyss got this gentle grin on his face and shook his head from right-to-left while slowly saying "Noooo!" I made a point to ask the question more than once along with Margrit Jacob, making sure there was no mistake about his response and unequivocal answer.

In short, Hermann Wyss seemed *amused* by both Billy Meier's Fuchsbüel "UFO" photos and the "Pleiadian spaceship" they purport to show.

• Curiously, *none* of Meier's proponents such as Brit and Lee Elders, Gary Kinder, Guido Moosbrugger, Wendelle Stevens, or Randolph Winters has ever interviewed the Wyss family! This writing represents the *first time* that their remarks and reactions to Meier's UFO pictures have ever been published.

• Wendelle Stevens claims that the "tree" at the Fuchsbüel location was approximately "80 feet tall by 50 feet [in] outside diameter."[135] In addition, Billy Meier's followers include the detail (as does Stevens) that after Semjase flew her "spaceship" around the tree, the tops of it glowed "bright red" for several nights afterwards, because of the radiation to which it had been supposedly exposed.[136] This is also extremely unlikely, since from its location at Fuchsbüel, the tree would have been visible not only to the Wyss family through the windows of their house,[137] but to the hundreds of people who drive daily in both directions on the main road from Wetzikon to Hofhalden.[138]

A bright red, glowing tree would have been *impossible to miss,* especially since there are no streetlights at the Fuchsbüel site, and it is extremely dark there at night, typical of the Swiss countryside.[139]

• Of the ten Fuchsbüel "UFO" photos, only *two* were taken toward the south, where not only the Wyss family but any passersby driving in a car would have seen Meier taking his photographs.[140] One can only speculate, but this is probably why Meier *moved his small potted tree* and the UFO model further up the hill so he could face west, where it would be far more difficult to see him.

• The final "smoking gun" that *proves conclusively* there was *never* a tree at the Fuchsbüel location can be found, ironically, in Meier's photo number 27, which was analyzed earlier in this chapter. Since we now know that Billy Meier's photo number 27 was taken also at Fuchsbüel and that this picture *predates* Meier's Fuchsbüel "tree" photos by some *4.5 months,* it's interesting to note that in this photo no tree is visible either!

Figure 63 (page 193) shows a digital superimposition of Meier's two Fuchsbüel photos taken both on February 27, 1975, and July 7, 1975. Notice that the "tree" appears *only* in the picture taken on July 7! This is objective evidence that Billy Meier was careless when he confabulated his "contact" stories, and also probably explains the reason(s) why Moosbrugger and Stevens incorrectly state that this earlier picture was taken at Jakobsberg-Allenberg, rather than Fuchsbüel. By listing the *wrong* location, Moosbrugger and Stevens help insure that no one would ever notice the Meier deception.

Conclusion

Billy Meier's ten Fuchsbüel "UFO" photos are hoaxes. The directions from which they were taken, and the story behind them, do not fit the facts when the location is investigated firsthand.

Fig. 55. The Wyss family farm located at the *bottom of the hill* at the Fuchsbüel am Hofhalden location where Meier claims to have taken his ten "UFO" photographs.

Figs. 56 and 57. (*Top*) Meier's seventh Fuchsbüel "UFO" photograph, taken above the Wysses' residence, well within their view. (*Bottom*) A picture I took of the *same* site, showing no tree! The arrow in both photos has been added to show the terrain matching I used to frame the shot. Today, the Wyss family grows corn in what used to be a barren field where Billy Meier created his ten Fuchsbüel "UFO" photographs. (Top photo courtesy: Margrit and Claudia Jacob.)

Figs. 58 and 59. (*Top*) A photo of the Fuchsbüel site taken by UFO researcher Major Colman VonKeviczky during his visit with Hans Jacob and his family. Notice that the tree did not exist even back then. (*Bottom*) Meier's sixth Fuchsbüel "UFO" photograph for comparison. (Top photo courtesy: ICUFON, Inc./Bottom photo courtesy: Margrit and Claudia Jacob.)

Figs. 60 and 61. (*Top*) Billy Meier's last Fuchsbüel UFO photograph, facing west. (*Bottom*) A photo I took while standing in the *same approximate spot* where Billy Meier snapped his last Fuchsbüel photo. Notice once again, in spite of having turned 90° to the right in order to get Lake Pfäffikon in view, there still exists no tree! (Top photo courtesy: Margrit and Claudia Jacob.)

Fig. 62. A digital superimposition overlaying Meier's tree on top of my own picture taken at the same location where Meier stood at the Fuchsbüel site when he made his tenth photograph of this series.

Fig. 63. My digital montage overlapping Billy Meier's two Fuchsbüel photos taken on February 27, 1975 and July 7, 1975. Notice that while the tree appears in the July 7 photo, it is not visible in the February 27 picture, which was taken approximately 4.5 months earlier! (Bottom two photos courtesy: Margrit and Claudia Jacob.)

Bachtelhörnli-Unterbachtel "UFO" Photographs

Date(s):   March 8, 1976, according to the
                        Verzeichnis[141]
                        March 28, 1976, according to Stevens[142]

Time(s):   0938 hrs. according to Stevens[143]
                        0938 hrs. according to Billy Meier[144]

Location(s):   Bachtelhörnli-Unterbachtel/Unterbach-
                        Orn, Switzerland[145]

Meier Photo   182–242[146]
Number(s):

Photographer(s):   Eduard "Billy" Meier[147]

Background Details

According to Wendelle Stevens, the "Pleiadians" had forbidden Meier from taking photographs of their ships for a period of "nine months" following his "tree sequence" photos at Fuchsbüel. Eight months later, on March 8, 1976, they finally relented.[148] What followed was a very long contact with Billy Meier and scores of photographs, with up to three objects seen in them at any one time, evidence, according to Meier's supporters, that he could not possibly be faking the photographs.

Analysis of the Bachtelhörnli-Unterbachtel Photographs

• Computer edge enhancements I conducted on Meier's photographs numbers 199, 207, 225, 230, and 231 reveal the existence of strings or supportive devices above each of the

"UFO" images visible in these pictures. Although, admittedly, no photographic negatives were available for these enhancements, there is very strong evidence that the supportive structures visible in these pictures are indeed wires or strings, and not simply "scratches," which is another possibility. But if these apparent suspension lines were truly "scratches," and showed up *only* in one or two of the Bachtelhörnli-Unterbachtel sequence photographs, then this would be weak evidence indeed.

The curious fact about Billy Meier's Bachtelhörnli-Unterbachtel "UFO" photographs is that the number of suspension lines that appear under edge enhancement processing always equals the number of "UFOs" in his pictures! In other words, where there's only one "UFO" visible, there's one suspension line. Where there are two supposed "spaceships" visible, there are two suspension lines. And where there are three "Pleiadian ships" in his picture, there are indeed three such supportive devices, like strings or wires! To explain or rationalize this fact as just a coincidence, or to dismiss these lines as just a "coincidence" is absurd, since the mathematical odds of this happening repeatedly are astronomical.

• Not only are there supportive structures visible in several of Billy Meier's Bachtelhörnli-Unterbachtel "UFO" photographs, but they are also in the correct positions just as if they are supporting small models! This fact makes it unlikely that they are not what they appear to be: wires or strings used by Billy Meier to suspend his "UFO" models.

Conclusion

Billy Meier's sixty Bachtelhörnli-Unterbachtel "UFO" photographs show small models suspended by wires or strings. These supportive devices are easily visible under computer edge enhancement processing and can be revealed with such commercial software for personal computers such as Adobe

Systems' Industry-standard PhotoShop® and Aldus's® Gallery Effects®. For those who have access to these software programs, feel free to try the "Emboss"* filters (featured in both these popular programs) on Meier's Bachtelhörnli-Unterbachtel photographs numbers 199, 207, 225, 230 and 231. After doing so, you will be able to see these various supportive structures for yourself.

---

*Although Adobe Systems, Inc., and Aldus Inc., which followed Adobe's lead, call their filter "Emboss," it is really an edge enhancement algorithm and should have been named as such originally. However, the name difference is irrelevant, since the respective filters in these two programs are sufficient for the task. PhotoShop® and Gallery Effects® are available on both the IBM and Macintosh® computer platforms, and will run under the Macintosh OS™ System 7.x or MicroSoft Windows™, version 3.1 or later. The software is also compatible with IBM's OS/2™ operating system, and OS/2 Warp™. Similar or equivalent computer enhancement filters are also available on Unix-based platforms and other workstation environments.

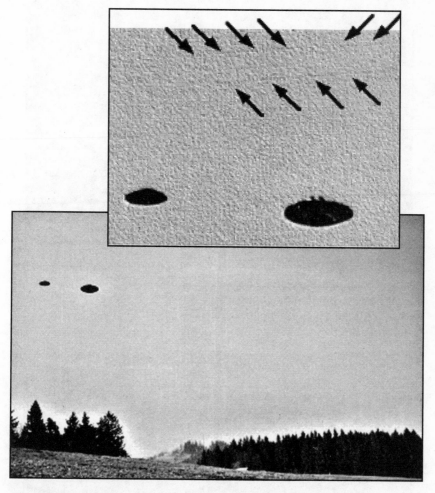

Fig. 64. (*Bottom*) One of Billy Meier's Bachtelhörnli-Unterbachtel photos, purportedly taken at 1638 hours according to his *Verzeichnis*. (*Inset photo, top*) A computer edge enhancement that I conducted which reveals what appear to be strings or wires above Billy Meier's two "UFOs." (Bottom photo courtesy: Margrit and Claudia Jacob.)

Figs. 65. and 66. (*Above*) Another one of Billy Meier's Bachtelhörnli-Unterbachtel photographs. (*Below*) My edge enhancement showing a supportive device or what appears to be a suspension line above the "UFO" as it exists in Meier's photo number 199. (Top photo courtesy: Margrit and Claudia Jacob.)

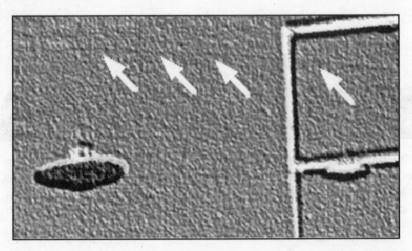

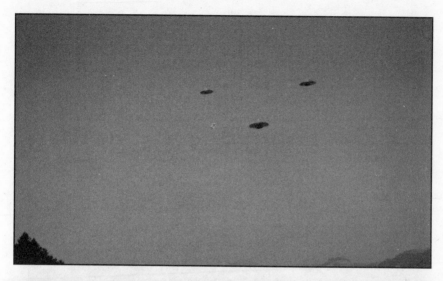

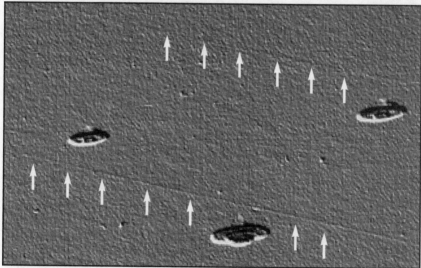

Figs. 67 and 68. (*Top*) Another one of Billy Meier's Bachtelhörnli-Unterbachtel pictures, purportedly taken at 0940 hours according to the listing in the *Verzeichnis*. (*Bottom*) A computer edge enhancement that I conducted which reveals what appear to be strings or wires above the three "UFOs" shown in Billy Meier's photograph. (Top photo courtesy: Margrit and Claudia Jacob.)

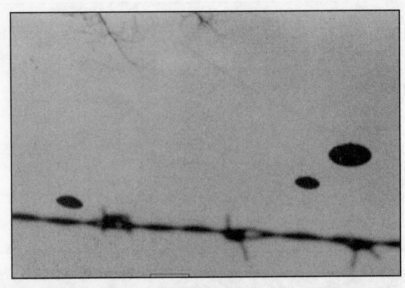

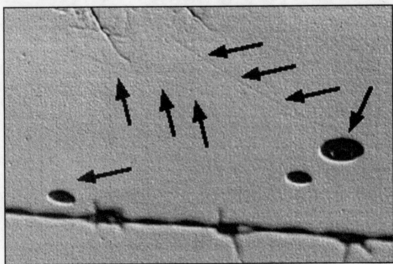

Figs. 69 and 70. (*Top*) Billy Meier's Bachtelhörnli-Unterbachtel photograph number 240, allegedly taken at 1645 hours. (*Bottom*) Arrows point to what appear to be supportive strings or wires above the"UFOs." (Top photo courtesy: Margrit and Claudia Jacob.)

The Hasenböl-Langenberg "UFO" Photographs

Date(s):	March 29, 1976, according to the *Verzeichnis*[149] March 29, 1976, according to Stevens[150]
Time(s):	1710 hrs.–1820 hrs. according to Meier[151] 1810 hrs. according to Stevens[152]
Location(s):	Hasenböl-Langenberg, Switzerland[153]
Meier Photo Number(s):	148–181[154]
Photographer(s):	Eduard "Billy" Meier[155]

Background Details

The next day after Meier successfully took his photos at Bachtelhörnli-Unterbachtel, he claims he was "telepathically summoned" once again for yet another photo opportunity. This time Meier traveled on his moped to a remote location called Hasenböl-Langenberg to take his pictures.[156] This was Billy Meier's fiftieth "contact" on record with the aliens.[157]

Although Wendelle Stevens claims that Meier exposed "four 36-shot rolls of diapositive color slides" during this alleged photo-encounter,[158] Stevens is mistaken, for Meier's *Verzeichnis* lists only *thirty-four pictures* as having been taken,[159] which is two short of a normal 36-exposure roll of 35mm slide film. Additionally, when I viewed all 1,058 UFO and UFO-related photos at the Meier compound, I noticed there were only thirty-four images in the Hasenböl-Langenberg series.

The Hasenböl-Langenberg photos, along with the Fuchs-büel "tree-sequence" pictures, are often cited by Meier supporters as being two of the most impressive series of UFO photographs ever taken.[160] While admittedly striking, the thirty-four pictures start by showing Meier's moped and his movie camera on a tripod, with what is supposed to be a Pleiadian ship coming in toward the camera from over the horizon. Each succeeding photo in the series shows the UFO approaching closer to the camera and moving toward the right, where it descends upon a large pair of trees, stopping to swing around and hover on the left side of the closest tree to Meier.

Unlike the "disappearing" tree in the Fuchsbüel am Hofhalden photos, the large trees visible in the Hasenböl-Langenberg series of pictures really do exist, and were later documented and measured by investigators.[161] Although at least one of these trees was later cut down,[162] there is no disputing the fact that the two trees visible in the photos not only existed, but were large ones typical for that region of Switzerland.[163]

Because the Hasenböl-Langenberg series of pictures shows the UFO first as a distant point in the sky, then continually approaching until it is at its closest point, supposedly hovering "beside" the large tree, the sequence is a good one for analysis since the alleged spacecraft can be compared to objects of known, quantifiable size.

In the five specific Hasenböl-Langenberg pictures where the UFO is seen next to the tree (Meier photos 164, 173–76[164]), Billy Meier and his supporters claim that the spaceship is hovering slightly *behind* the tree, and that the branches can be seen *partially obscuring* the *left rim of the spacecraft!*[165] Since the tree is 156 feet in the distance and 21 feet in diameter, and a steep valley drops off immediately behind it, Meier's proponents claim that this is proof the object really is a large spacecraft hovering some distance away; at least as far away as the tree, which rules out the use of a small model.[166]

While such reasoning is scientifically valid, the relevant question is, do the photos *really* show what Meier and his proponents claim, the image of a large seven-meter spacecraft hovering 156 feet from the camera?

Analysis of the Hasenböl-Langenberg Photographs

• In analyzing Meier's Hasenböl-Langenberg photographs, every copy obtained was scanned, including the color 4x5 inch prints and 8x10 enlargements which I purchased while at the Meier compound. After digitizing all copies into the computer, the images were subjected to a series of basic computer enhancements to see if anything could be learned starting at the rudimentary level.

Digital enlargements and other computer image processing techniques reveals that the "UFO" is positioned in *front* of the tree, and not *behind* it, contrary to what has been claimed. For example, the photos were subjected to false color contouring, a process in which the computer assigns a specific color to each object that has a unique density value in the photo. The resulting image can help determine depth and brightness (light value) issues, and distance factors. When viewing the color-contoured enhancements, it's obvious that the branches of the tree are behind the UFO, not in front of it. In addition, edge enhancement processing also confirmed this. (See figures 73 and 74.)

• Of the five Hasenböl-Langenberg photos which show the UFO hovering near the tree, two contain suspicious supportive devices or structures, which were detected under edge enhancement processing. Moreover, by digitally *increasing* the contrast and *lowering* the brightness values in the photos, the suspect lines are more visible.

One of these structures (see figure 75) appears to be some sort of "tether," whereas the suspicious vertical line visible in the other Hasenböl-Langenberg photo appears directly *above* the UFO image.

This second image was much less discernible, even under

computer processing, due to light from the sun partially obscuring the details of the "dome" on top of the saucer, which is where the "string" would normally be visible. While this faint linear structure is suspicious, without the original negatives to study, the issue of questionable methodologies cannot be resolved with absolute certainty.

Conclusion

Meier's Hasenböl-Langenberg "UFO" photos show a *small object* suspended *close* to the camera, in *front* of the large tree. The model appears to be rigged to an apparatus which allows it to be moved through the air for easy staging of the photographs. By shooting deliberately in the direction of the setting sun, Meier was able to use its glare to help obscure any supportive structures or "strings" that were used to suspend the model.

On the other hand, if the suspicious linear structures which were detected are not actually strings, then the photo is a darkroom montage since the computer enhancements clearly establish that the UFO is in *front* of the tree.

Should Meier's supporters ever produce a version of these photos where the tree branches appear to be in front of the UFO (which would establish that the object really is a large spacecraft), without original negatives such "versions" are scientifically useless and are not admissable as evidence even in a court of law.

Figs. 71. and 72. (*Top*) Hasenböl-Langenberg, 1810 hours. Meier and his proponents claim that the "UFO" is hovering behind the tree, which is 156 feet from the camera. If this is true, it would establish that the craft shown here is indeed a large object as claimed by Meier and his supporters. (*Bottom*) My enlargement shows close-up detail of the purported spaceship. (Top photo courtesy: Margrit and Claudia Jacob.)

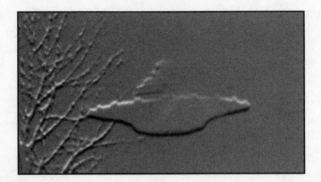

Fig. 73. Edge enhancement processing reveals that the "UFO" is in front of the branches of the tree and not behind it as claimed. This is proof that the "spacecraft" depicted here is a small model, due to the large size of the tree.

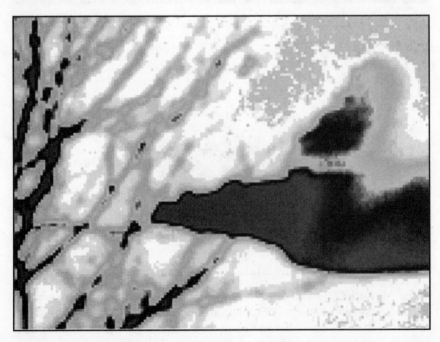

Fig. 74. Computer false color contouring verifies that the object is indeed in front of the tree.

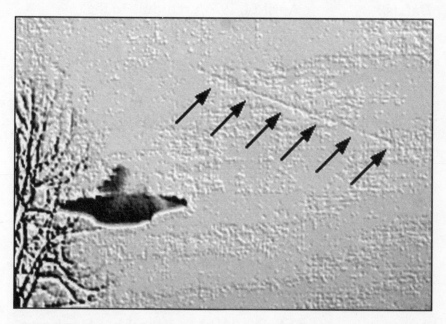

Fig. 75. In one of the color computer edge enhancements, this linear structure showed up. However, without original negatives to test, it is impossible to say for sure what it is. It could be a tethering line to suspend and/or move the small UFO model (its angle is consistent with one), or it could be just a scratch on the film or due to some other innocent artifact.

The Schmärbüel-Maiwinkle Photographs

Date(s):   April 14, 1976, according to the
                      Verzeichnis[167]

Time(s):   1611 hrs.–1624 hrs. according to Meier[168]
                      1611 hrs. according to Stevens[169]

Location(s):   Schmärbüel-Maiwinkle, Switzerland[170]
                      Schmarduel, Switzerland, according to
                      Gary Kinder[171]

Meier Photo   244–256[172]
Number(s):

Photographer(s):   Eduard "Billy" Meier[173]

Background Details

Approximately two weeks after he took the thirty-four Hasen-böl-Langenberg photos, Billy Meier claims that the Pleiadians summoned him again for yet another photo demonstration flyover. According to Wendelle Stevens, Meier was "telepath-ically guided to a hillside location between Schmarbuel (sic) and Maiwinkle, near Bettswill-Bäretswil in Canton Zürich. A Swiss military exercise was going on in that area and move-ment was controlled by military police."[174]

Most of the thirteen photos that Meier exposed at Schmär-büel am Maiwinkle purport to show a Swiss Mirage III jet fighter "attacking" Semjase's spacecraft.[175] This is the latest account of the photo incident by Stevens, who received this information from Billy Meier himself.[176]

Shortly after he (Meier) arrived (at Schmärbüel am Maiwinkle), Semjase, who may have already been there, turned off her screening shield and became visible to all, including the Army field radar in the military exercise. Meier began to hear the now familiar humming-whining sound associated with the ships under certain conditions and could see the ship clearly. He turned on his sound recorder and got his camera ready. Very soon a Swiss Army jet fighter was vectored in on the intruder by the ground units there. The pilot began making flight passes at the ship, apparently trying to get closer, but the ship would jump out of the way at the last moment. Meier began snapping 35mm color slide photos of the aerial skirmish, and was recording the sounds and shooting pictures of the action when two policemen drove up in a patrol car and asked what he was doing. About that time the strange circular craft swooped in and turned the sound up to a deafening level. The frightened policemen jumped back into their patrol car and sped out of there and away as the ET ship returned to position for interception by the jet fighter.

Meier resumed snapping pictures of the aerial display, always trying to get both the spacecraft and the jet fighter together in the viewing frame. He actually succeeded in 10 frames out of 14 frames exposed at this time. The jet fighter made 21 passes on the ET spacecraft and then broke off after starting the 22nd, and disappeared in the direction of Bettswil where there was a nearby airbase. Semjase told Meier that on that 22nd pass, the pilot had armed his fire control panel so that he could shoot if ordered, and that at that point she had had to neutralize the danger. The pilot's fire control panel began to smoke and failed completely. A mechanic at the base later reported that the fire control panel had melted down internally, and had to be completely replaced, including much of the wireing (sic).[177]

Analysis of the Schmärbüel-Maiwinkle Photographs

• The sun in Meier's Schmärbüel-Maiwinkle UFO photos is off to the right, as is evident by the angle of the illumination on the small tree branch visible in the foreground. The UFO is supposedly hovering over the field shown in the photo, and because of the angle and brightness of the sun, a shadow should be cast from the "Pleiadian ship" down to the grass on the field below. However, while every *other* object in Meier's Schmärbüel-

Maiwinkle photos show shadows visible in their proper directions, curiously, the "UFO" casts *no shadow at all!* This is suspicious.

Since Semjase's "spaceship" was fully "decloaked" and therefore visible to Meier and those "frightened policemen," her ship *should* have cast a shadow on the ground which would be visible in the picture. This is especially true if Semjase's spaceship really is a large 22.75-foot craft as claimed. Objects of such dimensions cast sizable shadows.

The absence of a visible shadow indicates that the photo is either a montage or that the "UFO" is really a small model and not a large craft as claimed.

• Although Meier and his supporters claim the Mirage fighter visible in the photos is "attacking" the Pleiadian ship, not a single picture in the Schmärbüel-Maiwinkle series actually shows such "Top Gun" maneuvers taking place. In other words, while the photos do indeed show *both* the jet aircraft and the "UFO," unless one were *told* that the plane is "attacking" the supposed spacecraft, no evidence of such a "dogfight" is visible! Indeed, analysis of relative distance factors, comparing the angular size of the UFO and the jet's position in relation to each other in three-dimensional space, indicates that no "attack" is taking place!

For example, the size of the Swiss Mirage fighter in most of Meier's Schmärbüel-Maiwinkle UFO photos varies between 1-2 millimeters, on a 4x6-inch print. By comparison, the size of the "UFO" is anywhere from *fifteen to twenty times* larger! This proves that the "UFO" is significantly *closer* to the camera than the jet aircraft is, and that the two objects are nowhere near each other in physical space.

The length of a Swiss Mirage III jet fighter is approximately 51 feet.[178] This means that the Pleiadian ship, at 22.75 feet in diameter, is 2.5 times *smaller* than the size of the Mirage jet. Therefore, the fact that the "UFO" is 2.5 times smaller proves that the two objects are nowhere near each other in real, physical space. In truth, *none* of Meier's Schmärbüel-Mai-winkle photos show the aircraft anywhere near the UFO, which is convincing evidence that it is not "chasing" the spaceship as claimed.

• Evidence that the "UFO" in Meier's Schmärbüel-Mai-winkle photos is a small model attached to a balloon lays in the fact that the object always drifts in the direction of the wind in all of the photographs! The direction of the wind is discernible because smoke can be seen coming from the chimney of a house in the background in a few of the photos. Based on the direction of this smoke, the wind is blowing from left to right, the same direction that the "UFO" is always flying.

One would expect that at least *one* of Meier's fourteen Schmärbüel-Maiwinkle photos would show either the "UFO" flying against the wind, or at least exhibiting *some* evidence of independent flight capabilities, especially since Stevens claims that in order to "elude" the jet fighter, which was supposedly in hot pursuit, the ship had to "jump" out of the way during the Mirage's alleged twenty-one passes at the object.

• If Meier's Schmärbüel-Maiwinkle photos were created by using a small model attached to a balloon, how is it that he managed to frame both the Mirage jet fighter and the "UFO" repeatedly in ten separate photographs? The task was relatively easy.

During my investigation in Switzerland, I discovered that the Swiss Air Force and various units in the armed forces regularly conduct their maneuvers in the areas in and around Schmärbüel-Maiwinkle. Whereas the artillery and tank corps often practice at the target range at nearby Frecht Nature Preserve,[179] the Swiss Air Force often flies in low through the valley at Schmärbüel-Maiwinkle, up all the way through Wetzikon and Hinwill, before circling back.[180]

Because the Swiss Air Force often flys the *same* aerial exercise routes repeatedly for as much as twenty to thirty minutes at a stretch,[181] and has done so for years, standing at *any* location along the plane's flight path one is able to frame any object in a picture. In fact, if one arrived during the beginning of such maneuvers, one would have repeated opportunities to frame several photos easily.

To prove this point, on September 2, 1991, Tina and I stood in a field in the town of Hinwill and observed a Swiss Mirage jet fighter make several passes over our heads. The location where we were standing was near the end of the plane's designated flight route, because shortly after passing overhead it would turn back and start its approach all over again. The plane would come streaking in from the direction of Schmär-büel-Maiwinkle and Bärettswil-Bettswil, ironically, following the *same flight path* and air "corridor" that the Mirage fighter in Meier's photos had flown sixteen years earlier![182]

After Tina and I observed the Mirage fighter make several passes, I took one of our plastic, silver-colored UFO models and attached it to some helium balloons.

As I filmed the object flying around, I waited for the Mirage fighter to pass overhead. When it did, Tina released the UFO model so it would appear in the same frames as the fighter aircraft. I then filmed the plane as it streaked by.

Highlights of the video footage Tina and I made during our experiments in Hinwill appear in the documentary *EX-POSED: The Billy Meier UFO Hoax*. Both the experiment and the results we obtained are proof that creating photos like Billy Meier's Schmärbüel-Maiwinkle sequence are easy to do.

Conclusion

Billy Meier's Schmärbüel am Maiwinkle photos are hoaxes. The method used to fabricate them most likely involved positioning a small UFO model in such a way that it would be able to be "framed" in the same photograph, along with the Swiss Mirage jet fighter as it flew by. There is no credible evidence visible in any of Meier's Schmärbüel am Maiwinkle photos that the Swiss Mirage fighter is "attacking" the UFO.

On a similar note, this is also true regarding aspects of Stevens's "account" of events surrounding Meier's Schmär-büel am Maiwinkle photographs. Other than Wendelle Stevens's verbal and written "assurance," there is *no credible evidence* to support his tales of either the "frightened police-men" or the fire-control panel system which allegedly "smoked" and "failed completely," due to the actions of Sem-jase. This is also true of the conveniently anonymous "mechanic" Stevens claims supposedly verified the damage to the Mirage fighter. Until Wendelle Stevens provides *any* evidence to substantiate his extraordinary claims, they must be considered useless hearsay.

Figs. 76 and 77. (*Top*) One of the ten Schmärbüel am Maiwinkle photos taken by Billy Meier which he claims shows the Swiss Mirage jet fighter "attacking" Semjase's spacecraft. (*Bottom*) My digital enlargement showing Mirage fighter and the alleged "Pleiadian" spaceship. (Top photo courtesy: Margrit and Claudia Jacob.)

The Hinterschmidrüti Photographs

Date(s):   October 22, 1980, according to the
        Verzeichnis[183]

Time(s):   1123 hrs.–1624 hrs. according to Meier[184]

Location(s):   Hinterschmidrüti, Switzerland[185]

Meier Photo 798–808[186]
Number(s):

Photographer(s): Eduard "Billy" Meier[187]

Background Details

Billy Meier claims that on October 22, 1980, the Pleiadians flew their brand-new, most advanced "spaceship" over Hinterschmidrüti and landed in the central parking lot of the Semjase Silver Star Center. Meier snapped eleven photographs of the craft as it sat in front of his house at the compound.[188]

Analysis of the Hinterschmidrüti Photographs

• The Hinterschmidrüti sequence shows a small model positioned close to the camera. This is evident by the fact that the background imagery in the photos are out-of-focus when they should not be.
• Detailed analysis of the construction features visible on the "UFO" in Meier's Hinterschmidrüti photos reveals evidence of manufacture consistent with the object being a small model. Items such as carpet tacks; an old-style metal, bendable water hose; and a bracelet are visible on the surface of the craft (see figures 79 and 80)!

• The hull of the "spaceship" is warped and bent, as figure 80 illustrates. This is further evidence that the object is a small model and not an extraterrestrial spacecraft.

Conclusion

Billy Meier's Hinterschmidrüti photos show a small "UFO" model positioned close to the camera.

Fig. 78. October 22, 1980, Hinterschmidrüti, Switzerland. Meier claims this photo shows the Pleiadians' most advanced spacecraft yet invented. (Photo courtesy: Margrit and Claudia Jacob.)

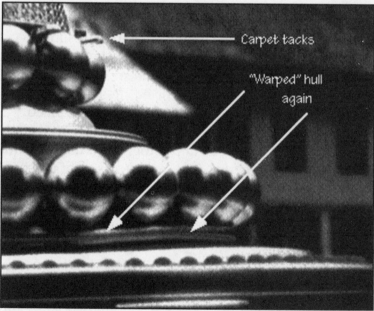

Figs. 79 and 80. My enlargements show its surface details. Arrows indicate how the hull of the "spaceship" is warped and coming apart at the seams!

General Comments about Meier's "UFO" Photos

As mentioned at the beginning of this chapter, because we have the luxury of knowing certain values regarding Meier's photos, such as the Pleiadian spaceship's purported size, the focal length of Meier's camera, the fact his lens is set at a fixed-focus, etc., the task of doing calculations to help determine the authenticity of Meier's UFO photographs is a relatively easy task. To illustrate this point, there is a mathematical formula one can use to determine *true object size and distance* in any photograph. The equation for determining these values is as follows:

$$Si/Fl \bullet D = As$$

Si represents the value for the *size* of the image as measured in millimeters on the *original* negative or slide.

Fl is the value for the *focal length* of the camera lens which was used, which in Meier's case is 42mm, as noted earlier.

D stands for *distance*, the reported distance to the object from the photographer, either known or hypothesized.

As is for the *actual size* of the object, either *theoretical* or *real*. For most of Meier's UFO photographs, the *As* value is 22.75 feet, or "seven meters," the reported size of most of the Pleiadian spacecraft.

Like virtually every equation, this formula can be manipulated to solve for any of the desired values. For example, if one wanted to determine *distance*, the equation would be as follows:

$$\frac{As \bullet Fl}{Si} = D$$

On the other hand, to calculate the *size* of the image in millimeters on the original film, the formula would be:

$$\frac{As \cdot Fl}{D} = Si$$

Finally, if one wanted to solve for the value to determine the *focal length* of the camera, this is the variation of the equation to use:

$$\frac{Si \cdot D}{As} = Fl$$

When one applies these basic formulas to Meier's UFO photographs, additional evidence of a hoax soon arises. The "UFOs" in Meier's photos *never* calculate out to be large objects "22.75 feet in diameter," nor do the distances of trees and other purported landmarks in his pictures ever pan out.

Feel free to try running some calculations yourself on Billy Meier's hundreds of UFO photographs, using these four formulas.

While Meier and his proponents continue to claim that his UFO pictures are genuine, as we have shown there is no credible evidence that this is true. Indeed, when applying basic photo-analysis techniques and methodologies, mathematics, computer enhancements, and on-site investigation, Meier's UFO photos come up sadly wanting.

How to Make UFO Movies and Photographs

Although Billy Meier is probably the only individual who can tell us *exactly* what techniques he uses to create his hundreds of "UFO" photographs, by analyzing his pictures some clues can be learned that provide insights into his methodologies.

In my earlier book on Billy Meier, I mentioned that he had used balloons and string or fishing line as one method to create at least some of the pictures published in Genesis III's original photo-journal, *UFO . . . Contact from the Pleiades, Volume I.*[189] UFO researcher Ray Stanford also noticed this fact[190] and indeed, balloons can be seen in the background of many of Meier's pictures—especially those published in *Pleiades, Volume I.*

As mentioned in chapter 2 of this volume, in order to prove how easy it is to produce convincing "UFO" pictures, Tina Layton and I brought several small "UFO" models made of plastic with us to Switzerland in 1991. After I assembled them in the Jacobs' backyard before a video camera, Tina and I later went to several of the exact locations where Billy Meier took his pictures, and successfully duplicated them. This also included the motion picture footage Meier had taken. The technique we used was a simple one: we simply attached the small models to helium balloons and filmed them *above* the trees so that there would be no point of reference.

Most of our successful duplications of Billy Meier's still photos and motion picture footage are featured in the Underground Video documentary *EXPOSED: The Billy Meier UFO Hoax.* Not only do you see me putting the models together, but you see Meier's cult as it really exists and the definitive results Tina and I obtained in replicating Billy Meier's photos and movies of "spaceships."

Duplicating Billy Meier's "UFO" photos was very easy. This was also true when we replicated his movie footage. Not only did our lightweight model "rock" back-and-forth in the wind like the "Pleiadian ships" can be seen doing in Meier's movies, but the act of even obtaining some helium turned out to be very easy.

Tina and I rented a tank from Pan Gas in Winterthur, where the company is headquartered. Winterthur is not that far from where Billy Meier used to live when he resided in Hinwill, and ironically, helium gas became available commercially for the first time ever in Switzerland in 1975, the *same year* that Billy Meier began taking his "Pleiadian" UFO pictures! Since helium is not natural to Switzerland and has to be imported, its arrival was a significant event for the country.

Figure 81 shows just one of several hundred "UFO" photos Tina and I were able to create. These particular shots were deliberately taken in Hinwill. Although our "Pleiadian" photos are admitted hoaxes, designed to prove the point that duplicating Billy Meier's "UFO" photographs is quite simple, *no* computer enhancement work done on them will ever find the fishing line we used to tether the model to the helium balloons. The fishing line was simply too fine and too far away to be picked up by the resolution of our 35mm film and single lens reflex camera. Indeed, by carefully shooting the pictures with the right amount of light and distance to the model, we were able to *hide* our support lines, which brings me back to one important point: Just because a computer can't find a "string" in a purported "UFO" photo via edge enhancement processing or other techniques does not mean that such a string does not exist! The limitation, as always, is the resolution of the film grain, which is true for any camera that uses conventional film.

While Billy Meier's "UFO" photographs are fabrications, what about his other pictures that allegedly support his claim of being in contact with Pleiadians? Are they genuine? Let's find out.

Fig. 81. (*Top*) One of some 200 fake "UFO" photos I took in Switzerland. Enlargement (*Bottom, left*) and computer edge enhancement of our fake "UFO" (*Bottom, right*); notice no string is visible!

Fig. 82. A close-up view of one of the transparent "UFO" models Tina and I brought with us to Switzerland.

Fig. 83. These models were made by Steve Horsch using clear plastic poured over an upside-down dinner plate with a cereal bowl inverted on top of it. By painting the *insides* of the models, the sun shines *through* the translucent plastic and reflects back extremely bright, just as if they were made of metal! When we assembled and attached them to helium balloons, we were able to use these models to replicate every significant aspect of Meier's "UFO" photos and motion picture films, easily proving how Meier created his pictures.

Fig. 84. A close-up view of two of the "UFO" models Tina Layton and I brought with us during our undercover trip to Switzerland. The bottom model has been painted on the *inside* of the clear plastic shell, which allows the sun's rays to penetrate the translucent surface and reflect back up off of the thousands of fine silver particles in the paint. By painting such a translucent surface on the inside in such a manner, one can obtain highly reflective, metallic-looking surfaces from normal bright, sunlit days. The top model has been painted on just the outside, and while reflective when the sun's rays strike it, its reflection is nowhere near as smooth or bright as the translucent model that was painted on the inside of its shell.

Notes

1. Wendelle Stevens, "Kal Korff and the 'Meier Hoax'—A Response Part 1," *MUFON UFO Journal*, October 1981, p. 4

2. Dr. Bruce S. Maccabee, United States Navy Optical Physicist and Photographic Expert, Bethesda, Maryland, in a letter to Kal K. Korff dated January 6, 1982

3. Jim Dilettoso, tape-recorded personal interview for the record with Kal K. Korff, Al Reed, and Barbara Reed, at the offices of Publication Professionals, Sunnyvale, California, September 6, 1980.

4. *UFO . . . Contact from the Pleiades, Volume I,* rev. ed. (Phoenix, Ariz.: Genesis III Productions, Ltd., 1979), p. 62.

5. Stevens, "Kal Korff and the Billy Meier 'Hoax'—A Response Part 1," p. 4.

6. Claudia Jacob and Margrit Jacob, personal interviews with Kal K. Korff and Tina Layton, Wetzikon, Switzerland, August 15, 1991.

7. Wendelle Stevens, "Kal Korff and the Billy Meier 'Hoax'—A Response Part 2," *MUFON UFO Journal,* November 1981, p. 11.

8. Elisabeth Gruber, personal interviews with Kal Korff and Tina Layton, Semjase Silver Star Center, Hinterschmidrüti, Switzerland, August 18, 1991.

9. Billy Meier, *Verzeichnis Authentischer Farb—Photos* (Hinterschmidrüti, Switzerland: Eduard Meier, 1975–1991), p. iii.

10. Wendelle Stevens, *UFO . . . Contact from the Pleiades—A Preliminary Investigation Report—The Report of an Ongoing Contact* (Tucson, Ariz.: Wendelle Stevens, 1983), Appendix V, p. 400.

11. Stevens, "Kal Korff and the Billy Meier 'Hoax,'—Part 1," p. 4.

12. Dr. Bruce S. Maccabee, United States Navy Optical Physicist and Photographic Expert, Bethesda, Maryland, personal correspondence with Kal K. Korff, letter dated January 6, 1982. *Also* William L. Moore, personal conversation with Kal K. Korff, Union City, California, May 1981. (Author's note: Bill Moore used to run his own professional photo service and is quite versed on camera optics.)

13. Meier, *Verzeichnis,* p. iii.

14. Ibid., p. 1.

15. Ibid.

16. Wendelle Stevens, *UFO . . . Contact from the Pleiades—A Supplementary Investigation Report—The Report of an Ongoing Contact* (Tucson, Ariz.: Wendelle Stevens, 1989), p. 387.

17. Ibid.

18. Meier, *Verzeichnis,* pp. 1, 5, 6.

19. Ibid., p. 1.

20. Kal Korff and Tina Layton's personal observations driving time from Hinwill to Frecht Nature Preserve, driving car slowly to simulate Meier's estimated moped speeds.

21. Stevens, *Supplementary Investigation Report,* p. 304.

22. Ibid.

23. Wendelle Stevens, *Message from the Pleiades, the Contact Notes of Eduard "Billy" Meier, Volume I* (Phoenix, Ariz.: Wendelle C. Stevens and Genesis III Publishing, 1988), p. 24.

24. Meier, *Verzeichnis,* p. 1.

25. Ibid., pp. 1, 5, 6. Also, author's personal observation (before hidden video camera with Elisabeth Gruber) viewing every Meier photobinder containing all 1,058 pictures at the Meier compound, Hinterschmidrüti, Switzerland, August 18, 1991.

26. *UFO . . . Contact from the Pleiades, Vol. I,* rev. ed., pp. 62–63.

27. Stevens, *Message from the Pleiades, Volume I,* p. 24.

28. Ibid.

29. Guido Moosbrugger, . . . *und sie fliegen doch! UFOs: Die größte Heraus-forderung des 20 Jahrhunderts* (München, Germany: Michael Hesemann Verlag, 1991), p. 411.

30. Meier, *Verzeichnis,* pp. 6–7.

31. Stevens, *Preliminary Investigation Report,* p. 302.

32. Meier, *Verzeichnis,* pp. 6–7.

33. Stevens, *Preliminary Investigation Report,* p. 302.

34. Meier, *Verzeichnis,* pp. 6–7.

35. Stevens, *Preliminary Investigation Report,* p. 304.

36. Moosbrugger, . . . *und sie fliegen doch!* p. 411.

37. Meier, *Verzeichnis,* p. 7.

38. Author's personal observation (before hidden video camera with Elisabeth Gruber), August 18, 1991.

39. Meier, *Verzeichnis,* pp. 6–7.

40. Stevens, *Preliminary Investigation Report,* p. 302.

41. Moosbrugger, . . . *und sie fliegen doch!,* p. 411. *See also* Stevens, *Preliminary Investigation Report,* p. 304.

42. Elisabeth Gruber, personal interviews with Kal Korff and Tina Layton, Hinterschmidrüti, Switzerland, August 18, 1991. *Also* Stevens, *Preliminary Investigation Report,* p. 304.

43. Elisabeth Gruber, personal interviews with Kal Korff and Tina Layton, August 18, 1991. *See also* Stevens, *Preliminary Investigation Report,* pp. 302–304.

44. Ibid., p. 304.

45. Moosbrugger, . . . *und sie fliegen doch!* p. 411.

46. Elisabeth Gruber, personal interviews with Kal Korff and Tina Layton, August 18, 1991.

47. Wendelle Stevens, "A Most Remarkable Recurring UFO Case!" *Argosy UFO* magazine, May 1977, p. 38.

48. Stevens, *Preliminary Investigation Report,* p. 302.

49. Meier, *Verzeichnis,* p. 4.

50. Ibid.

51. Ibid.

52. Ibid.
53. Ibid.
54. Ibid.
55. Ibid., pp. 14–15.
56. Ibid.
57. Ibid.
58. Stevens, *Supplementary Investigation Report,* pp. 85–89.
59. Moosbrugger, . . . *und sie fliegen doch!* p. 416.
60. Meier, *Verzeichnis,* pp. 14–15, 21–23.
61. Ibid.
62. Stevens, *Supplementary Investigation Report,* pp. 84–88. *See also* Stevens, *Message from the Pleiades, Volume I,* pp. 155–63, 175–79.
63. Stevens, *Supplementary Investigation Report,* pp. 85, 87. *See also* Stevens, *Message from the Pleiades, Volume I,* p. 155.
64. Cornelia Jacob, personal interviews with Kal K. Korff and Tina Layton, Wetzikon, Switzerland, August 19, 1991.
65. Stevens, *Supplementary Investigation Report,* p. 84. *See also* Stevens, *Message from the Pleiades, Volume I,* p. 155. *Also* Margrit Jacob, personal interviews with Kal K. Korff and Tina Layton, Wetzikon, Switzerland, August 19, 1991.
66. Claudia Jacob, personal interviews with Kal K. Korff and Tina Layton, Wetzikon, Switzerland, August 19, 1991.
67. Cornelia Jacob, personal interviews with Kal K. Korff and Tina Layton, Wetzikon, Switzerland, August 19, 1991.
68. Margrit Jacob, personal interviews with Kal K. Korff and Tina Layton, Wetzikon, Switzerland, August 19, 1991.
69. Claudia Jacob, Cornelia Jacob, Margrit Jacob, personal interviews with Kal K. Korff and Tina Layton, Wetzikon, Switzerland, August 19, 1991.
70. Meier, *Verzeichnis,* p. 8.
71. Stevens, *Supplementary Investigation Report,* pp. 381–84.
72. Meier, *Verzeichnis,* pp. 8, 10.
73. Ibid.
74. Ibid.
75. Ibid., p. 8.
76. Ibid., p. 10.
77. Ibid.
78. Ibid., p. 10.
79. Elisabeth Gruber and Simone, personal interviews with Kal Korff and Tina Layton, Hinterschmidrüti, Switzerland, August 18, 1991.

80. Elisabeth Gruber and Simone, personal interviews with Kal Korff and Tina Layton, Hinterschmidrüti, Switzerland, August 18, 1991.

81. Ibid.

82. Ibid.

83. Stevens, *Preliminary Investigation Report*, pp. 330–33.

84. Meier, *Verzeichnis*, p. 11.

85. Elisabeth Gruber and Simone, personal interviews with Kal Korff and Tina Layton, Hinterschmidrüti, Switzerland, August 18, 1991.

86. Ibid.

87. Meier, *Verzeichnis*, pp. 10–11.

88. Ibid., p. 10.

89. Ibid.

90. Ibid., p. 8.

91. Ibid., p. 10.

92. Ibid., p. 8.

93. Ibid.

94. Ibid., pp. 10–11.

95. Personal interview by Kal K. Korff with the Schweiz Meteorologische Zentralanstalt, May 1980.

96. Meier, *Verzeichnis*, pp. 8–10.

97. Stevens, "Kal Korff and the Billy Meier 'Hoax'—A Response Part 2," p. 14.

98. Wanderkarte (1:25000) Tösstal Zürcher Oberland, Orell Füssli, RV Verlag, Photoglob AG, 1988.

99. Stevens, *Preliminary Investigation Report*, p. 331.

100. Stevens, *Supplementary Investigation Report*, p. 375.

101. Personal interview by Kal K. Korff with the Schweiz Meteorologische Zentralanstalt, May 1980. *Also* Kal Korff's and Tina Layton's personal observations at the Fuchsbüel location, Fuchsbüel am Hofhalden, Switzerland, August and September 1991.

102. Personal interview by Kal K. Korff with the Schweiz Meteorologische Zentralanstalt, May 1980.

103. Ibid.

104. Stevens, *Preliminary Investigation Report*, p. 333. *See also* Stevens, Messages from the Pleiades, Volume I, p. 277. *See also* Stevens, *Supplementary Investigation Report*, pp. 375–84.

105. Meier, *Verzeichnis*, pp. 8, 10.

106. Elisabeth Gruber, personal interviews with Kal Korff and Tina Layton, Hinterschmidrüti, Switzerland, August 18, 1991.

107. Moosbrugger, . . . *und sie fliegen doch!* p. 411.

108. Kal Korff's and Tina Layton's personal observations at the Fuchsbüel location, August–September 1991, Fuchsbüel am Hofhalden, Switzerland.

109. Ibid.

110. Ibid.

111. Ibid.

112. Ibid.

113. Ibid.

114. Stevens, *Supplementary Investigation Report*, p. 380.

115. Kal Korff's and Tina Layton's personal observations at the Fuchsbüel location, August–September 1991, Fuchsbüel am Hofhalden, Switzerland.

116. Stevens, *Supplementary Investigation Report*, pp. 375–84.

117. Kal Korff, *The Meier Incident—The Most Infamous Hoax in UFOlogy* (Prescott, Ariz.: Townescribe Press, 1981), pp. 30–33.

118. Colman VonKeviczky, personal telephone conversation with Kal K. Korff, September, 1980. *Also* Claudia Jacob and Margrit Jacob, personal interviews with Kal K. Korff and Tina Layton. Wetzikon, Switzerland, August 15–18, 1991.

119. Colman VonKeviczky, personal telephone conversation with Kal K. Korff, September 1980.

120. Ibid.

121. Wendelle Stevens, "Billy Meier Is No Hoaxer!" letter to Kal Korff and readership of magazine, published in *Frontiers of Science*, March–April 1981, p. 9.

122. Colman VonKeviczky, personal phone conversation with Kal K. Korff, Jackson Heights, New York, September 5, 1981.

123. Ibid. *Also* Claudia Jacob and Margrit Jacob, personal interviews with Kal K. Korff and Tina Layton, August 15–18, 1991.

124. Colman VonKeviczky, personal telephone conversation with Kal K. Korff, September 1980.

125. Colman VonKeviczky, personal telephone conversation with Kal K. Korff, September 1980. *Also* Claudia Jacob and Margrit Jacob, personal interviews with Kal K. Korff and Tina Layton, August 15–18, 1991.

126. Meier, *Verzeichnis*, pp. 8, 10.

127. Moosbrugger, . . . *und sie fliegen doch!* pp. 259–62.

128. Stevens, *Preliminary Investigation Report*, p. 333. *See also* Stevens, *Supplementary Investigation Report*, p. 376.

129. *UFO . . . Contact from the Pleiades, Volume II*, 1st ed. (Phoenix, Ariz.: Genesis III Productions, Ltd., 1983), p. 66.

130. Elisabeth Gruber, personal interviews with Kal Korff and Tina Layton, Hinterschmidrüti, Switzerland, August 18, 1991.

131. Claudia Jacob and Margrit Jacob, personal interviews with Kal K. Korff and Tina Layton, Wetzikon, Switzerland, August 30, 1991.

132. Ibid.

133. Kal K. Korff's and Tina Layton's actual average driving times more than twelve times during six on-site visits to the Fuchsbüel am Hofhalden site, August and September 1991.

134. Claudia Jacob and Margrit Jacob, personal interviews with Kal K. Korff and Tina Layton, August 18, 1991. *Also* Kal K. Korff's and Tina Layton's personal observations, accompanying Margrit Jacob to the Wyss family farm at Fuchsbüel am Hofhalden, Switzerland, August 30, 1991.

135. Stevens, *Supplementary Investigation Report*, p. 375.

136. Elisabeth Gruber, personal interviews with Kal Korff and Tina Layton, Hinterschmidrüti, Switzerland, August 18, 1991.

137. Kal K. Korff's and Tina Layton's personal observations, accompanying Margrit Jacob to the Wyss family farm at Fuchsbüel am Hofhalden, Switzerland, August 30, 1991.

138. Ibid.

139. Ibid.

140. Ibid.

141. Meier, *Verzeichnis*, p. 32.

142. Stevens, *Supplementary Investigation Report*, p. 387.

143. Ibid.

144. Meier, *Verzeichnis*, p. 32.

145. Ibid.

146. Ibid., pp. 27–32.

147. Ibid.

148. Stevens, *Supplementary Investigation Report*, p. 387.

149. Meier, *Verzeichnis*, pp. 23–27.

150. Stevens, *Supplementary Investigation Report*, p. 429.

151. Meier, *Verzeichnis*, pp. 23–27.

152. Stevens, *Supplementary Investigation Report*, p. 429.

153. Ibid., pp. 23–27.

154. Ibid.

155. Ibid., p. 25.

156. Stevens, *Supplementary Investigation Report*, p. 429.

157. Stevens, *Message from the Pleiades, Volume II*, p. 238.

158. Stevens, *Supplementary Investigation Report*, p. 429.

159. Meier, *Verzeichnis*, pp. 23–27.

160. Jim Dilettoso and Wendelle Stevens, statements at the UFO '80 conference, Oakland, California, August 23–24, 1980.

161. Stevens, *Preliminary Investigation Report*, pp. 351–53. (Author's note: This reference by Stevens is accurate, since photos and video footage of the Hasenböl-Langenberg site independent of Meier have appeared in numerous other sources over the years.

162. Elisabeth Gruber, personal interviews with Kal Korff and Tina Layton, Hinterschmidrüti, Switzerland, August 18, 1991.

163. Author's personal observation, Canton Zürich region, Switzerland, August 15–September 2, 1991.

164. Meier, *Verzeichnis*, pp. 25–27.

165. Stevens, *Preliminary Investigation Report*, p. 352.

166. Ibid., pp. 351–53.

167. Meier, *Verzeichnis*, p. 32.

168. Ibid.

169. Stevens, *Supplementary Investigation Report*, p. 443.

170. Meier, *Verzeichnis*, p. 32.

171. Kinder, *Light Years*, fourth color photo (hardcover edition).

172. Meier, *Verzeichnis*, pp. 25–27.

173. Ibid.

174. Stevens, *Supplementary Investigation Report*, p. 443.

175. Ibid., p. 457.

176. Stevens, *Messages from the Pleiades, Volume II*, p. 6.

177. Ibid., p. 265.

178. *Jane's All the World Aircraft 1977 Edition* (London, England: 1977), p. 54.

179. Kal Korff and Tina Layton's personal observations, Canton Zürich region, Switzerland, August 15–September 2, 1991.

180. Ibid.

181. Ibid.

182. Ibid.

183. Meier, *Verzeichnis*, p. 115.

184. Ibid.

185. Ibid.

186. Ibid., pp. 115–16.

187. Ibid.

188. Elisabeth Gruber, personal interviews with Kal Korff and Tina Layton, Hinterschmidrüti, Switzerland, August 18, 1991. *See also* Meier, *Verzeichnis*, pp. 115–16.

189. Kal Korff, *The Meier Incident—The Most Infamous Hoax in UFOlogy* (Prescott, Ariz: Townescribe Press, 1981), pp. 45–62.

190. Ibid.

5

Smoking Guns: Analyzing Meier's "Time-Travel" Photographs

> If you travel into space, you will find humans wherever you go.
> And when they start to think, they need a teacher. If they have
> never seen a flower before, never heard anything about a flower,
> the one who knows the flower can teach them. And this is the way
> over the whole universe. The (UFO) photographs are only to make
> people think, to show them something; people shall come for
> these pictures, but they shall study the teachings, and they shall
> come to know.
>
> Eduard "Billy" Meier[1]

In chapter 7 of his *Preliminary Investigation Report*, Wendelle
Stevens presents the details of Billy Meier's "31st contact," a
period of *five days* during which Meier purportedly left the
Earth and ventured into outer space on board a Pleiadian
spacecraft with Semjase.[2] During this alleged journey, Meier
claims he visited the planets Venus[3] and Mercury,[4] and personally witnessed (along with four other extraterrestrial races)
the historic American Apollo and Soviet Soyuz space capsule
link-up of July 17, 1975.[5] As if this weren't exciting enough,
Meier also says that he returned for a *second* visit to the Pleiadian *Grossraumer* or "mother ship,"[6] where he met an alien
named "Ptaah," who was Semjase's father.[7]

233

After being given a tour of the mother ship and conversing at length with Ptaah, Meier says he traveled to the Pleiades star cluster[8] and what he calls the "DAL Universe,"[9] where he visited more alien worlds, observing different life forms in various stages of evolution.[10]

Billy Meier claims he took the majority of the photographs from his incredible trip while on board the spaceship by either aiming the lens of his camera out the porthole of the craft,[11] or by shooting off of a color flat panel display screen.[12]

Did Billy Meier really leave the Earth as claimed? What do the pictures he took during his alleged journey tell us, if anything?

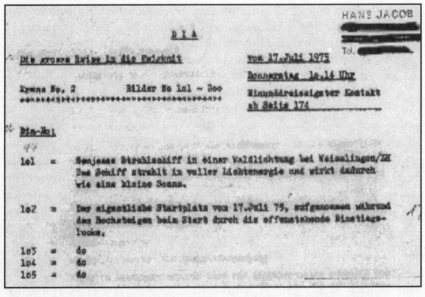

Fig. 85. This is the first page of the photo catalog Hans Jacob typed up which lists all of Billy Meier's UFO and time-travel photos. Jacob worked very closely with Meier to document each picture listed and the details of how they were supposedly taken. Most of the photos listed in Jacob's catalog, curiously, do not appear in Billy Meier's *Verzeichnis*, the official photo catalog published by the Semjase Silver Star Center. (Photo courtesy: Margrit and Claudia Jacob.)

The photo-binder kept by Hans Jacob documents in painstaking detail not only all of the locations Meier claims he visited, but contains first- and second-generation photographs of each of these places. What follows now is an examination and analysis of this material and the various claims that are associated with them. Please keep in mind that many of these photographs have never been published until now and that Meier and his supporters claim that these photographs have been "recalled" by the Pleiadians![13]

Photographs of the Planet Venus

Date(s):   July 17, 1975[14]

Time(s):   Not stated[15]

Location(s):   Inside Semjase's spacecraft, on the way
                    to the planet Venus[16]

Meier Photo   Not listed in the *Verzeichnis*, "recalled"
Number(s):   by the Pleiadians[17]

Photographer(s): Eduard "Billy" Meier[18]

Background Details

After Meier boarded Semjase's spacecraft, the first place she flew her spaceship was to the planet Venus, where Billy Meier got to see and "photograph" Venus while they were in orbit above it.[19]

Meier's photographs of the planet Venus originally appeared in Wendelle Stevens's unpublished manuscript for his *Preliminary Investigation Report*. When Stevens later released his *Preliminary Investigation Report* to the public, virtually *all* of the Meier time-travel photos were omitted! Thus, very few people have seen these images.

Unless otherwise indicated, all photographs analyzed in this chapter are from the Jacob collection.

Analysis of the Venus Photographs

• Meier reported that the alien view screen from which he took his photographs from inside the ship measured some "50 centimeters by 50 centimeters" or 19 inches by 19 inches in size, and was perfectly square. Meier also described the resolution of the images on this alien view screen as a *"finely scanned (sharpened image), similar to (laser) scanned photographs."*[20]

While it is not possible to determine the size or shape of this alleged alien view screen by examining Meier's Venus photos, the images nonetheless are out-of-focus and do not reflect the quality and clarity one would expect from a display device that was described as a *"finely scanned (sharpened image), similar to (laser) scanned photographs."*

• Billy Meier's "photographs of Venus" match *exactly* those taken by the NASA Mariner 10 spacecraft from its mission of *February 1974!*[21] As illustrated in figures 88 and 89, a simple visual examination of these photographs proves this.

• The cloud formations visible in Meier's version of his "photographs of Venus" are *identical* to the cloud formations in NASA's Mariner 10 pictures! This proves conclusively that Meier's photos are out-of-focus copies of the Mariner 10 images, taken seventeen months *before* his alleged "contact."

• Even if Meier's images were not a precise match with the NASA photographs, the pictures could *not* have been taken as Meier claims. The atmosphere of Venus is extremely dense and severely reflective in nature. Normal light from a camera lens cannot penetrate it. Thus, any picture taken of Venus without special filtering to compensate for this denseness will reveal no atmospheric details whatsoever.[22]

When Mariner 10 filmed Venus, NASA used a *special ultra-violet filter,* which allowed scientists to see the "atmospheric bands" of the planet, providing both better contrast and superior resolution. If NASA had used no filters, as Billy Meier did, their pictures of Venus would have been virtually useless.[23] Thus, the images of Venus visible in Billy Meier's photos show the planet as it appears when viewed by an *ultraviolet filter.* Since neither Billy Meier's camera nor the "Pleiadian view screen" were equipped with such a filter, Meier's images and how he claims he obtained them are an impossibility.

Conclusion

Billy Meier's photographs of Venus are really NASA Mariner 10's spacecraft images.

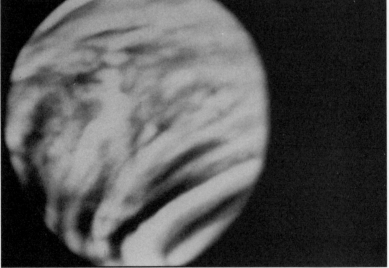

Figs. 86 and 87. These are the photographs of Venus Billy Meier claims he took on July 17, 1975, with his camera while "in orbit" above the planet on board the Pleiadian spacecraft. These photos have never been published until now! (Photos courtesy: Margrit and Claudia Jacob.)

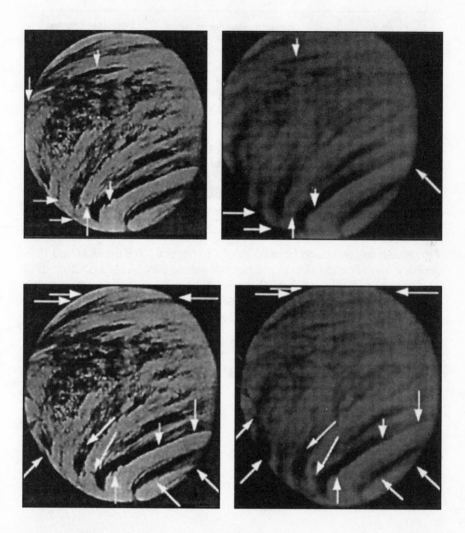

Figs. 88 and 89. The photos on the left are Mariner 10's ultraviolet-filtered image of Venus from its February 1974 flyby. The photos on the right are Billy Meier's pictures of Venus, which he claims he took on July 17, 1975, while on board a Pleiadian spaceship. I added numerous arrows to point out cloud formations which are identical in both photos, *proving* conclusively that Meier's pictures are really those taken by the NASA Mariner 10 spacecraft! (Left top and bottom photos courtesy: NASA/bottom photos courtesy: Margrit and Claudia Jacob.)

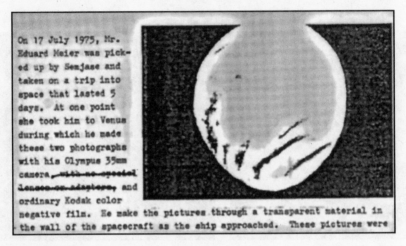

On 17 July 1975, Mr. Eduard Meier was picked up by Semjase and taken on a trip into space that lasted 5 days. At one point she took him to Venus during which he made these two photographs with his Olympus 35mm camera, ~~with no special lenses or adapters,~~ and ordinary Kodak color negative film. He make the pictures through a transparent material in the wall of the spacecraft as the ship approached. These pictures were

Fig. 90. An excerpt page from Wendelle Stevens's 1978 unpublished *Preliminary Investigation Report* manuscript where Billy Meier's photographs of Venus were first mentioned. Curiously, when Stevens later published his *Preliminary Investigation Report* in 1982, virtually every time-travel photograph taken by Meier was deliberately omitted!

Apollo-Soyuz Link-up Photos

Date(s):   July 17, 1975[24]

Time(s):   Sometime after 1630hrs. Swiss time[25]

Location(s):   Semjase's spacecraft, after visiting
                    Venus and Mercury[26]

*Meier Photo   Not listed in Meier's *Verzeichnis* catalog[27]
Number(s):*

Photographer(s): Eduard "Billy" Meier[28]

Background Details

Meier claims that after visiting the planets of Venus and Mercury, Semjase flew her ship over the Earth so that he could witness and photograph the historic American Apollo 18 and Soviet Soyuz space capsule link-up of July 17, 1975.[29]

According to Meier, as he hovered above the Earth to observe the docking of the two space ships, his watch read 1630 hrs.,[30] which means that the total time elapsed on Semjase's ship had been up to this point, seven hours.[31]

Although Billy Meier's Apollo-Soyuz space photographs have received minor coverage in the pro-Meier literature, in Switzerland copies can be purchased easily when visiting the Meier farm. The Semjase Silver Star Center sells them for five Swiss francs each per color print.

Do Billy Meier's photographs show the real Apollo-Soyuz space capsule link-up?

Analysis of the Apollo-Soyuz Link-up Photographs

• Meier claims that when he photographed the Apollo-Soyuz link-up, he aimed his camera at the alien view screen and snapped his pictures.[32] Although Meier says that the Pleiadian viewing screen was flat, square-shaped, and measured "50 centimeters by 50 centimeters" or 19 inches on each side,[33] a close examination of the *far right corners* of Meier's pictures reveals that the screen from which they were taken was *rectangular* in shape and *curved*, not flat and square-shaped as claimed. The screen in fact looks similar to a standard color television monitor, curvature and all.

• All of Meier's photographs of the Apollo-Soyuz link-up are slightly out-of-focus, off-color, and bear no resemblance to the *"finely scanned (sharpened image), similar to (laser) scanned photographs"*[34] quality as previously claimed.

• Billy Meier's Apollo-Soyuz space docking photographs

are *animation simulations* and are not *real pictures* of the historic event. The animation simulations are distinguishable from real images of the Soyuz spacecraft taken by Apollo 18 because of errors in the way the solar panel arrays were drawn by the artists on the Soyuz ship. For example, in the animations, the solar panel arrays on the Soyuz spacecraft appear "folded" and are not fully extended or in the "locked" position. This is precisely what we see in Billy Meier's version as well. However, in genuine photographs taken of the *real* Soyuz spacecraft by Apollo 18, one finds just the *opposite* to be true: the Soyuz spaceship's solar panel arrays are perfectly straight and are in the "locked" position. (See figure 92, page 244, for an illustration of this.)

According to NASA, when the Apollo-Soyuz spaceships docked, the Soyuz's solar panels were *fully extended and in the locked position.* This was normal for the Soyuz craft since the solar arrays served as an extra power source for the ship and had to be extended fully in order to function properly. Thus, the Soyuz spacecraft regularly flew with its solar arrays fully extended.[35]

• A close examination of the Meier prints which purport to show the docking reveals that the individual solar panel segments on each array of the Soyuz spacecraft *differ in size and proportion* when compared with real photos taken of the Soyuz by Apollo 18. (See figure 92.)

• The time that Meier claims he witnessed the Apollo-Soyuz link-up is incorrect, despite the fact that Meier says he *checked his watch first,* which supposedly read 1630 hrs.[36]

According to both official records at NASA and the *TRW Space Log* for 1975, the Apollo-Soyuz space docking took place at 1115 hrs. central daylight time,[37] which is 1915 hrs. Swiss time. Since Meier's watch would have shown what time it was back in his home country of Switzerland when he supposedly glanced at it, his statement about the time of his "experience" is in error by approximately two hours and forty-five minutes!

Conclusion

Billy Meier's photographs of the Apollo-Soyuz space capsule link-up are really out-of-focus stills from animation simulating the historic space docking. A comparison of the Soyuz spacecraft image in Meier's photos versus real pictures taken during the actual mission by Apollo 18 reveals significant discrepancies, which prove that Meier's versions do *not* show the real Soyuz craft!

Fig. 91. One of Meier's thirty photos of the Apollo-Soyuz space capsule link-up, which he claims he witnessed while in space aboard Semjase's spaceship. Arrows indicate the screen Meier shot these pictures from was *curved* and *rectangular* in shape, not flat and square-shaped as he claimed. (Photo courtesy: Margrit and Claudia Jacob.)

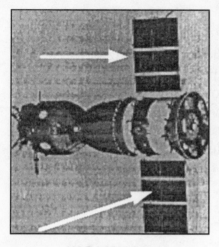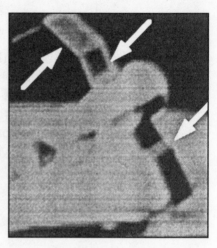

NASA Version   **Billy Meier's Version**

Fig. 92. (*Left*) The *real* Soviet Soyuz spacecraft as photographed by Apollo 18, July 17, 1975. The arrows point to obvious differences between the two Soyuz images, proving that Meier's version is not the real thing. (Left photo courtesy: NASA/Right photo courtesy: Margrit and Claudia Jacob.)

"DAL Universe Cosmonaut" Photographs

Date(s):   July 17–18, 1975, according to Stevens[38]
                        June 26, 1975, according to Billy Meier[39]

Time(s):   Not specified by Wendelle Stevens
                        2100 hrs. according to Billy Meier[40]

Location(s):   On board the Pleiadian "mother ship"
                        in the "DAL Universe"[41]

Meier Photo   109, 110, 111[42]
Number(s):

Photographer(s):   Eduard "Billy" Meier[43]

Background Details

After Meier was on board the Pleiadian mother ship for some time, he asked if he could take some pictures of the three "cosmonauts" he was conversing with: Asket, Nera, and Semjase. The Pleiadians supposedly relented, so Meier took three photographs. Do Billy Meier's pictures really show genuine aliens from the "DAL Universe" as claimed?

Analysis of the "DAL Cosmonaut" Photographs

• Contrary to what Meier claims, his three photographs of the "DAL cosmonauts" are *not* images of real people standing in physical space, nor are they of three-dimensional objects. Indeed, computer edge enhancements reveal that they are faint images and are two-dimensional, taken from a curved screen, just like virtually every other "time-travel" photograph Meier claims to have shot with his camera.

• The photographs supposedly showing the alien cosmonauts are out-of-focus and are *optically backwards* from the alleged characteristics of Meier's camera.

Remember, Meier's camera is jammed just short of the infinity setting, which means that objects *farthest* away from his lens will be in *better focus* than those objects closer to him. Since this is supposed to be the case, then how does one explain the fact that the "cosmonaut" *closest* to Meier is in better focus than the one standing farther away? Unfortunately, cameras don't work this way.

When I confronted Wendelle Stevens with these optical discrepancies at the 1983 National UFO Conference in Tucson, Arizona, he never responded. One could tell from the shocked look on his face that he had never even thought of this obvious point!

• Analysis of the background "wall" behind the two alleged "aliens" reveals that it is covered with a curtain! This is intriguing, since nowhere among the thousands of "contact notes" by Billy Meier is there any mention that the "Pleiadians" or "DALs" decorate the interior of their ships with terrestrial-looking "curtains."

• Meier describes the clothing of these alleged aliens as "rather different from those I know of Earth women's fashions."[44] However, the clothes are typical of the 1970s style, right down to the wide collars that were popular for that decade. In fact, the clothing these "cosmonauts" are wearing is indistinguishable from that of ordinary Earth fashions!

• Jim Dilettoso claims that the Pleiadians have what he calls "elongated earlobes" that extend all the way down to the jaw line, unlike Earthlings. Dilettoso has even stated that in Meier's alien photographs you can see that the ear-lobes are longer than those of human beings.[45] This is not true, as figure 94 proves. What Jim Dilettoso *claims* is an "elongated earlobe" is in fact a *lock of hair!*

Conclusion

The "cosmonaut" photographs were taken from a television monitor and are not genuine pictures of real beings standing in three-dimensional space.

Fig. 93. According to Meier and his supporters, this is a photo of "Asket and Nera," two aliens from the "DAL Universe."

Fig. 94. Another photo from Billy Meier that purportedly shows the "DAL cosmonaut" named Asket. According to Jim Dilettoso, this is a real photo of an alien because "elongated earlobes" are visible. This is simply not true. Indeed, a close examination of this picture clearly proves that what Dilettoso *claims* are two earlobes are actually locks of hair! (Photos courtesy: Margrit and Claudia Jacob.)

Other Meier "Time-Travel" Photographs *Never* Published Before!

The photo-binder that was meticulously kept by Hans Jacob is dominated by dozens of pictures Meier claims he took during his five-day "trip" into outer space. These photos have conveniently been "recalled" by the "Pleiadians"[46] and have been *omitted* in every pro-Meier book yet released. No examination of the Meier case is complete without addressing these images. Since there are more than sixty such pictures in the Jacob photo-binder, what is included here for analysis is a thorough cross-sampling.

The Dinosaur Photographs

Date(s):   July 17, 1975, according to Hans Jacob/
                   Billy Meier photo-binder[47]

Time(s):   Not specified by Hans Jacob/
                   Billy Meier photo-binder[48]

Location(s):   The planet "Neber"[49]

Meier Photo   N/A—"recalled" by the Pleiadians[50]
Number(s):

Photographer(s): Eduard "Billy" Meier[51]

Background Details

One of the planets that Billy Meier claims he visited is allegedly called "Neber," which Meier says is 1.2 million light-years from Earth.[52] While visiting this planet, Meier said that he observed pyramids, dinosaurs, and a primitive "cave-man" walking around![53]

Analysis of the "Dinosaur" Photographs

• The photos of the dinosaurs are out-of-focus, thus obscuring potentially important details. This makes no logical sense when one considers the purported optical characteristics of Billy Meier's camera and the "fact" that the lens is supposed to be jammed in such a way that images located at a distance will be clearer. Dinosaurs are very large creatures and Meier had to be more than *seventy feet away* from these large reptiles in order to fit them in the frame of his pictures.

• In Meier's second "dinosaur" photo, the creatures are equally out-of-focus, which is not possible since his second picture was taken from a distance which was at least fifty percent *closer* than his first picture. If Billy Meier had really stood on the surface of a planet and walked toward these dinosaurs (or they to him) to take this second picture, the focus level in the photo would have changed accordingly. Instead, both photos are equally out-of-focus when in fact they should not be.

Conclusion

While there is no way to prove that Billy Meier's pictures do not show real dinosaurs (there are no live ones in existence today with which to compare the images), the fact remains that Meier could *not* have taken his photos as claimed under the conditions he describes.

Figs. 95 and 96. Two of Meier's "dinosaur" photos taken during what he claims was a "visit" to the planet "Neber." This is the first time that these Meier "dinosaur" photographs have ever been published. The pictures appear in the Jacob photo-binder and are part of a collection of over 60 images taken during Billy Meier's five-day "trip" into time/space. (Photos courtesy: Margrit and Claudia Jacob.)

Fig. 97. A page from Wendelle Stevens's unpublished *Preliminary Investigation Report* manuscript showing still more "dinosaur" pictures. For reasons that have yet to be explained, Stevens omitted these damaging photos when his book was published.

"Cave-Man" Photographs

Date(s):   July 17, 1975, according to Hans Jacob/
                     Billy Meier photo-binder[54]

Time(s):   Not specified by Hans Jacob/
                     Billy Meier photo-binder[55]

Location(s):   The planet "Neber"[56]

Meier Photo   N/A—"recalled" by the Pleiadians[57]
Number(s):

Photographer(s):   Eduard "Billy" Meier[58]

Background Details

Billy Meier claims that while visiting the planet "Neber,"[59] he
observed primitive life forms of various kinds,[60] including
what he described as a "cave-man" walking around.[61] He then
took two photographs of this alleged primitive being.

Analysis of Billy Meier's "Cave-Man" Photographs

• A careful examination of Meier's "cave-man" pictures
proves once again that they were shot from a visual monitor
and not in a real, physical, outdoor environment. As the
arrows in figure 100 on page 255 clearly illustrate, the curvature of the monitor can be easily seen.

• Although Billy Meier's two pictures of this "cave-man"
are supposed to have been taken consecutively and only a
few seconds apart, a careful examination of his photos reveals
that the human-like figure visible in them actually *changes*
from the first picture to the next. In the first photo of his "cave-

man" series, the figure is obviously an ape-like creature. However, in his second "cave-man" picture, the figure suddenly changes into what paleontologists would call a Neanderthal man. How and why this figure changes suddenly from ape to man is never explained by Billy Meier, and this discrepancy is not accounted for in any of the pro-Meier books and literature. In fact, the very existence of these incriminating pictures are ignored entirely and no mention of them is ever made!

• Meier's two photographs are out-of-focus once again, and there is no logical reason for this. The images in his pictures also indicate motion blur, which is illogical as well, since his film speed was ASA 100 and his shutter speed was $\frac{1}{100}$th of a second,[62] taken in daylight hours while allegedly on the planet "Neber."

Conclusion

Billy Meier's two "photographs" of the alleged "cave-man" do not show any such creature. His first picture shows an ape, the second a man. The images are out-of-focus and could not have been taken outdoors on the surface of a planet (alien or otherwise) as claimed. The curvature of a monitor, visible in the lower right-hand corner of his second picture, proves this. See figure 100 for illustration revealing discrepancies between the two photos.

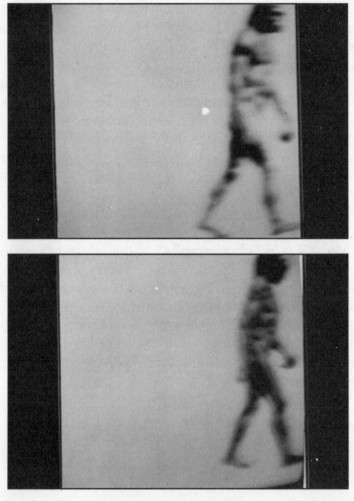

Figs. 98 and 99. These pictures show an alleged "cave-man" as "photographed" by Billy Meier during his five-day "trip" into outer space. Like most of Meier's "time-travel" images, this picture has never been published before, until now. (Photos courtesy: Margrit and Claudia Jacob.)

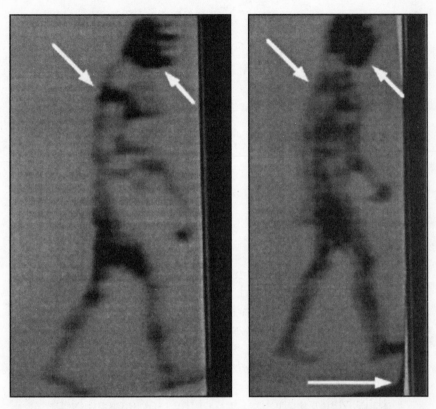

Fig. 100. Arrows at the top of each image point to discrepancies between Billy Meier's two "cave-man" photographs. The bottom right arrow points to the edge of a monitor screen from which Meier most probably shot the image from. (Photos courtesy: Margrit and Claudia Jacob.)

Billy Meier's Picture of the Horse Head Nebulae

Date(s):   July 17, 1975, according to Hans Jacob/
                        Billy Meier photo-binder[63]

Time(s):   Not specified by Hans Jacob/
                        Billy Meier photo-binder[64]

Location(s):   On board Semjase's spacecraft[65]

Meier Photo   243 according to Hans Jacob/
Number(s):   Billy Meier photo-binder[66]

Photographer(s):   Eduard "Billy" Meier[67]

Background Details

Another astronomical wonder Billy Meier claims he photographed when he passed within a "few thousand kilometers"[68] of it is the Horse Head Nebulae. Figure 101 on page 258
from the Jacob binder shows the picture that Meier took.

Analysis of Horse Head Nebulae Photograph

• Billy Meier's photograph of the Horse Head Nebulae is
out-of-focus when it should not be, due to the reported optical characteristics of his camera. Since the nebulae was more
than thirty to fifty feet away, it should have been in much better focus than his picture shows.
• The Horse Head Nebulae is several light-years across
and several light-years deep.[69] Since one light-year is nearly
six trillion miles,[70] if Billy Meier had flown within "a few thousand kilometers" of the nebulae as he claims, it would have
been indistinguishable from his reported distance. In fact, he
would have been *inside* the nebulae itself!

• Billy Meier's photograph of the Horse Head Nebulae is yet another Earth-based astronomy photo taken from a large telescope. Indeed, the background stars and other points of comparison prove this.

• Billy Meier shot this image from a monitor, as the curvature of the screen on the right side of his picture proves. See arrow on photo in figure 101.

Conclusion

Billy Meier's "photograph" of the Horse Head Nebulae is an Earth astronomy observatory photo.

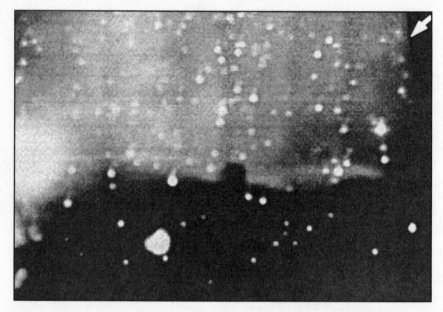

Fig. 101. This is a photo of the Horse Head Nebulae, which Billy Meier says he shot in outer space from a distance of a "few thousand kilometers." Since the Horse Head Nebulae is several light-years across, Meier could not possibly have taken the picture as claimed, since at this close range the nebulae would not have even been visible! In truth, the orientation of Meier's photo of the Horse Head Nebulae is from an Earth observatory picture and was shot from a television monitor (see arrow on upper right side of photo). (Photo courtesy: Margrit and Claudia Jacob.)

Photo of the *Grossraumer* or "Mother Ship"

Date(s):   July 17, 1975, according to
                    Wendelle Stevens[71]

Time(s):   Not specified by Wendelle Stevens[72]

Location(s):   On board Semjase's spacecraft[73]

Meier Photo   N/A—"recalled" by the Pleiadians[74]
Number(s):

Photographer(s): Eduard "Billy" Meier[75]

Background Details

After "witnessing" the Apollo-Soyuz link-up, Meier claims
that Semjase flew him in her ship to see what he calls the
Grossraumer or Pleiadian "mother ship," a craft 10.6 miles in
diameter[76] which houses "143,000 inhabitants."[77]

Analysis of the Grossraumer *or "Mother Ship"*

• Although Wendelle Stevens claims in his *Preliminary
Investigation Report* that the object in Meier's photo (see figure
100 on page 255) is seen "near a strange planet,"[78] my analysis of this picture proves that the "strange planet" is in fact the
planet Jupiter, and the "Pleiadian mother ship" is none other
than the NASA Pioneer 10 space probe!
• Figure 103 on page 260 shows a NASA animation with
arrows added pointing out features of the Pioneer unmanned
spacecraft for comparison. Notice once again that they are *virtually identical,* right down to the red "spot" in Jupiter's
atmosphere!

Conclusion

Meier's photograph of the "Pleiadian Mother Ship" is from an animation showing the Pioneer 10 unmanned spacecraft.

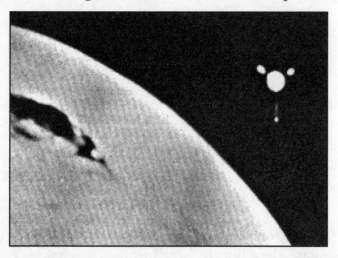

Figs.102 and 103. (*Above*) Billy Meier claims this picture shows a "Pleiadian Mother Ship" orbiting a "mysterious planet." (*Below*) Arrows show similarities between Meier's photo and a NASA animation. (Top photo courtesy: Margrit and Claudia Jacob/Bottom photo courtesy: NASA.)

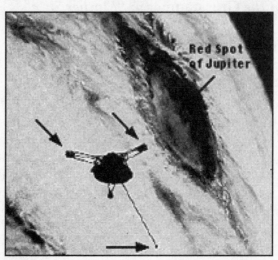

Photos of "God's Eye"

Date(s):   July 17, 1975, according to Hans Jacob/
                      Billy Meier photo-binder[79]

Time(s):   Not specified by Hans Jacob/
                      Billy Meier photo-binder[80]

Location(s):   On board Semjase's spacecraft[81]

Meier Photo   236–239 according to Hans Jacob/
Number(s):   Billy Meier photo-binder[82]

Photographer(s):   Eduard "Billy" Meier[83]

Background Details

Billy Meier says that while he was "in outer space for five days" he was fortunate enough to photograph one of God's eyes![84]

When I mentioned Meier's claim of having "photographed" God's eye in my 1981 book, the reaction by Meier's supporters (especially Wendelle Stevens) was most peculiar. They *denied* not only that Billy Meier had ever said such a thing,[85] they also *ignored* the fact that I had received copies of these actual photos from Colman VonKeviczky, who had received them from Hans Jacob.

Analysis of "God's Eye" Photographs

• Billy Meier's four pictures which purport to show the "Eye of God" are really out-of-focus copies of *Earth-based astronomy pictures* of the Ring Nebulae, located in the constellation of Lyra!

Figure 105 shows the Ring Nebulae as it appears when photographed *from Earth* through a telescope. Figure 107 on page 264 illustrates what happened when I took the *same* Earth-based picture of the Ring Nebulae, turned it upside down, flipped it backwards, rephotographed it deliberately out-of-focus, and enlarged it. The result is *identical* to Meier's pictures of what we are told is "God's Eye."

• Although Guido Moosbrugger,[86] Wendelle Stevens,[87] and other pro-Meier supporters now *deny* that Billy Meier ever claimed that he saw the "Eye of God" and took pictures of it, figure 106 from the Jacob photo-binder *proves* conclusively that Billy Meier did indeed make this claim.

Conclusion

Billy Meier's pictures of "God's Eye" are really out-of-focus copies of Earth astronomy photos of the Ring Nebulae.

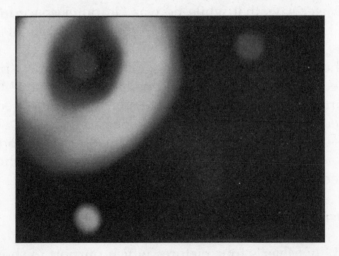

Fig. 104. One of Billy Meier's "God's Eye" photos allegedly taken during his five-day "trip" into outer space. Like many others of Meier's "time-travel" pictures, this one can also be definitively identified as showing anything *but* what Meier and his supporters claim. (Photo courtesy: Margrit and Claudia Jacob.)

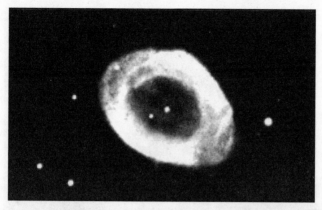

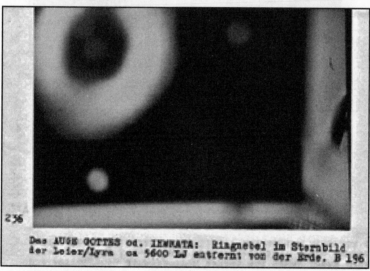

Das AUGE GOTTES od. IHWRATA: Ringnebel im Sternbild
der Leier/Lyra ca 5600 LJ entfernt von der Erde. B 196

Figs. 105 and 106. (*Top*) The Ring Nebulae in the constellation of Lyra as photographed from Earth through a large telescope. (*Bottom*) A page from the Jacob photo-binder showing one of the four "God's Eye" photos. The words "Das Auge Gottes" are German for the "Eye of God," disproving Wendelle Stevens's claim that there was a "translational error" by those who have criticized Billy Meier over the alleged authenticity of these "God's Eye" photographs. The words "Das Auge Gottes" are evidence that Billy Meier did indeed make the outlandish claim that he had traveled into space and was able to "photograph" one of "God's Eyes." (Top photo courtesy: Lick Observatory/Bottom photo courtesy: Margrit and Claudia Jacob.)

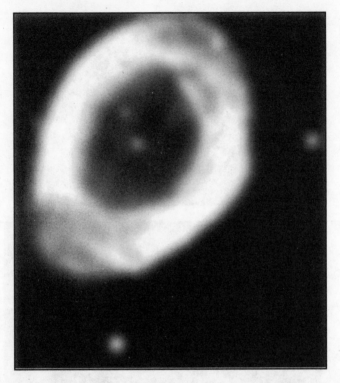

Fig.107. My recreation of Meier's "Eye of God" showing how Meier faked his photo by manipulating an astronomical photograph which was commonly available.

Where and How Billy Meier Obtained Some of His "Time-Travel" Photos

Now that we have conclusively proven that Billy Meier's "time-travel" photos are unimpressive hoaxes, where might he have obtained his images? What was Meier's "source"?

On April 27, 1976, Hans Jacob wrote a letter to *Fernsehen*, a major Swiss television station located in Zürich. Jacob included with his letter one of Billy Meier's "Apollo-Soyuz link-up" photos and asked the station if they had any idea where the image might have originated. On May 4, 1976, Mr. Heinz Schollenberger replied to Jacob and conclusively identified Meier's photo as originating from an artist's animation of the space docking that his station had aired on TV![88]

Copies of Jacob's and Schollenberger's letters are on file at TotalResearch and Underground Video, and appear in the original Jacob photo-binder.

Photographs of Another "Extraterrestrial" Spacecraft

Date(s):   July 17, 1975, according to Hans Jacob/
                    Billy Meier photo-binder[89]

Time(s):   Not specified by Hans Jacob/
                    Billy Meier photo-binder[90]

Location(s):   On board Semjase's spacecraft[91]

Meier Photo   183–185 according to Hans Jacob/
Number(s):   Billy Meier photo-binder[92]

Photographer(s): Eduard "Billy" Meier[93]

Background Details

According to Billy Meier, while orbiting the Earth in Semjase's spacecraft, he claims he observed several extraterrestrial ships from different planets in our galaxy,[94] and even took three pictures of these other purported "UFOs." These photographs have never been published before.

Analysis of "Alien Ship" Photograph

• In the lower left-hand corner of Meier's picture, one can see the reflection of a window and a tree! This proves that Billy Meier was not in "outer space" when he took these pictures.

• To settle any dispute over this issue, figures 109 and 110 on pages 267–68 show various computer enhancements I conducted revealing in more detail the window and tree reflection.

Conclusion

The existence of the reflection of a window and tree in Meier's "alien craft" photos conclusively proves that Billy Meier did not take these pictures while in outer space. Actually, Meier shot them from a television screen and in all likelihood never had to leave his living room to do so.

Finally, there is an interesting contradiction in Wendelle Stevens's account of just how long Meier's space-travel adventure supposedly lasted. In Stevens's *Preliminary Investigation Report*, he claims that Meier left the Earth for a period of five days.[95] However, in his later book, *Message from the Pleiades, Volume I*, Stevens claims that Billy Meier left the Earth on his "trip" for a period of only "30 hours."[96] Whether it was "30 hours" or "five days" is irrelevant since the analyses presented in this chapter conclusively demonstrate evidence of fabrication on the part of Billy Meier.

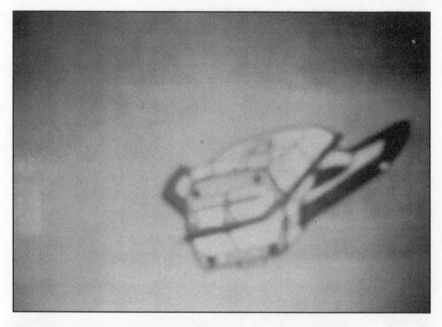

Fig. 108. One of the photos by Billy Meier which he claims shows an extraterrestrial craft. (Photo courtesy: Margrit and Claudia Jacob.)

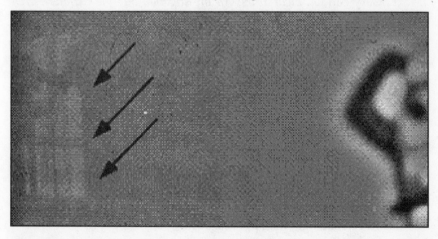

Fig. 109. I conducted a high-pass band filter computer enhancement with the contrast heightened: it revealed the window and tree reflection more clearly. This is definitive evidence that these "UFO" photographs by Billy Meier are hoaxes.

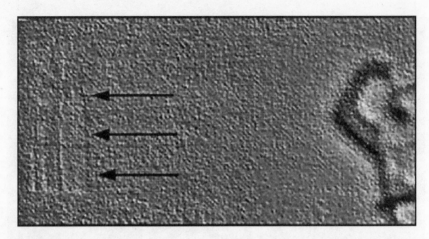

Fig. 110. Edge enhancement processing verifies the existence of this incriminating reflection, proving that Meier shot this picture off of a screen, and was not in "outer space" at the time.

Notes

1. Gary Kinder, *Light Years: An Investigation into the Extraterrestrial Experiences of Eduard Meier* (New York: Atlantic Monthly Press, 1987), p. 185.

2. Wendelle Stevens, *UFO . . . Contact from the Pleiades—A Preliminary Investigation Report—The Report of an Ongoing Contact* (Tucson, Ariz.: Wendelle Stevens, 1983), p. 98.

3. Ibid., p. 102.

4. Ibid., p. 103.

5. Ibid. *See also,* Ibid., p. 105.

6. Elisabeth Gruber and Simone, personal interviews with Kal Korff and Tina Layton, August 19, 1991, at the Semjase Silver Star Center, Hinterschmidrüti, Switzerland.

7. Wendelle Stevens, *Message from the Pleiades, the Contact Notes of Eduard "Billy" Meier, Volume I* (Phoenix, Ariz.: Wendelle C. Stevens and Genesis III Publishing, 1988), pp. 303–304.

8. Ibid., p. 318.

9. Hans Jacob, Meier Photo-binder, p. 5, col. 2.

10. Ibid., p. 6, col. 1.

11. Stevens, *Message from the Pleiades, Volume I*, p. 318.

12. Ibid., p. 286.

13. Ibid., p. 338

14. Ibid., pp. 285–86.

15. Ibid., pp. 285–91.

16. Ibid., pp. 285–87.

17. Billy Meier, *Verzeichnis Authentischer Farb—Photos* (Hinterschmid-rüti, Switzerland: Eduard Meier, 1975–1991), see entire publication.

18. Ray Stanford, tape-recorded deposition to Kal K. Korff, September 1980. *See also,* Stevens, *Message from the Pleiades, Volume I,* p. 338.

19. Stevens, *UFO . . . Contact from the Pleiades—A Preliminary Investigation Report,* p. 101.

20. Stevens, *Message from the Pleiades, Volume I,* p. 285.

21. *TRW SpaceLog 1974, Volume 13* (Redondo Beach, Calif.: TRW Systems Group, TRW Inc., 1974), p. 43.

22. Edward G. Danielsen, Jr. (Member of JPL's Mariner 10 Television Experiment Team), "Mariner 10 Results, Our Present View of Mercury and Venus," *TRW SpaceLog 1974, Volume 13* (Redondo Beach, Calif.: TRW Systems Group, TRW Inc., 1974), p. 41.

23. Ibid.

24. Stevens, *Message from the Pleiades, Volume I,* pp. 287–88.

25. Guido Moosbrugger, . . . *und sie fliegen doch! UFOs: Die größte Herausforderung des 20 Jahrhunderts* (München, Germany: Michael Hesemann Verlag, 1991), p. 417.

26. Stevens, *UFO . . . Contact from the Pleiades—A Preliminary Investigation Report,* p. 103.

27. Billy Meier, *Verzeichnis Authentischer Farb—Photos* (Hinterschmid-rüti, Switzerland: Eduard Meier, 1975–1991), see entire publication.

28. Stevens, *Message from the Pleiades, Volume I,* p. 291.

29. Ibid., p. 288.

30. Stevens, *UFO . . . Contact from the Pleiades—A Preliminary Investigation Report,* p. 103.

31. Ibid., p. 100.

32. Stevens, *Message from the Pleiades, Volume I,* p. 289.

33. Ibid., p. 285.

34. Ibid.

35. James Oberg, personal phone conversation with the author, June 1981.

36. Stevens, *UFO . . . Contact from the Pleiades—A Preliminary Investigation Report,* p. 103.

37. *TRW SpaceLog* (Redondo Beach, Calif.: 1975), p. 4.

38. Meier, *Verzeichnis,* pp. 16–17.

39. Stevens, *Message from the Pleiades, Volume I*, p. 328.

40. Meier, *Verzeichnis*, pp. 16–17.

41. Ibid.

42. Ibid.

43. Ibid.

44. Stevens, *Message from the Pleiades, Volume I*, p. 329.

45. Jim Dilettoso, tape-recorded personal interview for the record with Kal K. Korff, Al Reed, and Barbara Reed, at the offices of Publication Professionals, Sunnyvale, California, September 6, 1980.

46. Stevens, *Message from the Pleiades, Volume I*, p. 338.

47. Hans Jacob, *DIA—Die große Reise in die Ewigkeit von 17. Juli 1975 Donnerstag 10.14 Uhr Einunddreißigster Kontakt ab Seite 174* (Wetzikon, Switzerland), p. 10.

48. Ibid.

49. Ibid.

50. Stevens, *Message from the Pleiades, Volume I*, p. 338.

51. Hans Jacob, *DIA—Die große Reise in die Ewigkeit von 17*, p. 10.

52. Ibid.

53. Ibid.

54. Ibid.

55. Ibid.

56. Ibid.

57. Stevens, *Message from the Pleiades, Volume I*, p. 338.

58. Hans Jacob, *DIA—Die große Reise in die Ewigkeit von 17*, p. 10.

59. Ibid, pp. 10–11.

60. Stevens, original *Pleiades* unpublished manuscript, Appendix IV, 11 and 12th page sheet.

61. Hans Jacob, *DIA—Die große Reise in die Ewigkeit von 17*, pp. 10–11.

62. Stevens, original *Pleiades* unpublished manuscript, Appendix V.

63. Hans Jacob, *DIA—Die große Reise in die Ewigkeit von 17*, p. 6.

64. Ibid.

65. Ibid.

66. Ibid.

67. Ibid.

68. Anonymous source, private correspondence, May 24, 1980 and June 23, 1980, Switzerland. (Name, address and complete unedited letter from this source on file with Kal K. Korff, since he was an associate of Hans Jacob. In addition, Walt Andrus, MUFON, and TotalResearch also have unedited copies. At author's request in Switzerland, his name has not been used.)

69. Thomas M. Gates, astronomer, UFOlogist, NASA spokesman, personal conversation with Kal K. Korff, Sunnyvale, California, June 1981.

70. Ibid.

71. Stevens, *UFO . . . Contact from the Pleiades—A Preliminary Investigation Report*, p. 106.

72. Ibid., pp. 104–106.

73. Ibid.

74. Stevens, *Message from the Pleiades, Volume I*, p. 338.

75. Stevens, *UFO...Contact from the Pleiades—A Preliminary Investigation Report*, p. 106.

76. Ibid., p. 108.

77. Ibid., p. 107.

78. Ibid., p. 106.

79. Hans Jacob, *DIA—Die große Reise in die Ewigkeit von 17*, p. 6.

80. Ibid.

81. Ibid.

82. Ibid.

83. Ibid.

84. Ibid.

85. Stevens, *Message from the Pleiades, Volume I*, p. 282.

86. Guido Moosbrugger, *. . . und sie fliegen doch!*, pp. 267–68.

87. Stevens, *Message from the Pleiades, Volume I*, p. 282.

88. Heinz Schollenberger, letter to Hans Jacob, May 4, 1976.

89. Hans Jacob, *DIA—Die große Reise in die Ewigkeit von 17*, p. 4.

90. Ibid.

91. Ibid.

92. Ibid.

93. Ibid.

94. Ibid.

95. Stevens, *UFO . . . Contact from the Pleiades—A Preliminary Investigation Report*, p. 98.

96. Stevens, *Message from the Pleiades, Volume I*, p. 283.

6

Analyses of Billy Meier's "Alien" Metal Samples

She (Semjase) cautioned him (Meier) that Earth experts who would analyze them (the mineral and crystal samples) would find nothing particularly strange.

Wendelle Stevens[1]

It (the sample) does not look like anything that we've made here (on Earth).

Marcel Vogel, IBM Chemist[2]

Billy Meier claims that during his 105th contact with Semjase he was given "four metal, one biological, and nine mineral and crystal specimens" as proof of the Pleiadian visitations.[3] Moreover, Meier's supporters would have us believe that Billy was even lucky enough to have this milestone contact during Wendelle Stevens's second visit.[4] Meier immediately turned over the alleged "Pleiadian" samples to Stevens so they could be scientifically analyzed.

According to Genesis III's *UFO . . . Contact from the Pleiades, Volume II*, Gary Kinder's *Light Years*, Wendelle Stevens's *Preliminary Investigation Report*, and Guido Moosbrugger's *. . . und sie fliegen doch!*, scientific analysis and testing of

Meier's physical evidence has shown that one of the metal specimens *"is not of Earth origin"* (emphasis added).[5]

Let us now examine these particular claims by Meier's proponents.

As of this writing, there have been a total of four separate analyses conducted on the physical samples Billy Meier claims he was given by the Pleiadians.

Analysis I

The first of these was performed in Zürich in March of 1978 by the Eidgenössische Materialprüfungs und Vorsuchsanstalt für Industrie, Bauwesen und Gewerbe (Federal Material Examination Experimental Lab for Construction, Industry, and Business).[6] According to the firm's report, the samples analyzed consisted of aluminum, calcium, chlorine, copper, lead, phosphorus, potassium, sulfur, silicon, silver, and titanium, all of which can be obtained here on Earth.

Since the Swiss laboratory was never told about the alleged "Pleiadian" origin of the samples, they rendered no comments in their report other than simply listing the elemental contents.

Analysis II

Two months later, on May 12, a second analysis was conducted in the United States by Dr. Walter W. Walker, a metallurgist at the University of Arizona, Tucson.[7] According to Dr. Walker's report (Professional Paper Number 78–100), the samples were even more mundane, consisting of bismuth, calcium, copper, lead, and silver. Once again, not the slightest shred of evidence was found to indicate an origin other than Earth. In fact, one observation Dr. Walker noted is that *all* of the specimens were "most unsuitable for high performance vehicle structural use due to low strength and [their] tending to react with the atmosphere" (emphasis added).[8] More importantly, Dr. Walker specifically stated on page 4 of his report: "They (the specimens) are unusual in nature but nothing was found to indicate that they are of extraterrestrial origin."

Dr. Walker is one of the few scientists who has analyzed purported UFO fragments over the past few decades[9] and unlike the Swiss laboratory, he took the scope of his investigation beyond just listing the elemental contents of the specimens.

In the pro-Meier literature, only two books mention Dr. Walker's analysis, Wendelle Stevens's *Preliminary Investigation Report*[10] and Moosbrugger's . . . *und sie fliegen doch!*[11] How both of these books address the issues in Walker's report is most revealing.

In Stevens's *Preliminary Investigation Report*, he mentions Walker's analysis. However, while paraphrasing Walker's report, Stevens *omits* Walker's *negative comments* about the Meier specimens, especially the notation that nothing was found to indicate that they were extraterrestrial in nature![12] Moreover, while Walker's four-page report appears in its *entirety* in the unpublished manuscript for his *Preliminary Investigation Report*, Stevens *omits* this document from the *published* version, although he includes the Swiss laboratory's analysis, which also totals four pages![13]

Guido Moosbrugger's "treatment" of the Walker analysis is limited to *one sentence*, where he states that "Dr. Edwin Walker" (sic) and Dr. Marcel Vogel were two "specialists for metal analysis" who examined the Meier samples.[14] The rest of the two pages in Moosbrugger's book covering the metal analysis focuses on the controversial work of "Dr." Vogel.[15]

Analysis III

In late 1979 and early 1980, a third analysis was carried out at the request of Wendelle Stevens by Dr. Marcel Vogel, a senior research chemist for IBM Incorporated in San Jose, California. Dr. Vogel's analysis of Billy Meier's Pleiadian metal samples are quoted by the Meier faithful because Vogel claimed that they could not be manufactured by any technology here on Earth.[16]

This is what Marcel Vogel said he discovered when he analyzed the Meier samples. His comments concern the same "small specimen of one of the four states of metal" that both the Swiss laboratory and Dr. Walker analyzed,[17] which found nothing "extraterrestrial" at all about them.

> Right now, I could not explain the type of material that I have and its discreteness by any known combination of materials. I could not put it together myself as a scientist. To get a combination of thulium, silver, and silicon in discrete areas . . . but their discreteness is what intrigues me. You understand what I am saying? Because, you see, if I would take these combinations of materials and put them into a furnace, melt it, and pour it out and pull a little ingot, I would see all of these elements present there in any one area, but I don't [in these]. I see these discrete bits of material. Now it can only happen by some form of a cold fusion process where you have the elements present, and you fuse them together so they still maintain their (pure) identity but they interpenetrate into one another.
>
> Now we, with any technology that I know of, could not achieve this on this Earth planet. It is very exciting when you can get specimens like these, and have the opportunity of looking at and examining them . . . it does not look like anything that we've made here (on Earth).[18]

In May 1980, Sarah Shalley, a colleague of mine, and I met Dr. Vogel at his home in San Jose for an interview. During our three-hour meeting, the chemist revealed many details which proved to be of interest. Almost everything Marcel Vogel told us *contradicted* his earlier statements as reported by Genesis III and their associates.

When I asked if the samples were found to be of extraterrestrial origin, Vogel replied: "No. All I said is that the first sample was unique, which it is. I reported nothing else. The samples were comprised of aluminum, silver, and thallium; each of which have a high degree of purity."

At this point, Vogel left the room and returned with several objects.

"These," he said, "are the samples."

As Sarah and I viewed them, Vogel told us that the particular specimens we were holding were composed of amethyst, citrine, quartz, and silver solder. Thus, for the third time no evidence had been detected that Meier's samples originated from anywhere else but Earth.

Dr. Vogel then showed us what was supposed to be a lock of Semjase's hair! Being curious, I examined the hairs very carefully. They appeared to me to be human, coming from a blonde, split-ends and all!

"Is it—" I started to ask.

"It's human," Vogel replied, interrupting.

This conclusion also agrees with an analysis by Dr. Walter Birkby, a forensic scientist at the Arizona State Museum in Tucson who also examined the same hair specimens before Vogel did.[19]

Before the evening was over, Vogel showed us even more material: five volumes of Meier's "correspondence" with the Pleiadians and a videotape on the case that had been personally prepared and narrated by Wendelle Stevens.

While Vogel's remarks were enlightening, one of them was particularly puzzling regarding the discovery of the element thallium. Thallium (also spelled sometimes as thulium[20]), is an extremely rare, malleable, and highly toxic metal. It is unlikely that Meier would have been able to secure even a small sample.

Analysis IV

The riddle of the thallium was to go unsolved until the fourth analysis was conducted, this time by Dr. Robert Olgilvie, a metallurgist for the Massachusetts Institute of Technology in Cambridge. Dr. Olgilvie (with a grant from *Omni* magazine) analyzed the *other half* of the sample Marcel Vogel claimed was so unique.

When I checked with UFO researcher Harry Lebelson, the writer for *Omni* who did the article on the Meier case, I found out that there was *no thallium* in the Meier metal sample at all. Marcel Vogel had simply misinterpreted the graphs on the spectranalyzer![21]

Dr. Marcel Vogel and the "Disappearing" Sample

In addition to the mention of thallium and other alleged extraordinary properties of the Meier samples stated by Vogel, another claim often cited by Meier's proponents is the fact that while in the possession of Marcel Vogel, one of the metal samples "mysteriously" disappeared due to its unique properties. This claim appears in virtually every Billy Meier book, including *UFO . . . Contact from the Pleiades, Volume II*, which says this on page 57 about the metal's disappearance: "The specimen vanished without a trace from its container while being hand carried by Vogel to a new testing laboratory. To this day the metal's whereabouts remains an unsolved mystery."

The fact that the sample disappeared is considered additional evidence by the Meier faithful that there was "something unusual" or "extraterrestrial" about the metal samples Billy Meier turned over to Wendelle Stevens for analysis.

While it is true that *one* of the Meier specimens in Vogel's possession did end up "lost," there is no credible evidence whatsoever that its disappearance is a bona fide mystery. Indeed, the account of the metal specimen's "disappearance" as it appears in Volume II of *UFO . . . Contact from the Pleiades* is a deliberate confabulation by Brit and Lee Elders (who wrote the text of the book[22]), and does not square with either Marcel Vogel's account of how the sample "vanished" or that of Dr. Richard F. Haines, the *other* person who was present at that time! Ironically, Brit and Lee Elders's claim as to how the sample disappeared also contradicts the accounts in other pro-Meier books where this incident is mentioned,[23] as well as the Elderses' *own* video documentary titled *Beamship: The Metal*, which features Marcel Vogel recounting the incident on camera as it purportedly happened.[24]

After Vogel completed his initial testing of the Meier samples, allegedly detecting properties that he believed indicated an extraterrestrial origin, he wanted to share the results of his findings with a few of his colleagues. One of them was Dr. Richard F. Haines, a UFO researcher and scientist at NASA-Ames Research Center in Mountain View, California. When Vogel told him about this "astounding" piece of metal, he invited Haines to come over to his laboratory at IBM to take a look for himself. Dr. Haines agreed to see the specimen, as any scientist would.[25]

When Dr. Haines arrived at the IBM facility, he was met by Vogel who said that he could not find the specimen! Dr. Haines then spent the next twenty minutes or so retracing Vogel's steps, trying to help him locate the "mysterious" metal that had suddenly vanished.[26] Unfortunately for Billy Meier and his supporters, the sample which Vogel claimed had so intrigued him would never be found.[27]

The disappearance of the mysterious metal specimen means that it cannot be independently studied. Thus, by any reasonable criteria of evidence, whether it be legal or scientific, Vogel's conclusions are not credible evidence of anything since they cannot be independently verified.

These facts also *refute* what Brit and Lee Elders wrote on page 57 in Volume II of their *Pleiades* photo-journal, where they claim: "The specimen vanished without a trace from its container while being hand carried by Vogel to a new testing laboratory." As we have just shown, Vogel had the sample at his own laboratory at IBM and was not carrying it to a new testing facility when it allegedly vanished. Dr. Haines had come to visit Vogel, not the other way around.

An even greater distortion of this account can also be found on page 57 of *Pleiades, Volume II,* when Brit and Lee Elders write: "This was to be the last statement made (by Vogel) on the remarkable metal sample that had taken the scientific community by storm."

Since Marcel Vogel is the *only* person who ever claimed that the Meier samples were unique and extraterrestrial in origin, a conclusion which cannot be verified, the claim by Brit and Lee Elders that the sample had "taken the scientific community by storm" is an obvious exaggeration.

How the Meier Metal Sample Most Likely "Disappeared"

Let's assume that Marcel Vogel is telling the truth when he claims that the sample "disappeared." Is there a plausible explanation for its disappearance? The answer is yes.

When Sarah Shalley and I were at Vogel's home for our interview, he showed us four other "UFO fragments" that had been sent to him by various researchers around the world. He even let Sarah and me hold them in our hands, something a prudent scientist would never do. While this potential contamination was bad enough, what was even worse was where and how Vogel "handled" his alleged UFO fragment collection.

When Vogel asked Sarah and me if we wanted to see his collection of UFO fragments, we naturally said yes. Vogel then reached into the pocket of his trousers and pulled out a black rubber coin pouch, the kind which opens up via a slit in the middle when squeezed in the palm of one's hand. Normally, such a coin pouch is kept for small change or keys. I had never before seen anyone use one for alleged UFO fragments! I was amazed then, and still am today, at how casually he treated these potentially valuable samples, some of which he considered to be "unique," to use his own phrase. In all likelihood, if Vogel is telling the truth, he probably *lost* the small piece of "Pleiadian" metal that is still an article of pure faith among Billy Meier's proponents.

Additional evidence that Vogel simply lost the specimen can be found, ironically, in Genesis III's own *Beamship: The Metal* video documentary. Marcel Vogel makes this startling statement, recounting his "experiences" with other "lost" specimens:

> I've had this happen before to me. And when I've worked with crystals like this. [Author's note: Vogel then holds up an amethyst crystal in his hand.]
>
> I'd work with a crystal, study it, as I have over the last ten years, and suddenly the next day I went, go to reach for it and (it) will be gone! It will have disappeared.
>
> I first accused myself of being negligent and not paying attention, and finally I put it aside and said if it happens, it happens. I won't let it bother me.
>
> I don't know how to explain it, I have no way of giving any rational explanation. And at this moment I must categorize it as a mystery.

"Dr." Marcel Vogel's Questionable Scientific Integrity

Just what kind of scientist was Marcel Vogel? How credible was his work and what kind of scientific qualifications did he possess to make some of the extraordinary statements he did concerning the Meier samples he analyzed? Although Marcel

Vogel's "analysis" of the "Pleiadian" samples are considered the truth by Billy Meier's proponents, there is every reason to question the very integrity and accuracy of much of Vogel's work, especially his "analysis" of the supposed "unique" metal sample.

Marcel Vogel, who died on February 12, 1991, was a very unusual individual and a controversial figure. Aside from being a brilliant chemist, he also delved into most of the areas of the paranormal, especially "psychic" phenomena.[28] For example, Vogel claimed for many years that he could "bend" metal spoons with his mind, using what he called his "mental energies" (à la Uri Geller). Vogel was even featured in the *National Enquirer* and other sensational publications for these alleged abilities (see figure 112).

While Billy Meier's proponents are quick to cite Marcel Vogel's "analysis" of the metal samples as "proof" of the extraordinary nature of the Meier evidence, what they don't say is how *unreliable* Vogel's research and conclusions have been whenever they've concerned the areas of paranormal research or the subject of UFOs.

The first concern about Marcel Vogel's credibility pertains to the very title which much of the Meier literature uses. Contrary to what Guido Moosbrugger and Wendelle Stevens's books claim,[29] Vogel does not hold either a real Ph.D. or a legitimate doctorate. Instead, Vogel was awarded an *honorary doctorate* from the *International College of Spiritual and Psychic Sciences in Montreal, Quebec, Canada!*[30]

These are excerpts from the obituary notice for Marcel Vogel as it appeared in the February 13, 1991 edition of the *San Jose Mercury News*, which chronicles some of the controversial areas of his life:

A Funeral Mass will be celebrated Thursday for Marcel Joseph Vogel, 73, a former materials scientist at IBM Corp. in San Jose who became known worldwide for his research in communication between humans and plants.

Mr. Vogel died Sunday in a San Jose hospital of a heart attack suffered at his San Jose home.

Born in San Francisco, Mr. Vogel attended the University of San Francisco and the University of California, Berkeley. He held an honorary doctorate of humanities in spiritual and psychic sciences from the International College of Spiritual and Psychic Sciences in Montreal, Quebec.

Interested in luminescence and phosphorescence since he was in grammar school, he collaborated with his professor at Cal on a book about luminescence that was published in 1943. Later, he started Vogel Luminescence Corp., which manufactured a variety of products used in lettering and display graphics.

Mr. Vogel sold the business in 1957 and started his 27-year career with IBM, during which he obtained patents in magnetic recording media, liquid crystals, and rare earth phosphors. He also developed a magnetic coating for hard disks still used in IBM computers today.

After leaving IBM in 1984, Mr. Vogel concentrated initially on plant research, measuring reactions of plants with electrodes attached to their leaves and to scientific instruments.

He claimed plants can read people's minds, will respond to spooky stories, can sense emotions of humans miles away, react more readily to children than to adults, and thrive on human love and kindness.

Mr. Vogel's research and a book dealing with the subject, *The Secret Life of Plants,* brought him worldwide renown.

At the time of his death, Mr. Vogel was running Psychic Research Inc. in San Jose, described in its literature as a "nonprofit corporation using scientific research and education to aid mankind."

A second issue with "Dr." Vogel's credibility has to do with the fact that he is a *chemist* and not a *metallurgist.* By comparison, Drs. (who have real Ph.D.s) Walker and Olgilvie are metallurgists; they are experts in the study of metals. It is curious that only Marcel Vogel found anything "extraordinary" about the Meier samples even though the Swiss laboratory and Drs. Walker and Olgilvie were unable to, despite analyzing the *same sample.*[31] These other analysts were far more qualified than "Dr." Vogel to render an opinion, and none of them concluded that Meier's samples were either extraterrestrial in origin or came from anywhere else other than Earth.[32]

A third issue concerning Marcel Vogel's credibility is his demonstrable record of *fraud* in his experimental work, especially when it involved psychic research. On June 7, 1980, "Dr." Marcel Vogel was tested for his alleged psychic abilities under controlled conditions. The three men who tested Vogel were paranormal researcher and professional magician Bob Steiner; Charles Nyquist, another paranormal researcher who is also a practicing attorney; and Dr. John Palmer, the director of the Parapsychology Department for John F. Kennedy University in Orinda, California.[33]

Vogel was also observed in how he interacted with others, especially children, while conducting his "psychic" feats, since Vogel had claimed that he could "teach anyone to bend metal bars."[34]

Here are some unedited excerpts from Bob Steiner's report on the outcome of the numerous experiments that were conducted on "Dr." Vogel, including observations made concerning his methodologies:

> On June 6, 1980, I telephoned Dr. Vogel to confirm the appointment [to test his alleged psychic abilities] for June 7. All systems were go. He cautioned me to eat lightly.
>
> I inquired if he was serious. He assured me that he was, and informed me that the vibes get very intense—sometimes people even vomit. (I resisted my knee-jerk reaction to reply that I could already feel it coming on.) . . .
>
> June 7, 1980, was the day of the event. I took with me two observers: John Palmer, Ph.D., Director, Department of Parapsychology, John F. Kennedy University, and Charles W. Nyquist, Esq.
>
> Charles W. Nyquist has considerable skill and credentials in both mental magic and exposure of psychic frauds.
>
> We (Palmer, Nyquist, Steiner) arrived at Dr. Vogel's home at 9:55 A.M.; the starting time had been indicated as 10:00 A.M.

Dr. Vogel was warm and cordial in welcoming us. We three observers had decided that, other than the formal protocol on our experiment and the carrying it out, we would allow Dr. Vogel free rein to conduct the day as he saw fit. We had even decided not to push him into signing the protocol if he chose not to. . . .

Guests (subjects) started arriving. Many apparently knew Vogel quite well. It was a beautiful day. Everything was held in Vogel's back yard. Benches were lined up for the children to sit on. Present were the following:

9 children, ages 5 to 11, all of whom were subjects J. B., M. B., D. E., S. E., S. G., G. D., C. W., S. W., and "H."*

5 adults, sitting in the yard (parents/grandparents)

Video cameraman, with a video camera

A photographer

John Palmer, Charles W. Nyquist, Bob Steiner, Marcel Vogel.

The video cameraman kept his camera going throughout the proceedings.

Around this time, *while Vogel had diverted the attention elsewhere, he took a spoon and quickly bent it. I looked quickly over to Nyquist, whose quick glance to me confirmed that he, too, had seen this move. In later discussion, we verified that we had both seen the move.* This bent spoon was not used in any later part of the day, as far as I can tell. [Emphasis added]

After everybody was settled, Vogel explained how to bend a spoon. He closed his eyes, exhaled noisily through his nose, and bent the spoon which he was holding in his two hands.

He then introduced telepathy, and gave a brief description of it.

He then mentioned Randi, a magician who debunks. He introduced Palmer, Nyquist, and Steiner as "three very important gentlemen."

He next vividly described a make-believe orange in his hand. He peeled it, smelled it, pulled off sections, gave a section to each child, and requested that they eat it. He graphically narrated throughout this procedure. He described how good the orange

---

*The names of the children have been withheld because they are minors. Their full names, and all other supportive documentation, are in Steiner's report, and are on file at TotalResearch, Underground Video, and with professional magician James Randi.

tasted. He inquired how many of the children had experienced the orange, and could actually taste it. All nine children raised their hands: some immediately, and some after noticing the other hands in the air.

Next he introduced a make-believe cookie, in a similar manner.

Much later, Dr. Palmer, who has his Ph.D. in Psychology, observed that these were *hypnotic induction techniques.* [Emphasis added] I told him that I agreed, and requested that he put that in his report. He said that he preferred not to.

After the cookie, Vogel introduced me and my test, telling the children that I would conduct a test. However, before turning the floor over to me, he launched into his metal-bending. He dramatically took a spoon in his two hands, closed his eyes, exhaled noisily through his nose, and explained relaxation.

Then he said: "When you're ready, just SMASH it up!" On the loud word "SMASH," the spoon in Vogel's hands bent, *as he brought his hands together beneath the center of the spoon. It was done just the way I would bend a spoon without any intent to deceive anyone.* [Emphasis added]

Then the children tried, as he coached and coaxed them through the experience. Eight of the nine children were able to bend the forks or spoons; the younger ones were obviously straining to do so—physically, that is. One child was unable to bend his fork. Dr. Vogel stood that child in front of him, with Vogel seated. *Vogel reached around, grabbed the child's fists in his own hands, and bent the fork.* [Emphasis added]

The children then followed instructions and all stood up proudly with their bent silverware, as the photographer snapped their picture.

Then, before proceeding in his "telepathy" (experiment), Vogel discussed energy in plants and stones.

He next explained water divining.

Next he had each child handle a stone and describe its source. He said archeology is now done this way.

Then Vogel started on his telepathy. He mentioned that he does this in his "mind-boggling" class. He had 10 envelopes. He opened envelope number 9, showed the picture to the cameramen, and he concentrated on it. The children were to draw what they perceived.

He then revealed that the picture was a U.S. flag. He inquired how many drew a square or a flag. He considered the drawing of a square to be a hit. He did not control the drawings at all during this. He moved along quite rapidly.

Next he followed the same procedure with envelope number 4, which was a house with trees near it. Needless to say, a house OR trees would have been considered a hit.

The same procedure was followed with envelope number 10, which was a face with "I love you" written on it.

Notwithstanding the commonplace and multiple targets on each trial, there were no corresponding pictures (negative psi?).

The children were given a break.

Dr. Vogel ranked the Hits, Partials, and Misses on Randi's experiment. It was now noon, and Nyquist, Palmer, and Steiner were ushered out.

We left, while everyone else stayed.

CONCLUSION ON RANDI EXPERIMENT:
In the opinions of all three observers (Dr. Palmer, Nyquist, Steiner), nothing took place which warrants any further investigation. *There was no indication of any psychic or paranormal abilities.* [Emphasis added]

CONCLUSION ON OTHER EXPERIMENTS:
In the opinions of all three observers (Palmer, Nyquist, Steiner), nothing took place which warrants any further investigation. *There was no indication of any psychic or paranormal abilities.* [Emphasis added]

OVERALL EVALUATION:
In my opinion, to end with the above conclusions is not sufficient. There must be an evaluation of what took place during the course of these events.

John Palmer's comments: The brevity of Mr. Palmer's comments is partially explained by his view of the proceedings. He explained to me that nothing paranormal seemed to have taken place and, since he knew I would detail the observations, he believed that it would be an unnecessary duplication for him to do the same. I accept his sincerity in this matter, though I would have preferred that he detail his observations, and told him so.

In order to advance the science of parapsychology, if it is a science, it is necessary that experiments be published in journals
read by parapsychologists. This is necessary whether the experiment demonstrates or fails to demonstrate psychic ability. Absent
that, those who fail will be able to impose upon the professional
time of other dedicated researchers in the future, because those
researchers will have no source from which to learn what has
been happening in the field.

Furthermore, without publicity of those who have failed in
tests of psychic ability, nationwide claims of such ability will go
unrefuted even after they have been tested and failed to produce.

It would seem in order for Dr. John Palmer, who observed the
entire proceedings detailed above, to publish those results in the
journals of parapsychology, if for no other reason than to save
another dedicated researcher from rerunning the same no-results
day which Dr. Palmer did with Dr. Vogel.

Effect on the Children: To me the most important evaluation
of this proceeding is to assess the effect on the children. *In my
opinion, Dr. Vogel gently, calmly, warmly, and pleasantly led these children down the path toward irrationality.* [Emphasis added]

He (Marcel) led them to believe that, by holding a stone in
their hands, they could "receive" where it came from. He made
them believe that they had some mystical power to bend silverware, when in fact they simply used their physical strength.

He led them to believe that they could receive telepathic
impressions of pictures, when in fact the results showed that they
did not. Even though the results showed that they did not receive
impressions, I believe that the children nonetheless left with the
impression that they did and could.

At a very tender, malleable age, when children should be
learning how to address, accept, and deal with the realities in life,
Dr. Vogel is instructing them in "receiving" impressions of things
which, according to the best knowledge that science has been able
to produce, simply do not exist.

The destruction of introducing this type of non-thinking into
the mind of a young child is incalculable.

Although perhaps nicer terms are available to describe the
case of an adult doing this to little children, the one which occurs
to me as most appropriate is "mind-fucking."

SINCERITY AND BELIEF STRUCTURE OF MARCEL VOGEL: To evaluate the sincerity and belief structure of Dr. Marcel Vogel is at once both difficult and exceedingly important. Is he sincere and does he truly believe in what he is doing? Or does he know better?

We have here a 63-year-old brilliant scientist. He is a chemist, for IBM. He had his picture in the newspaper showing that he had literally broken an iron bar with his mind. I personally saw him applying pressure to the clenched fists of a little child, so that a fork could bend.

When a target picture is a dollar sign, and a little child scribbles all over the paper and labels it "A Design," does the brilliant Dr. Vogel honestly consider that to be a direct hit?

If Dr. Vogel were sincere, and truly believed that these effects were what he represented them to be, why did he duck our attempts at meeting for so long? . . .

From conversations with Dr. Vogel, and based partially upon the apparently responsible position he holds at IBM, I conclude that he is a learned, intelligent man. And he is a trained scientist.

In order to assure technical accuracy in this report, I just telephoned Marcel Vogel to inquire if he properly bears the title "Dr." Although in all my correspondence I addressed him as "Dr. Vogel," and *he never notified me to the contrary* [emphasis added], he informed me today that he is not a Ph.D., and is not entitled to use the title "Dr."* (For convenience, I will not rewrite everything. Just be aware that Marcel Vogel is Mr. Marcel Vogel.)

An evaluation of the sincerity and belief structure of Mr. Vogel must necessarily evaluate whether he has dealt with us in a sincere manner. *Clearly he has not.* [Emphasis added] We must also evaluate whether, in our opinion, this obviously brilliant, trained scientist can physically bend metal with the strength of his hands and arms, while actually believing that it is being done by his mind alone. To me that is unbelievable.

And that is my evaluation of Mr. Marcel Vogel: The idea that he is sincere and believes what he purports to believe is, in my opinion, unbelievable—I do not believe it! I do not believe that he sincerely believes the

---

*During the entire time Sarah Shalley and I interviewed Vogel at his home, we also addressed him as "Dr." not knowing Vogel did not possess a legitimate degree. Marcel Vogel, as with other people, never once bothered correcting us, nor did he ever correct me during subsequent conversations!

things he states, nor the things on which he instructs little children. People who thus manipulate the minds of others should be held accountable for it. Children must not be allowed to be fair game for the Marcel Vogels of the world. [Emphasis added]

Respectfully submitted,

Robert A. Steiner
6/16/80

In addition to Marcel Vogel's chicanery with "spoon-bending," he also claimed that he could "heal" people with the touch of his hands. When I talked with one of the persons who "Dr." Vogel supposedly had healed, UFO researcher Paul Cerny, on June 22, 1994, I was told that, "if Marcel Vogel healed me, I wasn't aware of it. In fact, as I recall, my ankle got *worse* after he got through touching it!"

Yet another reason to question Dr. Vogel's integrity has to do with an incident that took place while Sarah Shalley and I were visiting him. When I asked Vogel what he thought of Meier, he replied, much to my amazement, that while he considered Billy Meier to be a fraud, a liar, and an "anti-Christian," he was certain that "Semjase" existed. Vogel even claimed that he had talked with her!

"Would you like to meet her?" Vogel asked. Stunned, I asked him how this was possible and he replied that he could "contact" Semjase by meditating over the large amethyst and quartz crystal which was positioned on the coffee table in his living room!*

Still not knowing what to make of this, I told Vogel that I would love to meet Semjase, provided that she showed up *before* it was time for me to leave. During my three-hour stay, Semjase never arrived.

---

*While I was working with the production crew taping an episode of FOX TV's "Encounters," producer Bob Kiviat told me that Vogel had invited *him* to "meet Semjase" as well. Of course, she never appeared!

Vogel's allegedly "unique" Meier metal specimen is no longer available for independent testing, thus reducing this portion of the Meier evidence to triviality. However, the observations and background information concerning Vogel's questionable methodologies and lack of integrity stand on their own, independent of the Meier case.

Finally, for those people who still wish to believe that Vogel's "analyses" of the Meier specimens are credible, and that Meier's "Pleiadian" metal samples constitute "hard evidence" of extraterrestrial visitations, I close this chapter by disclosing the following facts, along with an offer.

In yet another display of his peculiar behavior, Marcel Vogel gave me an actual piece of one of the Meier metal specimens he had examined. I have had this alleged "Pleiadian" metal sample now since May 1980, and over the years my fellow UFO research colleagues such as Jim Borden, Paul Cerny, Thomas Gates, Dr. Richard F. Haines, Glen Hoyen, William Moore,[35] Al and Barbara Reed, and Dr. Jacques Valleé have all seen it.

The sample Vogel cut for me was from the "fourth state of Pleiadian metal," and photographs of this larger specimen can be seen on page 56 of Genesis III's *UFO . . . Contact from the Pleiades, Volume II*; page 416 of Wendelle Stevens's *Preliminary Investigation Report*; and on page 174 of Genesis III's *Message from the Pleiades, Volume II*.

There are some unexplainable contradictions from Meier's proponents concerning this specimen. For example, Wendelle Stevens says in his *Preliminary Investigation Report* that this sample was the one that mysteriously "disappeared" in Vogel's IBM office the day that my colleague, Dr. Richard Haines, visited him.[36]

In addition, Brit and Lee Elders claim in *UFO . . . Contact from the Pleiades, Volume II*: "This mysterious specimen created an uproar within the scientific community because of its unusual bonding techniques. It showed a combination of both crystalline deposits and metal without evidence of cross breeding, which is unheard of in our present technology. This piece mysteriously vanished while in the possession of Marcel Vogel."[37] However, in their own book, *Message from the Pleiades, Volume II,* Brit and Lee Elders and Wendelle Stevens contradict themselves, making the claim that the "mysterious" metal specimen was "never tested."[38]

While we have already disproven Brit and Lee Elders' statement about the specimen having created *"an uproar in the scientific community,"* the fact remains that a piece of this "Pleiadian fourth state of metal" still exists and is in my possession as of this writing.

Here is my offer: If *anyone* wishes to pay for a nondestructive analysis of this sample, I will make it available on the condition that the results of any test be made public regardless of their outcome. As Marcel Vogel told me when he gave me the specimen, the sample is merely ordinary silver solder and is nothing special! This is also what Dr. Olgilvie told Harry Lebelson of *Omni* magazine after he completed his analysis of the *other half* of this same sample before it was cut.[39] Although Stevens and his associates would later claim that Olgilvie's sample also "disappeared,"[40] the specimen Vogel gave me has never vanished nor has it ever behaved in any unusual way over the past fifteen years. (Figure 111 shows the specimen.)

The "hard evidence" for Billy Meier's "Pleiadian" rock and metal samples being of extraterrestrial origin simply does not exist. Although one sample was "analyzed" by "Dr." Marcel Vogel and found "not to be from this Earth," Vogel's conclusions are not supported by any other scientist, including Drs. Olgilvie and Walker, as well as the Swiss Laboratory in Zürich. Only those individuals who *ignore the facts* behind this aspect of the Meier case or have a vested interest at stake continue to cite Vogel's "analysis" as if it were valid.

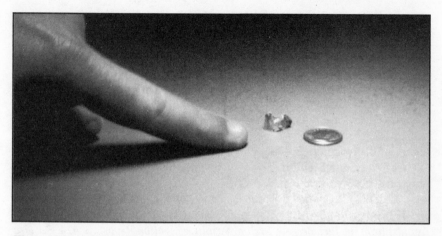

Figs. 111 and 112. (*Above*) The alleged "fourth state of Pleiadian metal" sample Marcel Vogel gave to me in May 1980. This "Pleiadian metal specimen" is really ordinary silver solder. (*Below*) A photo of the story in the June 12, 1980 issue of the *National Enquirer* featuring "Dr." Marcel Vogel. (Top photo courtesy: Underground Video, from the documentary *EXPOSED: The Billy Meier UFO Hoax*/Bottom photo courtesy: Bob Steiner.)

Scientist Breaks Iron Bar With the Power of His Mind

In a startling demonstration of psychic power, a top IBM scientist split an iron bar into two pieces using only the power of his mind.

And three stunned eyewitnesses — all scientists — admit they are completely baffled. They'd been watching IBM scientist Marcel Vogel demonstrate his ability to bend metal with mind power alone. After bending a spoon, he picked up the iron bar, concentrated on it — and the bar snapped off in his hand.

"I'm positive he did it with mental energy," marveled metals engineer Denise Laire. "It broke with a popping noise."

Even Vogel, 61, a brilliant scientist who helped develop the magnetic recording tape, was shocked.

"I have often bent bars of metal, but this

Notes

1. Wendelle Stevens, *UFO . . . Contact from the Pleiades—A Preliminary Investigation Report—The Report of an Ongoing Contact* (Tucson, Ariz.: Wendelle Stevens, 1983), p. 85.

2. *UFO . . . Contact from the Pleiades, Volume II,* 1st ed. (Phoenix, Ariz.: Genesis III Productions, Ltd., 1983), p. 57.

3. *UFO . . . Contact from the Pleiades, Volume I,* rev. ed. (Phoenix, Ariz.: Genesis III Productions, Ltd., 1979), p. 58.

4. Wendelle Stevens, *UFO . . . Contact from the Pleiades—A Preliminary Investigation Report,* p. 27.

5. *UFO . . . Contact from the Pleiades, Volume II* (Phoenix, Ariz.: Genesis III Productions, Ltd., 1983), p. 57. *See also* Wendelle Stevens, *UFO . . . Contact from the Pleiades—A Preliminary Investigation Report,* p. 424. *See also* Gary Kinder, *Light Years: An Investigation Into the Extraterrestrial Experiences of Eduard Meier* (New York: The Atlantic Monthly Press, 1987), pp. 249–53. *See also* Guido Moosbrugger, *. . . und sie fliegen doch! UFOs: Die größte Herausforderung des 20 Jahrhunderts* (München, Germany: Michael Hesemann Verlag, 1991), pp. 278–80.

6. Wendelle Stevens, original unpublished manuscript for *UFO . . . Contact from the Pleiades, The Report of an Ongoing Contact* [with dialogue correction by Eduard Meier] (Tucson, Ariz.: Wendelle Stevens, 1978).

7. Stevens, *UFO . . . Contact from the Pleiades—A Preliminary Investigation Report,* p. 415.

8. Dr. Walter W. Walker, *Preliminary Metallurgical Investigation of Swiss Metal Samples,* Professional paper Number 78–100 (not dated), p. 4.

9. Coral and Jim Lorenzen, *Flying Saucers and the Startling Evidence for the Invasion from Outer Space* (New York: Avon Books, 1967), pp. 104–45.

10. Stevens, *UFO . . . Contact from the Pleiades—A Preliminary Investigation Report,* p. 415.

11. Moosbrugger, *. . . und sie fliegen doch!* p. 278.

12. Stevens, *UFO . . . Contact from the Pleiades—A Preliminary Investigation Report,* pp. 415–20.

13. Ibid., pp. 420–23.

14. Moosbrugger, *. . . und sie fliegen doch!* p. 278.

15. Ibid.

16. *Beamship: The Metal. Beamship* documentary series trilogy, Genesis III Productions, Ltd., 1986, back video cassette box quote from "Dr." Marcel Vogel.

17. Stevens, *UFO . . . Contact from the Pleiades—A Preliminary Investigation Report,* p. 424.

18. *UFO . . . Contact from the Pleiades, Volume II,* p. 57.

19. Stevens, *UFO . . . Contact from the Pleiades—A Preliminary Investigation Report,* p. 428.

20. *Webster's New Twentieth Century Dictionary Unabridged,* 2d ed. (New York: Prentice Hall Press, 1979), p. 1904.

21. Harry Lebelson, telephone conversation with Kal K. Korff, New York City, June 1982.

22. *UFO . . . Contact from the Pleiades, Volume II,* p. 1.

23. Wendelle Stevens, *UFO . . . Contact from the Pleiades—A Supplementary Investigation Report—The Report of an Ongoing Contact* (Tucson, Ariz.: Wendelle Stevens, 1989), p. 528. *See also* Kinder, *Light Years,* pp. 249–53.

24. *Beamship: The Metal,* Genesis III Productions, Ltd., 1985.

25. Dr. Richard F. Haines, personal interview with Kal Korff, Henry Parker, and Dr. Tina Seelig for the video documentary *EXPOSED: The Billy Meier UFO Hoax,* Palo Alto, California, September 14, 1993.

26. Ibid.

27. Ibid.

28. "Marcel Vogel, Scientist and Psychic Researcher," Obituary article for Marcel Joseph Vogel, *San Jose Mercury News,* Morning Final Edition, February 13, 1991, p. 5B.

29. Moosbrugger, *. . . und sie fliegen doch!* p. 278. *See also* Stevens, *Preliminary Investigation Report,* p. 424.

30. "Marcel Vogel, Scientist and Psychic Researcher," *San Jose Mercury News,* Morning Final Edition, February 13, 1991, p. 5B.

31. Stevens, *UFO . . . Contact from the Pleiades—A Preliminary Investigation Report,* p. 424.

32. Ibid.

33. Bob Steiner's file on Marcel Vogel, loaned to Kal K. Korff on September 2, 1994.

34. Marcel Vogel, personal interview with Kal K. Korff and Sarah Shalley, Marcel Vogel's home, San Jose, California, May 1980.

35. William L. Moore, *Focus,* Fair Witness Project, Incorporated, Volume 5, December 31, 1990, p. 35.

36. Stevens, *UFO . . . Contact from the Pleiades—A Preliminary Investigation Report,* pp. 424–26.

37. *UFO . . . Contact from the Pleiades, Volume I ,* rev. ed. , p. 56.

38. *Messages from the Pleiades, the Contact Notes of Eduard "Billy" Meier, Volume I* (Phoenix, Ariz.: Wendelle C. Stevens and Genesis III Publishing, 1990), p. 174.

39. Harry Lebelson, telephone conversation with Kal K. Korff, New York City, June 1982.

40. Stevens, *UFO . . . Contact from the Pleiades—A Supplementary Investigation Report* , p. 529.

7

Other Meier "Evidence"

We have little kids, eight years old, going outside on videotape saying "and here's where they [the Pleiadians] landed last winter and melted a big ring in the snow. And then it froze, and then Daddy [Billy Meier] came out and put a garden hose on it." And they were thrilled because it was a little ice skating ring for them, 25 feet in diameter.

Jim Dilettoso[1]

The individual tracks are quite large, being about two meters (6.5 feet) in diameter.

Wendelle Stevens[2]

Although most of the evidence in the Meier case is by far photographic in nature, rounding out the other claims of "hard evidence" in the case are alleged "landing-tracks"[3] by the Pleiadian craft; independent "eyewitness" testimonies which recount sightings of the spaceships;[4] and the "pilfering" of Meier's UFO pictures by the CIA, KGB, and unnamed nefarious intelligence agencies.[5] These latter organizations are also said to often "spy" on Meier and monitor his various activities.[6]

While such sweeping declarations make for interesting

reading, is there any credible evidence to support these interesting claims? Let's investigate these allegations by Meier and his supporters and see what we can determine.

The Pleiadian "Landing-Tracks"

In addition to various rock, metal, and mineral samples, another form of physical evidence presented as a testament to Billy Meier's claims of alien contact are the "landing-tracks" purportedly left behind by the Pleiadian spacecraft. According to the book *UFO . . . Contact from the Pleiades, Volume I*, we are told that: "To the experts, these tracks represent a curious phenomena not easily duplicated or explained."[7]

Of course, none of these "experts" are ever named, nor are we told just what it was about the tracks themselves that was supposedly so baffling; Genesis III just assures us that they are.

The claim that the Meier "landing-tracks" are even a "curious phenomena" is a strange remark indeed, *since I am the only one who has ever bothered obtaining any soil samples from these tracks for scientific analysis!* This is why it is doubtful that the unnamed "experts" and "scientists" Genesis III refers to in Volumes I and II of the *Pleiades* photo-journals ever existed. Without any soil or vegetation samples from these sites, what could these "experts" have studied?

According to Meier, the Pleiadian ships seldom land; instead they supposedly hover just above the ground and create three circular impressions of flattened grass 120 degrees apart.[8] Each of these imprints are two meters in diameter (roughly 6.5 feet) and the grass inside them swirled down in a counterclockwise fashion.[9]

Moreover, Genesis III (specifically Brit and Lee Elders) make the additional claim that "Gamma [radiation] testing" at the set of three landing-tracks located behind Meier's house "revealed a RAD count well above normal almost two years after"* the tracks were first made by the "Pleiadians" in 1978.[10]

It should be noted that other than the word of Genesis III that abnormal "Gamma levels" were detected, there is no proof that this is true! Verbal assurances, regardless of the source, are not scientific proof of anything, and there is no logical or reasonable explanation as to why Genesis III failed to obtain any soil samples from these purportedly remarkable "landing-tracks." Genesis III also fails to mention that they never documented on either videotape or motion picture film any readings from the equipment they claim they rented to measure the radiation levels.[11]

Such "oversights" are inexcusable and bring into question Genesis III's professed competence as objective, scientific, and thorough investigators. In spite of these facts, the Meier faithful and his promoters continue to tout the "Pleiadian landing-tracks" as "hard evidence," when in truth they are not. They ignore the fact that merely *photographing* the purported "UFO" landing-tracks, without analyses of either vegetation or soil samples, isn't proof of anything.

Analysis of "Pleiadian" Landing-Track Samples

As mentioned in chapter 2, I obtained soil samples from some of these so-called Pleiadian landing-tracks.

When I arranged for scientific testing of the various Meier soil and vegetation samples I had collected, I asked that the laboratories report back to me only if there was any difference at all between the control samples I gathered and those obtained from the "landing-tracks." My reasoning was simple: I was not going to pay for a long-winded report telling me that

---

*A "rad" is a term in physics for a unit of energy absorbed from ionizing [charged particle] radiation, equal to 100 ergs per gram of irradiated material.

there was nothing special about the samples. I was only inter-ested if something worthy of scientific study were found.

In every sample analyzed (there were a total of four), there was *no discernible differences between any of the "UFO" soil samples and the ordinary dirt, grass, and rocks obtained as control samples!*

For those who still wish to believe that there is something "extraordinary" or "unique" about Meier's "Pleiadian land-ing-tracks," the remaining soil samples Tina Layton and I obtained are available to anyone who wants to have them tested. This offer is open to all takers, with my usual one con-dition attached: Whatever the test results, they must be released to the public.

How to Make "Pleiadian Landing-Tracks"

How does one manufacture purportedly "mysterious" circu-lar impressions as "UFO landing-tracks"? One of the easiest methods for making them is to take a round piece of plywood or pressboard and place it on top of some grass.

Circular-shaped pieces of plywood or pressboard can be purchased quite easily from any number of sources, such as a local lumber yard or any decent nursery, hardware, or garden store. Their sizes range from only a few inches in diameter up to several meters.

If you want to make it look like the UFO "swirled" the grass around in either a clockwise or counterclockwise direc-tion (thus duplicating Meier's alleged "vortice" effect), simply twist the board in whichever direction you want the grass to be "mysteriously" affected. Grass that is approximately one foot in height or roughly one-third of a meter tall is ideal for creating convincing "vortice effect" swirls. Be careful, for if the grass is too tall, it will be hard to control when you try to "swirl" it by rotating the pressboard. On the other hand, if the grass is too short, then you won't have enough to work with.[12]

Place lots of bricks or stones or anything else that creates a fair amount of weight on top of the round piece of board. Then leave the plywood or pressboard where it is for anywhere from one day to an entire month, depending on the severity of the impression you want to create. When you finally remove the round wooden board and whatever it was you used to weight it down with, you will have left behind a very convincing-looking "UFO landing-track," one with all the characteristics of Meier's own "Pleiadian" impressions!

If Billy Meier's landing-tracks were indeed fabricated in this manner, it would easily explain one of the alleged characteristics that Wendelle Stevens and other Meier proponents seem to find so enormously baffling: the "phenomenon" of insect infestation. Whenever plants are deprived of sunlight (as would be the case for those directly under the round pressboard) they cannot photosynthesize. When this happens, they begin to die. The resulting decay, not to mention the accumulated moisture, will always attract a good number of insects, especially in the damp climates in Switzerland.

While Brit and Lee Elders claim in *Pleiades, Volume II,* that "One scientist concluded that perhaps there is a residue of ultraviolet light attracting these creatures,"[13] such speculation by this supposed unnamed "scientist" is meaningless, since no soil or vegetation samples were ever analyzed until my investigation thirteen *years* after the fact!

In summation, the "hard evidence" for Meier's "UFO" landing-tracks simply does not exist. While the passage of time might account for the fact that nothing unusual was found in my samples of Billy Meier's "UFO landing-tracks," if the Genesis group had not been so haphazard in their investigation, we might know the answer to this aspect of the Meier case. Unfortunately, all we have today, other than the mundane samples Tina and I obtained, are photos of these tracks and nothing else that is scientifically credible to work with. This means that this portion of the Meier "evidence" is of no real value and cannot be used to legitimately substantiate the case as being credible.

Figures 113–115 show one of Meier's "landing-tracks" as they appear in photos from the Jacob binder, and my recreations of them using a round piece of pressboard I purchased for under twenty dollars.

Further examples of these simulated landing-tracks and how to create them, plus how to create other types of "UFO landing marks" often reported, appear in the video documentary *EXPOSED: The Billy Meier UFO Hoax.*

Fig. 113. One of the numerous "Pleiadian landing-tracks" allegedly made by Semjase's spacecraft, according to Billy Meier. (Photo courtesy: Margrit and Claudia Jacob.)

Fig. 114. Kal K. Korff holding a round piece of pressboard used to fake "UFO landing-tracks." (Photo courtesy: Underground Video.)

Fig. 115. This impressive-looking "UFO track" was created in a matter of hours by using the methods described in this chapter. It looks precisely like some of Billy Meier's "Pleiadian landing-tracks." (Photo courtesy: Underground Video.)

Other "Witnesses" to Meier's UFO "Contacts"

In all of the pro-Meier books, much is made of the supposed "fact" that there are "dozens of people" who have personally witnessed and occasionally independently photographed the Pleiadian spacecraft.[14] While this sounds impressive at first glance, the original version of *UFO . . . Contact from the Pleiades, Volume I* failed to include the *names* of any of these "witnesses." Also omitted were their accounts of what it was that they were supposed to have seen.[15]

Indeed, the only thing one finds on the pages of *Pleiades, Volume I,* are photographs of Meier sitting in a room full of unidentified people which, of course, proves absolutely nothing. In fact, some of the "witnesses" who are shown in the book gathered around Meier are clearly from Genesis and various reporters conducting interviews![16] But the photos of all these people looked nice, and with the caption heading at the upper right-hand corner of the book labeled "The Witnesses," Wendelle Stevens and Genesis III were able to use these photos to impress a gullible public.[17]

While the first edition of *Pleiades* failed to include this significant information, Stevens's original *Pleiades* manuscript and some of his later books did. However, as we shall see, what information *is* provided is not very impressive. Indeed, several curious but intriguing patterns emerge when these supposed "independent" eyewitness testimonies are examined carefully.

Though Wendelle Stevens boasts of "dozens of witnesses,"[18] his *Preliminary Investigation* book lists only fourteen, all of whom either were or are members of Meier's group. In other words, there are *no testimonies from any independent, outside observers.*[19] This fact is never mentioned by Meier's supporters; instead, they stress the "number of witnesses." By pumping up the number of these "witnesses," the more credible the "contacts" of Billy Meier appear to be.

The "Independent Eyewitnesses"

The first curious (and suspicious) aspect about all of these alleged "independent" sightings is that nearly all of them take place *during the night*, usually between the hours of 11:00 P.M. and 2:00 A.M.,[20] when most people are asleep. This is especially true in Switzerland where, even today, 24-hour grocery stores and all-night fast-food restaurants simply do not exist.[21] The fact that most of these "sightings" occur during the night is convenient for Billy Meier because, if he is behind this aspect of the hoax, then staging these events late at night greatly *reduces* the odds of him or any confederate(s) being caught.

It is obvious that visibility at night is extremely limited compared to daylight hours, and this is especially true in the Swiss countryside and in the surrounding areas where Billy Meier lives, as Tina Layton and I personally observed.

The second curious (and also suspicious) aspect of these allegedly independent "UFO" sightings is that the objects are *never seen at close range*. Indeed, even Wendelle Stevens concedes that the "spaceships" are always "500 meters to a mile away," at a minimum![22]

A typical "independent" UFO sighting that Meier stages to regale the uncritical faithful usually takes place via the following manner:

• Billy Meier announces sometime during the day that he will have a "contact" later that night. This means that for several hours everyone gradually gets worked up over the possibility that they may see the "Pleiadians."

• Between the hours of 11:00 P.M. and 1:00 A.M., a small group of these perspective "independent" witnesses (usually Billy Meier's devotees) either follow Meier out into the Swiss woods at night or they drive him to whichever location he insists the "Pleiadians" will make an appearance.

• Meier will suddenly announce for everyone to stop and

wait a *minimum of 500 meters (1,625 feet) from the actual point of contact*, which always takes place behind large clumps of forest trees that obscure him from view.

• Sometime after forty-five minutes, perhaps as long as two hours, a "mysterious light" will then be spotted rising from the clump of trees Billy Meier is hidden behind and the light will drift away, receding upward into the sky. Usually, this light is reddish in color, or sometimes whitish-orange.[23]

• Billy Meier will then emerge shortly thereafter and rejoin the group of "witnesses," asking them whether or not they had seen "Semjase's spaceship leaving." Naturally, the response from his followers is always yes.

If this sounds unimpressive, it is, because the modus operandi of these "independent sightings" is such that Billy Meier could simply be going into the woods and launching a balloon or other device with a flare or a light attached to it.

It is most curious that although these independent "observations" purportedly take place fairly frequently, *no one else* in the surrounding areas has ever reported seeing a UFO on these occasions, only those persons who Billy Meier takes out into the woods with him! Upon close examination, the fact remains that there is an *absence of reports* from the more than 60,000 people who live in the area! Why is it that if *real* "spaceships of the Pleiades" are literally rising up from the woods of Switzerland, that only Billy Meier and members of his group report them? As Elisabeth Gruber told me when I interviewed her, only Billy Meier has the "privilege" of seeing the "Pleiadians" during the day.

For those who are "impressed" with these "independent" sightings, observations of blobs of light rising in the night sky are not proof of anything, nor are photographs taken of the same "phenomena." In truth, the "hard evidence" for these purportedly "independent" UFO sightings of Meier's Pleiadian friends does not exist. Figure 116 lists the names of these alleged "independent" eyewitnesses. The data is from Moosbrugger's book; the chart speaks for itself.

Jacobus Bertschinger*	Atlantis Meier* (Billy Meier's son)
Eva Bieri*	Gilgamesha Meier* (Billy Meier's daughter)
Bernadette Brand*	Kalliope Meier* (Billy Meier's wife)
Madeleine Brügger*	Methusalem Meier* (Billy Meier's son)
Christina Gasser	Guido Moosbrugger*
Elisabeth Gruber*	Herbert Runkel*
Thomas Keller	Engelbert Wächter*
Brunhilde Koye*	Maria Wächter*
Bernhard Koye*	Conny Wächter*
Freddy Kropf	Hans Zimmermann
Silvano Lehmann	

Fig. 116. Chart showing the alleged "independent" witnesses, all of whom claim to have seen Billy Meier's "UFOs." The asterisk next to each name denotes those who are either members of Billy Meier's group or his immediate family.

Alleged CIA/KGB Involvement

Billy Meier's supporters claim that the elite intelligence agencies of several nations, including the Swiss government, have "raked over" contact sites and intercepted the development of Meier's photos.[24] The CIA, the former KGB, the former East German government,[25] and unspecified "men in black"[26] are all said to be responsible for pilfering Meier's "evidence" and generally spying on his activities and those around him. In an attempt to research these claims, UFO researcher Bill Moore and I asked not only the CIA, but the Swiss government as well, whether or not they had ever even heard of Mr. Meier or if these allegations were true. All of the answers we received were identical: No one seemed to know who Meier was!

In response to written inquiries, the Swiss Consulate General of Los Angeles replied:

> With reference to your letter, I very much regret not to be in a position to give you the desired information.
>
> *Eduard Meier is unknown to us, as well as his publications.* (Emphasis added)
>
> Yours faithfully,
>
> THE COUNCIL GENERAL OF SWITZERLAND
>
> J. Lustenberger

In the hope that at least some record could be found on Billy Meier, a Freedom of Information Act request was filed by Bill Moore with the U.S. State Department. This was their reply dated December 27, 1982:

> Re: Freedom of Information Act Request #8202708
>
> Dear Mr. Moore:
>
> This refers to Mr. Shiel's letter of August 10 that acknowledges your Freedom of Information Act request concerning Eduard Meier regarding UFO-type spacecraft and any claims generated about UFO's [sic] between the State Department and the United States Embassy in Bern.
>
> Any information pertaining to this topic would most likely appear in the Department Central Policy Records, Bureau of Oceans and International Environmental and Scientific Affairs Records, and Bureau Intelligence and Research Records. *However, thorough searches of those record systems failed to locate any information about your subject.* (Emphasis added)

If I may assist you with other questions regarding the Freedom of Information Act or the Department's record systems, please do not hesitate to contact me.

Sincerely,

Cindy R. Miller
Information and Privacy Staff

While pro-Meier supporters and assorted UFO conspiracy buffs will no doubt cry "cover-up," the fact remains that until *any* proof is provided by Meier and his associates (as opposed to unsupported claims and vague assurances) that such nefarious activities are taking place, the statements made by these agencies must stand since they have never been disproven. Indeed, the tales of all this purported "spying" on Meier are *unsubstantiated* and will remain so until the pro-Meier people provide solid evidence to give them legitimacy.

Notes

1. Jim Dilettoso, tape-recorded personal interview with Kal K. Korff, Al Reed, and Barbara Reed at the offices of Publication Professionals, Sunnyvale, California, September 6, 1980.

2. Wendelle Stevens, *UFO . . . Contact from the Pleiades—A Preliminary Investigation Report—The Report of an Ongoing Contact* (Tucson, Ariz.: Wendelle Stevens, 1983), p. 365.

3. Guido Moosbrugger, *. . . und sie fliegen doch! UFOs: Die größte Heraus-forderung des 20 Jahrhunderts* (München, Germany: Michael Hesemann Verlag, 1991), p. 159.

4. Elisabeth Gruber, personal interviews with Kal Korff and Tina Layton, Semjase Silver Star Center, Hinterschmidrüti, Switzerland, August 18, 1991.

5. Wendelle Stevens, *UFO . . . Contact from the Pleiades: A Supplementary Investigation Report—The Report of an Ongoing Contact* (Tucson, Ariz.: Wendelle Stevens, 1989), p. 444.

6. Jim Dilettoso, personal interviews with Kal K. Korff, Al Reed, and Barbara Reed, September 6, 1980.

7. *UFO . . . Contact from the Pleiades, Volume I,* rev. ed. (Phoenix, Ariz.: Genesis III Productions, Ltd., 1979), p. 61.

8. *UFO . . . Contact from the Pleiades, Volume II,* 1st ed. (Phoenix, Ariz.: Genesis III Productions, Ltd., 1983), p. 53.

9. Ibid.

10. Ibid.

11. Gary Kinder, *Light Years: An Investigation into the Extraterrestrial Experiences of Eduard Meier* (New York: The Atlantic Monthly Press, 1987), p. 216.

12. Experiments by Kal K. Korff, TotalResearch, 1991–1995.

13. *UFO . . . Contact from the Pleiades, Volume II,* p. 53.

14. *UFO . . . Contact from the Pleiades, Volume I,* 1st ed., pp. 44–45.

15. Ibid.

16. Ibid.

17. Ibid.

18. Stevens, *UFO...Contact from the Pleiades, A Preliminary Investigation Report,* pp. 126–60.

19. Ibid.

20. Ibid.

21. Author's personal observation while in Switzerland.

22. Stevens, *UFO . . . Contact from the Pleiades, A Preliminary Investigation Report,* p. 68. *Also* Wendelle C. Stevens, National UFO Conference, Tucson, Arizona, May 23, 1983.

23. Elisabeth Gruber, personal interviews with Kal Korff and Tina Layton, Hinterschmidrüti, Switzerland, August 18, 1991.

24. Jim Dilettoso, personal interviews with Kal K. Korff, Al Reed, and Barbara Reed, September 6, 1980.

25. Ibid.

26. Jim Dilettoso, personal interviews with Kal K. Korff, Al Reed, and Barbara Reed, September 6, 1980. *See also* Stevens, *UFO . . . Contact from the Pleiades, A Preliminary Investigation Report,* pp. 511–13.

8

Assorted Claptrap:
Jim Dilettoso on the Meier Case

Let me ask you a question, Jim, you went on record recently as saying you have, what, a Ph.D. from McGill University? Is that correct?

Kal K. Korff[1]

Yes, I went on record saying that.

Jim Dilettoso[2]

I have searched our files and have no record of anyone by the name of Jim Dilettoso (or any variation thereof) as having attended or graduated from McGill University between 1965 to the present.

Ms. Karen J'bari[3]

Jim Dilettoso is the individual the Genesis people uses to talk their way into various scientific and technical facilities in order to get access to state-of-the-art equipment. Jim Dilettoso has repeatedly misled the public about his involvement and activities in the Meier case. As we have seen, he also misrepresented the facts of the few tests that have legitimately been conducted on the Meier "evidence," especially Meier's "UFO" photographs, which he claims to have "tested and authenticated,"[4] a scientific impossibility. Indeed, as Jim Dilet-toso reiterated and kept stressing to me during our debate on FOX TV's "Encounters" television show on November 19, 1994, "I stand behind the testing that I've done."

This chapter contains excerpts from numerous tape-recordings of remarks Jim Dilettoso has made over the years which prove irrefutably that he is often less than forthcoming. Although Wendelle Stevens rationalizes Dilettoso's behavior by claiming that the latter was "often forced into half-truths, not of his own choice,"[5] the following excerpts from these tape-recorded conversations with Dilettoso prove otherwise.

My first encounter with Jim Dilettoso took place at the UFO '80 symposium in Oakland, California, on August 23. After what turned out to be a hostile first encounter and debate, Dilettoso called me two weeks later and said he wanted to meet with me and my associates, Al and Barbara Reed, who own the company Publication Professionals. Dilettoso also stated that he wanted to clarify some of the "interesting questions" that were raised during our discussion at UFO '80.

Dilettoso indicated he would bring a briefcase full of documents that would answer any questions we had concerning the scientific analysis and test procedures that had been performed on the Meier evidence. Moreover, he stated that he wanted to discuss plans to initiate further testing by "neutral and unbiased" laboratories in order to "get to the bottom of all this."

To show Genesis III's sincerity, he claimed they would go back and rerun tests, as well as any new test deemed necessary. "We are not trying to prove the case is real," said Dilettoso.

When I asked Dilettoso, "What if new testing proved that the case wasn't real, then what?" Dilettoso replied, "Well, then we will have done our job!"

Naturally, I welcomed this opportunity, and Dilettoso met with Al Reed; his lovely wife, Barbara Reed; and myself on

September 6, 1980. The first set of comments from Dilettoso that we shall examine are excerpted from this tape-recorded interview. Included after Dilettoso's remarks are my comments clarifying the facts for the record.

Many of these statements by Dilettoso first appeared in my original 1981 exposé book on Meier.

Dilettoso: We worked with a lot of people there [at Jet Propulsion Laboratory (JPL)] in doing this. Ranging from Bob Nathan, who was one of the people who invented image processing back in the sixties, and he has been at JPL on a daily basis since then.

And (Nathan) made available a lot of people to us. In fact, one day, he (Nathan) sent everybody home except for two lab technicians who worked with them, and we were there from two in the afternoon to near midnight, doing stuff after he gave everyone the day off.

COMMENT:
I spoke with Dr. Bob Nathan later the same evening to verify Dilettoso's comments. Nathan *denied* that such an event ever took place. According to Dr. Nathan, he did not send any employees home nor give them the day off. He also stated that the copies of the Meier photographs he had received were of such poor quality that no analytical data could be obtained from them.

Dilettoso: Eric von Jacobi shot through plastic and all, sent the pictures to Bill Spaulding. They also sent some super 8mm movie film that they had acquired from Billy and they sent it to Colonel VonKeviczky who they thought was a safe person to get it to Wendelle [Stevens]. Two months later Wendelle's talking to Jacobi, says "I don't have the photographs yet" and says "Oh I sent them to VonKeviczky." So Wendelle calls VonKeviczky who denies ever receiving the photographs.

Wendelle hears a month later that not only does VonKeviczky have the photographs, but he's selling slide sets.

COMMENT:
Jim Dilettoso is referring to a set of Meier photographs that was sent to Mr. Bill Spaulding, director of the civilian UFO group, Ground Saucer Watch (GSW), for analysis. GSW concluded that Meier's pictures were a hoax.

Bill Spaulding did not obtain any pictures from Eric von Jacobi. They were sent to him from Mr. Wilfried Falk of Mannheim, Germany. Falk's letter proving this is in my files.

There is no such person as "Eric von Jacobi." Dilettoso has confused the name of "Ilse von Jacobi," who is a Swiss female UFO researcher and, as explained in chapter 1, was one of the earliest investigators of the Meier case.

Colman VonKeviczky is not a colonel, but in fact is a major. VonKeviczky does not sell slides from the alleged 8mm movie footage that Dilettoso is referring to; however, he does sell slide copies of photographs that were supplied to him originally by Hans Jacob. In addition to the slides that VonKeviczky sells, he also provides a copy of his findings which states that the Meier case is a hoax.

A. Reed: [The slides are] taken off the frames then?

Dilettoso: Yes. In the movie film. So Wendelle has to get a court order to get the photographs back from VonKeviczky, which he did, and he got the super 8mm film spliced! It had been cut in two sections and not spliced back together again. So that started a feud going with VonKeviczky who was "bummed out" over Wendelle sending in a court action to get the photographs back. So he's out there selling Meier photographs to anyone who wants to walk in and pay some $30 for a set. And he says it's a hoax.

COMMENT:
Dilettoso's statement that Wendelle Stevens had to obtain a "court order" to secure the return of the motion picture footage from VonKeviczky is not true. Stevens never resorted to any "court action."[6]

VonKeviczky sells slide copies of the Meier photos that were supplied to him by Hans Jacob. The majority of these photos have been curiously omitted from publication by Genesis III and are featured in the present book.

Dilettoso: So Wendelle doesn't take a very strong stand in any of that. He says that if anyone's out there circulating the photographs to just let 'em do it. It puts photographs out there so that once the tests are conclusive, then people already have the photographs in their hands.

COMMENT:
If this statement is true, then Stevens should have no objections to the photographs that Colman VonKeviczky sells. Apparently Stevens's policy (if indeed he ever had one) changed. In August of 1980 Genesis III sent a letter through a Phoenix attorney ordering VonKeviczky to stop selling the photographs in question. VonKeviczky refused their request, pointing out the fact that Genesis III had no case, since the Meier photos he sells *predate* Lee Elders's "rights agreement" with Billy Meier.

Dilettoso: Plus looking at the film grain, you can get a pretty good idea of whether or not it's two slides sandwiched together. And his photos [Meier's] are not. When you're looking at the original, you can only do that with an electron microscope or a very detailed scanning method looking at the film grain.

A. Reed: Which electron microscopes were in use when you were testing?

Dilettoso: I think one was a Minolta, but the other begins with an H. I want to say Hammamatsu but that's an Array System. Maybe Hamminex.

A. Reed: I was wondering if it was Edex?

Dilettoso: No.

A. Reed: Because Edex is a firm in Hayward.

Dilettoso: [With apparent interest] Uh huh . . .

A. Reed: And one range they use X-, S-, or C-Bands. I don't know if you're into—

Dilettoso: Oh yeah, yeah.

A. Reed: —into that?

Dilettoso: Yeah. Yeah right! Two thousand diameters was our best resolution on the Minolta.

COMMENT:
This was a test question for Dilettoso. X-, S-, and C-Bands are *radar frequencies* and are unrelated to electron microscope technology! If Jim Dilettoso really knew anything about electron microscopes, he would not have fallen for this test question the way he obviously did.

Dilettoso: In the photograph that Bill Spaulding claims there is a string, it's not a string at all. Anyone who knows anything about photography knows that from handling the negative, it's a crease.

COMMENT:
Dilettoso has been greatly misinformed. Spaulding was given first-generation copies of Meier's photographs, not negatives. Therefore, no "crease" could have occurred handling the photos.

Dilettoso: Film grains swell when exposed to radiation. We learned this from Richard Dixon at Livermore Labs.

COMMENT:
When I checked with Richard Dixon of Lawrence Livermore National Laboratory (coincidentally, where I also used to work), I was told by Dixon, "I do not remember talking to such a person. If it concerned UFOs, I would certainly remember it."

When asked if film grains swell when exposed to radiation, Dixon replied, "I don't know if they do. I would need to check on that." Dixon then put the phone down and consulted with photographic expert Chuck Cook, a co-worker and scientist who often photographs the nuclear-related experiments at "Site 300" for Lawrence Livermore National Laboratory. Cook confirmed that film grains do *not* swell when exposed to radiation. "In fact," Cook said, "the silver nitrate doesn't even begin to move around until you put it in the developer!"

Dilettoso: It's a foregone conclusion that whatever UFOs are, they put off a lot of radiation and a lot of magnetism. So even if you're snapping pictures, film is being affected by the radiation.

COMMENT:
Once again, this is simply not true and it is up to Jim Dilettoso to prove otherwise.

Dilettoso: In all of Billy's film, the film grain is larger than the manufacturer says it should be.

COMMENT:
Since Dilettoso never studied *any* of Meier's *original negatives*, he is in no position to make this statement! Besides, as already established, film grains do not swell when exposed to radiation. This "radiation obsession" of Dilettoso's is pure nonsense.

Dilettoso: We went to De Anza [Systems], for example, with the floppy disk and said, "Here, would you show us how your equipment works?"

COMMENT:
According to Ken Dinwiddie of De Anza Systems, Dilettoso never offered any sort of floppy disk. This disproves an earlier comment by Dilettoso that they brought software equipment with them to De Anza.

Dilettoso: So we took the first-generation photographs, he (Nathan) sent his lab home, about fifteen people, [at] one o'clock in the afternoon.

COMMENT:
Dr. Nathan denied that such an event took place, and also denied that the prints he examined were "first generation."

Dilettoso: Nathan said that he couldn't find anything that was too out-of-character with the photographs.

COMMENT:
When Dilettoso's statements were fact-checked with Dr. Nathan, the latter said the copies he received were *too poor in quality* for running a proper evaluation. Dr. Nathan did, however, mention the fact that by simply looking at the Meier photos, he could tell that they were "obvious hoaxes."

Dilettoso: We have about ten hours of him (Marcel Vogel) and the entire lab proceedings. And we have about an hour of him discussing why the metal samples are not possible in earth technology; going into intrinsic [sic] detail of why it is not done anywhere on Earth, that type of chemistry.

COMMENT:
This scenario was fact-checked with Marcel Vogel while he was still alive. He stated that Dilettoso did not have ten hours of videotape as claimed. According to Vogel, all Dilettoso had of his "analysis" is one hour of tape, which Vogel himself supplied.

Dilettoso: When you meet Billy [Meier], and you see him trying to figure out how to feed his family, there's a lot of destitution in his area of people that just don't have anything. Nothing. Children without shoes in the wintertime is a reality in his town. And when you're talking to him, and you see that he is worried about how he's gonna feed his family, and how he's going to pay, get some money to buy rolls of film let alone pay to process the film. And never leaves the town; he hasn't left the town in eight years, and very few people come in and out of town. You realize that it just is not possible financially for him to set up anything to be sandwiching two pieces of film together.

COMMENT:
Since Billy Meier moved to Hinterschmidrüti in *1977*, and had been living there for only *four* years when Jim Dilettoso made this statement, the claim that he "hasn't left the town for eight years" is patently absurd.

Korff: You've met him, talked with him?

Dilettoso: No, but the videotapes of, you know of, uh, Wendelle went over there; was there for ten days and the video cameras were on twenty-four hours a day for ten days. Just on in the house. Psychological Stress Evaluations was done off the voice track of the tapes.

COMMENT:
The existence of these ten-day/twenty-four hour videotapes has yet to be proven. While Dilettoso may claim such tapes exist, one cannot help but remain skeptical as to the authenticity of this statement, especially when his previous claim of having some ten hours of videotape has also been refuted.

In truth, Billy Meier is far more financially secure than Dilettoso claims, and the town of Hinterschmidrüti is a typical middle-class farm community with Billy Meier being their "celebrity" neighbor. Dilettoso's claims of Meier being financially destitute are simply not true.

Dilettoso: Billy's considered a "witch" (in his home town), that's what they call him. He's a witch because he makes those "Satans" [UFOs] come here. Uh, as far as they're concerned, there's a lot of controversy over Billy's children having developed ESP. And some tests were done with one of the kids in one room coloring in a coloring book, while a kid in the other room has no idea of what the other child has done, but has said to find the objects in the room to emulate what your sister is doing. So the other kid goes over, takes out the crayons, opens up to the same page, and colors the same colors, the same time as the other kid is coloring the other one.

COMMENT:
These are more unfounded claims by Dilettoso. Tina Layton and I were unable to find *anyone* in Switzerland who could recall such "psychic demonstrations" or tests for such abilities taking place as described by Dilettoso.

Dilettoso: Meier's objective is not to make money. To him, his job is that his "vibrating field" so to say; his "tuning" of his body as a liquid crystal and his past genetics and his whatever, he cannot explain it. It is such that he can have physical contact with them and write down what they say, and get the evidence from them and keep it hidden in cardboard boxes in his barns. And when the right people come he turns over stuff to them. And uh, Wendelle is not the only investigator that he's turned stuff over to, for he has a real close alliance with an East German, that research has indicated is probably a Russian agent.

COMMENT:
What Dilettoso is referring to is how Billy Meier supposedly uses his body as a "liquid tuning crystal" in order to "channel" his messages from the "Pleiadians," when he is not having direct face-to-face contact with them. While this is an intriguing claim, there's no credible evidence to support it.

A. Reed: This is what I was getting at. Sooner or later we should think that the KGB or somebody—

Dilettoso: Yeah.

A. Reed: Would move in on this.

Dilettoso: Yeah, they've all been there, they've all been there.

A. Reed: Having, you know, possession of that kind of knowledge, they would simply take him, the data, the family, and everything else.

Dilettoso: Yeah.

A. Reed: If not them, our own CIA.

Dilettoso: Yeah, that's been attempted. That's why Wendelle brought in some outside security companies, international security companies, company retired military personnel, high-level personnel that now have their own security company who uh, take care of security on Billy. Billy's now been moved out of the town in the last six months, and is kept somewhere else.

COMMENT:
The "security company" that Dilettoso refers to is Intercep, which is owned by Lee Elders and Thomas K. Welch. Intercep is a two-person company, and is hardly the "international" security company Dilettoso claims it to be.

Dilettoso has also forgotten that earlier he said Meier had not left town for eight years. Now he has changed his story.

Korff: Who, then, owns Genesis?

Dilettoso: No one owns it. It's a foundation with a board of advisors and a board of trustees. All profits are assigned to various nonprofit foundations.

COMMENT:
This contradicts an earlier statement made by Genesis III documented in the June 1980 issue of the *APRO Bulletin* in which Genesis claimed that all of the profits from the book would be used for further research—not to be donated to any organization. Also, Wendelle Stevens sent a letter to me in which he stated that he is a one-fourth partner in Genesis III.

Finally, court papers on file in Pima County, Arizona, stemming from the lawsuits between Genesis III and some of their former partners such as Michael Osborn and Word Distributors Incorporated, prove that Brit Elders, Lee Elders, and Thomas Welch are some of the other legal owners of Genesis III Productions and that the company is not "nonprofit" as Dilettoso claims.

Dilettoso: Now Wendelle just selected the Meier case as one that could be a vehicle. There's at least a hundred other cases that he's working on that have this much evidence. It's just one that he picked. Almost like a rabbit out of his hat. There was an interesting combination of people there [at the UFO '80 Symposium] last weekend; Richard Miller and Wendelle used to do transchannelings for the Air Force back in the fifties. Richard Miller quoted the "space people" under strict Air Force control back in the fifties. They would fly up to Alaska because they were told that the magnetic fields there were proper for resonance induction, and we have hundreds and hundreds of hours of audio recordings of Richard and other CIA officers doing transchannelings of aliens. In the last few years, [UFO researcher] Leo Sprinkle has done work with two of those CIA officers who have developed serious personality aberrations.

Korff: Because of what?

Dilettoso: Because of being, and it seems like something consistent in people that do channeling, is that their so-called cell-salt structures change and they develop diabetes. There's also studies done that indicate that the last two popes developed diabetes, as do a lot of East gurus. So what's the correlation between transchanneling and cell-salts and diabetes, then diabetes going unchecked, developing into other neurotic and schizophrenic behaviors that usually show up as olfactory and motor-sense disturbances like Parkinson's disease? It's not where they become schizophrenic where their thinking is impaired, but where their body reactions are affected. And Billy shows signs of that also. His resistance is down so much that he almost has perpetual pneumonia. He goes to the hospital; it's hard to get him to the hospital every few months; the infection from the shotgun blast has not totally healed. But [w]hat seems consistent in the some thousand contactee cases that are being studied is that the vibrating field put out by the ship and by the beings themselves dominates the aura. The magnetic field that can be kirlian photographed dominates it so much that it appears to even get down and start reprogramming the DNA.

COMMENT:
While the United States government (and others) would undoubtedly be interested in studying anyone who could *legitimately* communicate with extraterrestrial intelligences, neither Wendelle Stevens nor Richard Miller has ever provided any documentation that they performed "transchannelings" of "space people" for the CIA or any other U.S. government organization. I also have yet to see any evidence indicating that cell-salt structures have been altered. As far as any "vibrating field altering or reprogramming of the DNA," again I have yet to see any proof that such a thing does, or even can, occur.

Richard Miller's "abilities" were exposed as groundless by UFO researcher Paul Cerny back in the late 1970s. While Miller *claims* he is in "contact" with aliens, he cannot prove it, and Cerny's work exposing him must stand until otherwise refuted.

Since there is no hospital in Hinterschmidrüti, although Dilettoso claims that Meier visits one every few months, this is yet another contradiction in his earlier claim that Billy Meier hasn't left his own hometown in some "eight years."

Finally, no one at the Meier farm could recall either to Tina Layton or me that Billy Meier was "wounded by a shotgun blast." In addition, there is no such injury or "assassination attempt" listed among any of the pro-Meier books of Genesis III, Gary Kinder, Guido Moosbrugger, Wendelle Stevens, or Randolph Winters. A simple check of these works proves it.

B. Reed: What about his wife?

Dilettoso: His wife just wants the whole thing to stop. His wife and kids, three little kids, talk about the space people coming to their house. We have little kids, eight years old, going outside on videotape saying "and right here's where they landed last winter and melted a big ring in the snow. And then it froze, and then Daddy came out and put a garden hose on it." And they were thrilled because it was a little ice skating rink for them, twenty-five feet in diameter.

COMMENT:
This is another truly remarkable claim, but like Dilettoso's countless others, it, too, lacks any supportive or substantive data. One interesting note, however, is the fact that Dilettoso claimed the ring was *twenty-five* feet in diameter. In contrast, the Meier books claim that the Pleiadian craft, with the exception of one, are *twenty-one* feet in diameter.

Dilettoso: And then Billy did some demonstrations of things which were very remarkable. You think Uri Geller does things with metals, bending things; Billy's kids do that instantly. They don't have to hold it and think about it, they just go "whoosht" and bend it. And videotape of Billy flipping like a Swiss silver dollar into the air and it just somewhere between going up and coming down, turned into just silver fragments, and just fragmentized and just shattered all over the floor. And he attributes it just like Uri Geller does; they're just latent abilities that are in everyone that are available once you tune into the higher vibrations. You have to tune into those vibrations to contact space people. So getting these other abilities is just a side effect of tuning into those vibrations.

COMMENT:
Once again there is no tangible evidence to support the authenticity of these claims.

B. Reed: Are the children tuned into 'em then?

Dilettoso: The children claim to be in telepathic contact with Semjase all the time. And their intelligence is incredibly accelerated.

COMMENT:
Again, these statements are not supported by tangible evidence, nor by anyone at the Meier farm. As Bernadette Brand, Elisabeth Gruber, and Simone reiterated and emphasized to me, *only Billy Meier* is in contact with Semjase and the "Pleiadians." Meier himself is on record as having made this same statement, branding others who claim they are in contact with the Pleiadians as "liars."[7]

Dilettoso: Though anyone who has worked on the evidence of the [Meier] case can't find anywhere where it's a hoax, and the only people who claim it's a hoax are those on the outside that are saying there can't possibly be this much evidence and verification.

COMMENT:
I know of *no one* who has ever claimed that this case is a hoax based upon the reasoning that there cannot "possibly be this much evidence or verification." The Meier case is a hoax because there is no credible evidence to indicate otherwise, and for the many other reasons outlined in this book.

Dilettoso: So in all the photographs we got the same thing. Twenty-two feet, three inches. No matter how big it was in the picture, and we did that on about forty photographs just popping 'em into the Hammamatsu System.

COMMENT:
Dilettoso claims that some forty photographs allegedly taken

by Meier were scanned through a Hammamatsu Array System. And as he stated, the dimensions of the craft always measured twenty-two feet, three inches. However, the given dimensions of the "Pleiadian" spacecraft that appear in the Genesis/Meier books measure out to 22.75 feet in diameter. Why is there this discrepancy?

If the dimensions of the Pleiadian craft as detailed in the pro-Meier books are correct, then the Hammamatsu Array System was in error. If one assumes that the Hammamatsu Array System is accurate, then the books are greatly in error. Which is the correct measurement and which source is in error?

Finally, in all of the pro-Meier books by Genesis III, Kinder, Moosbrugger, Stevens, et al., there is no mention of forty photographs having been analyzed. Indeed, these books mention only *four* photos having been analyzed and Dilettoso is on audiotape saying the same thing in his numerous conversations with Underground Video as well.

Dilettoso: [Billy Meier's alleged "transchanneling"] Works the same way that they teach levitation and TM [transcendental meditation]. They teach you to meditate on a mandala, a mind-light picture, and do an internal sound vibration called a mantra. And by the intersection of light and sound inside your body, you levitate. And now there's thousands of people in that program who have at least "hopped" up in the air a few times. And at their training center in the Midwest, they're now even in there on their on-campus book store selling "hopping pillows" that are these little round pillows that you sit on that have straps and with seat belts! To keep you on the pillow so that when you go up in the air and come down, you don't hurt your knees or ankles or anything.

COMMENT:
Again another truly remarkable statement that is completely unsubstantiated, as there is no scientific or other credible evi-

dence that people "levitate" on "hopping pillows." Indeed, an open invitation is hereby extended to Jim Dilettoso to produce *any* individual who can perform these "psychic feats."

Dilettoso: [Elaborating on some of the allegedly "advanced engineering propulsion technics of the Pleiadians" as stated by Billy Meier, and on a small scale model which Dilettoso claims he successfully tested and flew inside a vacuum.] You start with a battery operated phonograph, turntable, and you make a spindle that will go like a regular record spindle from the bottom all the way up to the top of the bell jar. And you make it by taking equal diameters of byrillium, titanium, and copper, and twisting them twenty-two times from end-to-end and putting them in as a spindle. Then you take a phonograph record and take sixteen bar magnets north pole and to the center, south pole to the outside, and glue them onto a phonograph record. And take another phonograph record, same bar magnets, and glue them north to the inside, south to the outside, and slip it down over the top of the spindles. Since north is on the inside they won't come together. They just stand there like that. [Dilettoso illustrates what he is talking about by holding his hands out and cupping them together.]

Without the bell jar on, glass bell jar, you turn the phonograph record on. The bottom one starts turning and the top one just kind of bounces up and down. And then it starts to turn really slowly.

Put the bell jar on, pump out the air, and the top of the phonograph record will start to spin in the opposite direction of what it was spinning before.

Then you turn on the ultraviolet light, in wide band, the vacuum, however you can set it up best. The top phonograph record will then rise up to the top of the bell jar. And that's the basis of the experiment.

COMMENT:
As is obvious, Dilettoso's description of this "advanced Pleiadian propulsion system" leaves a lot to be desired. It in fact is nothing more than a gussied-up version of basic principles of magnetism that have been known on this planet for over 100 years!

In addition to the fact that Jim Dilettoso has never provided any evidence that his "invention" exists, assuming that it does, the use of ultraviolet light under the circumstances he describes has no effect at all. In fact, Dilettoso's "Pleiadian propulsion system" statements reviewed above are still further examples of the pseudoscientific puffery he is well known for.

A. Reed: Wendelle said . . . he [Meier] couldn't focus, he had to "hip shoot" [take his photos shooting from the hip] because the mirror was also stuck.

Dilettoso: Right.

A. Reed: I took exception to that, because you understand—

Dilettoso: Well, it's a range-finder camera anyway.

A. Reed: Oh! It's a range finder!

Dilettoso: Right.

A. Reed: The mirror is stuck on it?

Dilettoso: The mirror, I believe, was the mirror that was on the light meter.

COMMENT:
Dilettoso, who is often billed as a "photographic expert,"

seems to be *unaware* that the operation of a light meter depends upon a *photo-electric cell or battery* rather than a mirror!

Finally, Billy Meier's camera is a standard Olympus 35mm ECR Single Lens Reflex, as can be easily proven when one examines page iii of Meier's own *Verzeichnis,* and Genesis III's *own* video documentary on the Meier case called *Contact.* In this documentary, there is a scene with Billy Meier at his home holding his camera and showing how he operates it with one hand. It is not a "range-finder camera" as Dilettoso claims.

Dilettoso: Wendelle's into brevity, he's into taking a whole bunch of information and making it as simple as possible for the mainstream to get.

A. Reed: From his service days no doubt.

Dilettoso: Yeah. He [Meier] was right-handed and lost his right arm at the shoulder, about a year before his contacts started.

COMMENT:
According to the book *UFO . . . Contact from the Pleiades,* Meier lost his *left* arm in a bus accident in 1963—not his right arm, as claimed by Dilettoso (look carefully at the photographs of Meier in the Genesis III books, this is obviously the case). In addition, when I saw Billy Meier briefly in person, Meier waved at me with his right hand; you could see that his left arm was clearly missing.

However, if one chooses to believe Dilettoso, then consider the following: Dilettoso stated that Meier's contacts started one year after he lost his arm. If this is true, then Meier's first contacts with alleged extraterrestrials began in 1964, eleven years *before UFO . . . Contact from the Pleiades* claims that they started. This is a most intriguing contradiction.

Dilettoso: We also went and talked with [Hollywood special effects expert] Doug Trumbull. Trumbull told us that he couldn't do that type of photography [duplicate the Meier photographs] let alone 8mm movies, for under a million dollars.

COMMENT:
As shown earlier in chapter 4, duplicating Meier's photographs for anywhere from twenty to one hundred dollars is quite easy. Besides, Dilettoso has yet to provide the slightest shred of evidence that Doug Trumbull actually said this. Instead, the only "proof" we have concerning these statements is Jim Dilettoso's "word" for things.

B. Reed: Why is it that he's never taken any pictures of any aliens?

Dilettoso: He has, oh, about a dozen I've seen. And two of them are quite remarkable photographs that have two aliens [women] in thin spacesuits, a man with a helmet on, and the whole control panel of the spaceship behind them. But VonKeviczky sells those photographs as pictures of Billy Meier's girlfriend.

COMMENT:
Colman VonKeviczky does not sell pictures of these "Pleiadian cosmonauts" under the façade that they show Meier's girlfriend. Indeed, the information stating that Semjase is Meier's "girlfriend" was supplied by Billy Meier himself.

B. Reed: Are they human-looking then?

Dilettoso: Yeah, really human-looking. Except in two of the closeup photographs, the earlobes come way down and attach onto the jawbone. But otherwise they look totally human, and they [the aliens] explained to him [Meier] that anyone whose earlobes are attached to their jawbones, their sense of hearing is tremendously improved. And told him to do an experiment of pulling on his own ears real hard, and seeing how their own hearing changed. And when I do it, I can definitely hear higher frequencies, all of a sudden just clicks in.

COMMENT:
As chapter 5 proves, when Billy Meier's "cosmonaut" photographs were analyzed, there were no "extended earlobes." Jim Dilettoso is mistaken, the "extended earlobes" are nothing more than hair which extends down to the side cheekbones of the human beings Meier's photos really depict.

As far as Dilettoso being able to hear "higher frequencies" when he tugs on his earlobes, he is imagining things (if not making them up), as any ear specialist will tell you.

A. Reed: Well, you said yesterday that you had brought enough data with you to possibly put to rest some of the questions that we would have, and I was wondering, or was it in the nature of the conversation we've just been having or are there some documents you can leave us or—

Dilettoso: There's a document package here in town that I left with Marcel [Vogel] a week ago, that I will pick up and get to you. What I'll have to do is have you sign a nondisclosure agreement that, you can contact the people whose names are in the report, but you can't discuss their names with any people on the outside, because those people would deny it. But you're free to contact the people whose names are in the report, and contact them directly.

COMMENT:
Dilettoso never did show up for another meeting, and *fifteen years after* he first made this promise, he still has not fulfilled it.

B. Reed: When they (the Pleiadians) communicate, how do they communicate?

Dilettoso: Most of them can talk if they want to, but they don't have to. . . . Yeah, well there's lots of those [aliens] throughout the universe and they range from looking almost insect-like to looking like "cat people," monkeys, and whatever.

COMMENT:
This is another unsubstantiated statement.

B. Reed: Do you have pictures of all of these? Do these people take pictures of the aliens?

Dilettoso: No. And a lot of pictures that are taken are so very inundated (with radiation) that it just becomes a blob.

A. Reed: The radiation just kind of scrambles the film grain.

Dilettoso: Yeah.

B. Reed: Then why was Meier able to get clear shots?

Dilettoso: Well, because they set that up with him. And see, they, do you know what astral projection is? Did you ever hear of that?

B. Reed: Yes.

Dilettoso: OK, they do something like that to get from one dimension to another. And the craft does that, too. So they're not fully in their full-materialized place, when they're having a lot of their contacts, that's why they appear to be "ghostlike."

B. Reed: So there's no radiation there?

Dilettoso: There is radiation, 'cause that radiation is what is able to go from one dimension to another. But if Billy can go to their dimension or they can meet in a middle ground, a vibrating field that may be as different than the vibrating ray of the body as a liquid crystal. The body viewed as a liquid crystal, then there's a tangible solidness there, when the two of them meet in a spectrum that might be out of the visible spectrum of human vision, and out of the material plains of this kind of concrete body, but something similar to when you do a séance and photograph ghosts. A lot of people do that, he can retune his "vibration" and they can retune theirs, so they meet exactly in a place.

B. Reed: So the radiation doesn't—

Dilettoso: Radiation is still there but he's able to raise his vibrations with a type of meditation.

B. Reed: So it [the radiation] doesn't ruin the film then, is this what you're saying?

Dilettoso: (Pause) Right.

COMMENT:
Radiation cannot "scramble" film grains as Dilettoso claims, which further demonstrates and establishes his lack of expertise in even basic photography. Al and Barbara Reed set him up with this test question.

With regard to his other claims, again there is no tangible evidence to support these statements.

Korff: I wanted to jump back to the paper (the exposé that I wrote on the Meier case you said you read). I was wondering if you could tell me specifically what was "off" about the paper that you saw or the one (you claim you saw) from Tucson?

Dilettoso: I didn't even get to read it, I got to look at it. And just scanned through it, and I don't even know the details of it that were in there. But I know that some of the people who had worked on the tests said that some of the stuff that was in there was just bullshit! You know, had nothing to do with the scientific procedures, and what's the basis of this information. And the objective, I mean I'm not even really interested in what's in the paper. I'm interested in telling you what really happened, you know, as opposed to going over it point-by-point.

COMMENT:
At the UFO '80 Symposium, Dilettoso said that he had read my exposé (my "little paper," as he put it) and that it made him "very angry." Now, two weeks later, he stated that he had not read my exposé. Which statement is true?

Dilettoso: Nobody even knows that I'm here except Wendelle, and Wendelle said that if they [Al Reed and Kal Korff] have that much desire to know what's going on, then let's give 'em some stuff to go do some tests, you know, and just let them find out for themselves, and if you can find something that isn't "kosher," well, then, we'd bring in the other people who have worked on it too, and then decide if that test should be done in another area, or it should be immediately publicized, or what. It's just the objective to let out the truth and publish it.

COMMENT:
If Dilettoso's objective is truly to find the truth and publish it, then why all the secrecy? Why don't these "200 scientists," which Jim Dilettoso claims have "authenticated" the Meier evidence, step forward and be counted? Where are all the lab

firms that proved beyond a shadow of a doubt that the Meier evidence is authentic? Where is, as I've stated repeatedly, the hard evidence, or, for that matter, *any* evidence? In truth, it does not exist.

Korff: I have a list of possible, oh these are people which in my opinion would have to have been involved with the enhancements at JPL. You don't have to say yes or no, but if you've ever heard of these people. What about Nathan Carter?

Dilettoso: No.

Korff: John Keiler?

Dilettoso: I think that Wendelle knows him. I'm not sure. I've heard that name, I don't know in what context I've heard it.

Korff: What about Jean Llore?

Dilettoso: No, not familiar.

Korff: Williard Gibbs?

Dilettoso: No.

COMMENT:
This was another "test question" for Dilettoso, and he failed it. The only *real* name on the list was that of Jean Llore, a scientist at JPL who is very prominent in their photo enhancement laboratories. If any extensive work on the Meier photos had really been conducted at JPL, as Dilettoso claims, then Jean Llore would have been involved.

Dilettoso: They know way more than they're leaking out. And even if they say that they're getting the information right now, they already have the information. They're just saying that they're getting it, they have all the stuff. They're just playing their waiting game.

B. Reed: What are they waiting for?

Dilettoso: The right atmosphere to release it internationally. Cause once it's released in America, it's released all over the world. And what about little villages in South America where some guy's gonna say he's in touch with the aliens and they've made him king of the country?

COMMENT:
To further explain Dilettoso's statement, Jim is saying that former military men such as UFO researcher Len Stringfield are merely "sitting" on extraterrestrial "hard evidence," but are just "waiting" for the "right time" to release it. This claim was fact-checked with Len Stringfield; he laughed and said this was not true.

Len Stringfield has specialized in the collection and reporting on cases involving alleged crashed UFOs and/or their occupants. Len has even published several papers on this subject, and both my associate Al Reed and I have helped him in his various endeavors. Reed and I were often privy *in advance* to much of the material that later made it into public release via Stringfield's papers.

Aftermath Note

The day after the interview with Dilettoso, I was invited by KGO radio in San Francisco to appear on the "Bob Trebor Show" to speak on the Meier case. On Sunday, September 7, 1980, I disclosed to millions of listeners my views that the Meier affair is a hoax.

The following morning, Al Reed received a phone call from Jim Dilettoso. Dilettoso stated that he was stunned, hurt, and couldn't believe the riddling that I had given him over the radio. As to why Dilettoso phoned Al and never once attempted to contact me (after all *I* was the guilty party, *not* Al Reed) remains a mystery. However, Dilettoso did state that he would show up the *next day* with all kinds of documentation that would substantiate the Meier case's authenticity. Mr. Reed waited and waited, and as of this writing, fifteen years later, Jim Dilettoso *still has not shown!*

In addition, in three subsequent telephone conversations with Dilettoso (two with myself and one with Al Reed), Dilettoso *freely admitted* that the supposed "film grain analysis" presented in the Genesis III book, *UFO . . . Contact from the Pleiades, Volume I,* did not show film grains at all, but rather, was simulated by dropping a *mezzotone screen** over an enlargement of a portion of one of the objects in Meier's photographs! This was additional corroboration of what Ken Dinwiddie had testified to earlier (see chapter 3) when he stated that the Genesis III "computer analysis" images "are not photos of the actual readouts"!

When asked why this deliberate fabrication was done, Dilettoso stated that it was to "simplify the analysis" so that the general public could understand it.

While Dilettoso may believe this rationalization, by any reasonable legal, objective, or scientific criteria this is deception. Indeed, Genesis III should have *admitted* the truth from the beginning, acknowledging the truth about their "computer analysis" instead of concocting their "facts" the way they did. Such truthful revelations, however, do not help sell books and are admittedly less sensational.

---

*A mezzotone screen is a sheet of plastic that graphic artists use to give an image a "textured" or "grainy" appearance.

More Groundless Claims by Jim Dilettoso

After nearly *twenty years* of being involved in the Meier scam, Jim Dilettoso has left a wide path in his wake of other misstatements of facts and claims that are without foundation. The following are some excerpts from other tape-recorded conversations he has made with such companies as Underground Video and in debates with this author.

Dilettoso: We developed the system that LucasFilm and many others are using for doing off-line editing of video systems. We are now the hub of the LucasFilm/Skywalker ranch fiber optics division.

COMMENT:
In September 1993, I checked with all relevant offices of George Lucas's two companies, Industrial Light and Magic and Skywalker Ranch in Marin, California. After several conversations with the many computer technicians and managers in the optics and optical special effects departments, Lucas-Film attorney Jim Kennedy informed me that "whoever this Jim Dilettoso is, he is not telling the truth. We would like to know where he said this, because we get this all the time. We always get these 'name droppers' and we prosecute them." Kennedy then asked for all the evidence Underground Video and TotalResearch has concerning any fraudulent claims Dilettoso was making regarding ILM and other George Lucas-owned business entities such as Skywalker Ranch.

Dilettoso: In Guido Moosbrugger's book, there's a photograph of a little toy station wagon with a little Barbie and Ken doll driving it and a little picture of a UFO that they shot at one of their lectures. And maybe they photograph them with fluorescent light.

COMMENT:
Obviously, Dilettoso has not read Moosbrugger's book very carefully, if at all, since he does not speak, read, or write German, the language that the book is written in! While there are indeed several hoax pictures of Meier's included in this work, the photos he is referring to are listed as illustrations 25, 26, and 27 in Moosbrugger's work. Although these pictures of Meier's are indeed double exposures involving miniatures, there is no "Ken and Barbie doll" anywhere in them.

Finally, the notion that these hoax pictures were not taken by Billy Meier, but by his own cohorts instead is thoroughly *refuted* by Billy Meier's own *Verzeichnis*, page 145.

Dilettoso: If my techniques [for photo analysis] are wrong, we're in trouble. Because I sell the same software to satellites, missile companies, medical companies, and imaging that's done which requires absolute precision. In a Cruise missile and a Tomahawk missile. Which require precise precision.

COMMENT:
Since I personally designed the Classified Viewgraph Tracking System software for both the Department of Defense and the United States Pentagon while working at Lawrence Livermore National Laboratory (1988–1991), I checked with my numerous contacts both at the LLNL and in Washington, D.C. *There are no records of Jim Dilettoso having sold any software to them!*

Dilettoso is hereby challenged to provide any valid evidence to support his claim.

Underground Video: If he [Marcel Vogel] lost them, how did you [Jim Dilettoso] get them [the metal samples]?

Dilettoso: I delivered them to him [Vogel]. I took them out of his [Vogel's] pocket.

Underground Video: Did he [Vogel] know that you took them out of his pocket?

Dilettoso: No. I sat in the backseat of the car with him, he was being totally irresponsible in the way he was handling the case. We were at a briefing; he took cellophane off a pack of cigarettes, dropped the metal samples into that, folded it up, and put it in his [Vogel's] wallet. I sat beside him in the backseat of the car, removed his wallet, removed that cellophane, had rolled up another piece of cellophane, put it back in his wallet, and put it back in his pocket.

Underground Video: Was this guy [Marcel Vogel] drunk or what?

Dilettoso: What do you mean was he drunk? No, he wasn't drunk.

Underground Video: You said he was irresponsible; maybe he was drinking or something.

Dilettoso: He's not irresponsible. The metal samples still exist. There are more samples than we even took to Marcel Vogel.

Underground Video: Can anyone test those? If we got a scientist that, uh—

Dilettoso: No.

Underground Video: —that you would recognize?

Dilettoso: Recognized by who?

Underground Video: Well, by you, as part of the scientific community. By you. You said—

Dilettoso: It's more involved than that.

COMMENT:
First Dilettoso says Vogel was behaving "irresponsibly," then he contradicts himself by saying that Vogel was not irresponsible.

It is hard to believe that Dilettoso could have picked Vogel's pocket without him knowing it, especially while sitting down in the backseat of a car. If anything, Dilettoso would have had an easier time when Vogel was standing.

When I checked with Marcel Vogel's widow on October 29, 1994, via telephone, she confirmed something I already knew from my previous meetings with Vogel when he was alive, namely, that he *never smoked cigarettes!* This is further evidence that Dilettoso's account is simply not true. Besides, his "story" totally *contradicts* every other account of the metal sample and its alleged "disappearance" in the books by Genesis III, Kinder, Moosbrugger, and Wendelle Stevens.

Dilettoso: I've diligently done my work and we, we operate in the circles that we operate in, which is certainly *not* inside the UFO community, for any other reason that I'm entertained by it.

I'm entertained by these weirdo people wearing pyramids on their heads, and everybody's channeling everybody and you know all of these wild claims of stories, and merchandising and books and lectures and workshops and just what a bunch of hoo ha. Those people do not have a *clue* what is going on in the UFO, uh, reality of them, the aliens, coming here. I don't think you'll find five people, of the *hundreds* which go to those events [UFO conventions such as UFO West Los Angeles and UFO West San Francisco], that really know what's happening.

COMMENT:
These remarks by Jim Dilettoso are included so that the numerous "New Agers" who associate with him, as well as the promoters of the various conferences he continues to give lectures at, to conduct his workshops at, and occasionally play music for, will now know what he really thinks of them.

Dilettoso: (There are) hundreds of pages of my diagrams and schematics on how we did it and what equipment and everything are in that [Wendelle Stevens's *Preliminary Investigation Report*] book.

COMMENT:
A simple examination of Stevens's *Preliminary Investigation Report* reveals that Dilettoso is wrong once again: in truth, in Wendelle's book there are only *nineteen pages* of information pertaining to the alleged "computer analysis" and only *two* diagrams![8] Indeed, Stevens's inclusion of this material is hardly new or original since it is a *verbatim reprint* of a pseudoscientific paper Jim Dilettoso presented years earlier at the UFO '79 Conference in San Diego! Thus, by the time Wendelle Stevens reprinted this material in his book, it was information that was outdated by four years.

Jim Dilettoso and His Imaginary Ph.D.

In addition to the many misleading and incorrect statements Jim Dilettoso has made, as reviewed in this chapter, Dilettoso has also misrepresented repeatedly his alleged "educational" background. The following are excerpts from some of Dilettoso's more recent remarks during the past few years concerning his claims of having a "Ph.D."

Dilettoso: [having been asked about his alleged Ph.D.] One was given to me for the work that I did. Some people don't recognize that as being achieved. I view it as a higher level than that.

Underground Video: Who gave it [the Ph.D.] to you?

Dilettoso: McGill University. Of course, you're going to make this into a big deal.

COMMENT:
Dilettoso, for once, is correct. It is a big deal. If Dilettoso did not go around the country making unsupportable statements about his "educational" background, specifically stating that he has a Ph.D. from McGill University, then the controversy would never have started in the first place.

Underground Video: So OK, so your final statement is you did get a Ph.D. from McGill University?

Dilettoso: Yes.

Underground Video: Where are they [McGill University] at?

Dilettoso: In Canada, Montreal, Canada.

Underground Video: Is there a year for that issuance of that degree?

Dilettoso: In [19]81.

COMMENT:
Once again, Jim Dilettoso is not telling the truth. He does not have a Ph.D. (honorary or otherwise) from McGill University. (See Figure 117 for additional information on this issue.)

More on Jim Dilettoso's Imaginary Ph.D.

The last exchange from Jim Dilettoso we shall examine took place on March 12, 1994, between Dilettoso and me on the cable radio show "UFOs Tonight," hosted by UFOlogist Don Ecker, who is sometimes referred to as the "Larry King" of the UFO interview talkshow circuit. Ecker also co-publishes with his wife, Vicki Cooper, *UFO Magazine,* which is widely read in the field of UFOlogy. While on Ecker's program, I took Dilettoso to task over his oft-repeated distortions concerning his "educational" background.*

Korff: Let me ask you a question, Jim. You went on record recently as saying you have, what, a Ph.D. from McGill University? Is that correct?

Dilettoso: Yes, I went on record saying that.

Korff: Well, I believe there are two faxes visible to Mr. Ecker from McGill that say that that's not true.

Dilettoso: Uh hum.

Korff: How do you explain that?

---

*When I first met Dilettoso at the UFO '80 Symposium in Oakland, California, on August 23, 1980, I asked him specifically what his educational background and academic credentials were. I did this because Dilettoso had been billed in both the convention's promotional and official program guides as a "photographic expert," something I suspected wasn't quite true after hearing his lecture. During his speech, Dilettoso made numerous technical errors to his audience! After his talk, Jim told me that he had attended the University of Connecticut for six years (never earning even an Associates degree, which normally takes just two years) and claimed that his "specialized field of expertise" involved hooking up lights to blink on-and-off via synthesizers! When I later checked with the University of Connecticut, I discovered that Dilettoso had *never* attended that school.

Dilettoso: Yeah, I contacted them myself and discovered that.

Korff: Oh, I see. Well, how do you explain that, Jim?

Dilettoso: Well, as I explained earlier, for the work that I had done in two specific research cases, in a very complex research case we were given honorary degrees.

Korff: Oh, so you have an *honorary* Ph.D! Why did you not use that term when you talked about your own background?

Dilettoso: Because it didn't seem to be a relative matter at the time because I was very proud of the work that I had done.

Korff: Don't you draw a difference between an honorary degree and a—

Dilettoso: (interrupting) Well, I certainly do now.

Korff: (finishing the sentence) —a legitimate one?

Dilettoso: But you know, when a number of people are given degrees for the complexity of work that they did, they stand by the degree and are proud of it. There's a lot of skepticism about what value these degrees have whether it's from Antioch College or a mail order university. So I no longer say it.

Korff: OK, would you be willing to supply Mr. Ecker with proof as to who you worked with at McGill and what you did there?

Dilettoso: Certainly.

Korff: And they'll [McGill University] verify that you were given an honorary degree?

Dilettoso: Uh-huh.

Korff: And who did you speak with at McGill?

Dilettoso: I don't think we need to do this publicly on the radio because all of my work is widely known in the people that work with our company.

Korff: Will you agree, Jim, to send Mr. Ecker a copy of your honorary degree?

Dilettoso: I'll send Mr. Ecker enough information that he will be able to understand where I have been educated and what it is that we actually do.

Korff: Do you have an honorary degree from McGill, yes or no?

Dilettoso: I will send the documents that will attest to what it is that I have been awarded by these universities and I interpret it by what the document says as a bona fide honorary degree.

Korff: Jim, you're not, it's a yes or no question. Do you have an honorary degree from McGill, yes or no?

Dilettoso: To me it's a yes.

Korff: OK, now, will you send a copy of that degree to Mr. Ecker?

Dilettoso: Well, of course. I'll send him a very good package of information.

Korff: Specifically your honorary degree? Because if you were awarded one, Jim, you have to have one somewhere.

Dilettoso: Yeah, yeah, we do. I have that.

Korff: You'll send it? Yes or no?

Ecker: OK, Kal, he said he'd send it.

Dilettoso: I said I will, we're uh—

Korff: (interrupting) I think we'd all like to see it.

Dilettoso: Yes.

COMMENT:
When I checked back with Don Ecker in October 1994, Dilettoso had not sent any package about his "educational background." This was at least the *twelfth such instance* where Jim Dilettoso had *promised* to send confirmatory "documentation" regarding his claims but never did.[9]

During my conversation with Ecker, I asked him why he thought Dilettoso had not sent any information to him. Ecker replied, while laughing, "Jim's long on promises but short on delivery."

On November 17, 1994, I checked with McGill University for what was the third time in thirteen months to definitively settle the issue of whether Jim Dilettoso had ever received *any* degree from them, honorary or otherwise.

Figure 117 shows the unedited reply I received from Ms. Karen J'bari, Secretary to the Registrar at McGill University, after her staff conducted yet another investigation, which included a check of their computerized records for various spellings of "Dilettoso." As J'bari's letter proves, Jim Dilettoso cannot support his claim that he was awarded a degree from McGill, "honorary" or otherwise.

In fact, between takes during the filming of my debate with Dilettoso for the FOX TV show "Encounters" on November 19, 1994, Jim was clearly both nervous and fidgety, concerned of course that I was going to raise this issue on camera. I refrained from doing so only because Dilettoso's wife was present on the set and Jim was already losing the debate. As the old saying goes, "truth will out."

Dilettoso tried to "explain" to me that my checking with McGill was not accurate, since I did not know how to spell his last name correctly. I then told Jim Dilettoso that even if this were true (which it is *not*), it was *irrelevant* since McGill University *does not issue* honorary doctorates and never has in their entire history, as their letter to me, reproduced in figure 117, confirms!

Dilettoso on Fellow UFO Researchers

Dilettoso: Kal Korff, that eighteen-year-old kid that Bill Moore had put up to slandering the Meier case.

COMMENT:
Bill Moore did not "put up Kal Korff to slandering the Meier case." Bill Moore helped edit my original book on Billy Meier and nothing more. My opinions of the Meier "evidence" have always been my own, and Bill Moore's opinions have either been based on the results of my research or have been derived through his own investigations.

Dilettoso: We decided amongst ourselves, "Hey, we don't want this out in a book, we don't want it out in a video." The Elders (Brit and Lee Elders) are turning this into a circus. We started withholding information. There was no reason to turn this over to the Elders so they could get into a fighting match with Bill Moore.

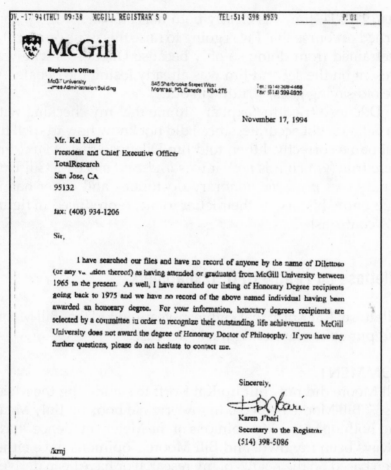

DV. -17 94 (THU) 09:38   MCGILL REGISTRAR'S O   TEL:514 398 8939   P. 01

McGill

Registrar's Office

McGill University
James Administration Building

845 Sherbrooke Street West
Montreal, PQ, Canada   H3A 2T6

Tel.: (514) 398-4466
Fax: (514) 398-8939

November 17, 1994

Mr. Kal Korff
President and Chief Executive Officer
TotalResearch
San Jose, CA
95132

fax: (408) 934-1206

Sir,

I have searched our files and have no record of anyone by the name of Dilettoso
(or any variation thereof) as having attended or graduated from McGill University between
1965 to the present. As well, I have searched our listing of Honorary Degree recipients
going back to 1975 and we have no record of the above named individual having been
awarded an honorary degree. For your information, honorary degrees recipients are
selected by a committee in order to recognize their outstanding life achievements. McGill
University does not award the degree of Honorary Doctor of Philosophy. If you have any
further questions, please do not hesitate to contact me.

Sincerely,

Karen J'bari
Secretary to the Registrar
(514) 398-5086

/kmj

Fig. 117. One of several FAXes I have received from McGill University in Montreal, Canada, regarding Jim Dilettoso. This letter, written for the public record by Ms. Karen J'bari, Secretary to the Registrar at McGill University, proves that Jim Dilettoso is not telling the truth when he claims he received either a "Ph.D." or an "honorary doctorate" from McGill. Since at least 1979, Jim Dilettoso has made numerous unfounded claims about both his purported "educational" background and supposed list of professional "accomplishments." Despite demonstrable evidence to the contrary this has never deterred either Genesis III, Gary Kinder, or Wendelle C. Stevens (as well as other Meier supporters) from citing Dilettoso's many fictional claims as if they were established scientific facts.

COMMENT:
Jim Dilettoso is correct, the Elders have indeed turned the Meier case into a "circus," figuratively speaking. However, it is *impossible* for Dilettoso to play the role of the "innocent victim" here since it is he who provided much of the "ammunition" and pseudoscience the Elders, Hesemann, Kinder, Stevens, Moosbrugger, and Randolph Winters use (along with other Meier supporters) to continue to mislead people. This is especially true where Genesis III's "photo analyses" are concerned, as was shown in chapter 3 of this book.

Dilettoso: My understanding is that Richard [Dr. Richard F. Haines] had observed it [the Meier metal sample] a day or two already [before the sample "disappeared" from Marcel Vogel].

COMMENT:
When I checked with Dr. Richard Haines regarding Dilettoso's claim, on October 27, 1994, Haines replied that Dilettoso's version was "an outright lie. I never got to see the sample, as you [Kal] very well know." Laughing, Dr. Haines ended his remarks by adding, "I don't know where he [Dilettoso] gets this stuff from."

Dilettoso: Harry Lebelson at *Omni* magazine, and he walked pieces through MIT. And, uh, allowed them to; they also "vanished." And those people (the scientists at MIT) are still working on them.

Underground Video: How do you know that they are still working on them?

Dilettoso: I just know that they are.

Underground Video: You mean it's not a matter of opinion; it's a matter of factual knowledge?

Dilettoso: I have not followed it [the alleged metal sample testing at MIT] for years. My mission was to place them at various places, to seed people to do very important work with them. End of mission for me. Johnny Appleseed. . . . It's just what they told me. I don't even know Harry Lebelson.

COMMENT:
Unfortunately, there's no way to tell just *what* Dilettoso is talking about here since he once again contradicts himself. Jim Dilettoso is hereby challenged once again to prove what he says is true about any alleged "secret" testing on the Meier metal samples still taking place, whether it be at MIT or any other location in the world.

Dilettoso: I have no desire to validate or invalidate the Meier case.

COMMENT:
If this is true, then Dilettoso would not have conducted himself the way he has, nor would he continue to appear in the media and on record defending both the Meier case and his self-proclaimed "scientific testing" of Meier's "UFO" photographs.

Dilettoso: I do not think Fred Bell is true. I do not support the activities of Fred Bell. I do not support the activities of Barbara Marchiniak.* Most of the people at those events [UFO conventions] I consider to be real goofy.

---

*Barbara Marchiniak claims that she "channels" the Pleiadians. Fred Bell claims he is in "contact" with Semjase. According to the Meier group, only Billy Meier is in contact with the Pleiadians and no one else. (Bernadette Brand, Elisabeth Gruber, Simone, personal interviews with Kal Korff and Tina Layton, August 18, 1991, Hinterschmidrüti, Switzerland).

COMMENT:
Fred Bell, like Billy Meier, claims he is also in contact with the "Pleiadians," specifically "Semjase." This comment of Dilettoso's has been included so that those who associate with him and appear at some of these same conferences (like Bell and Marchiniak) will know exactly what Jim Dilettoso *really* seems to think of them!

Underground Video: What do you think of the Paul Villa [UFO] photographs?

Dilettoso: Well, I've only looked at two photographs.

Underground Video: The large one where you're looking up in the trees?

Dilettoso: Yeah.

Underground Video: Have you done any analysis on it?

Dilettoso: I have, and that one tests out being a very large object. But the same object in another photograph, where it's in the middle of that farm area with the truck, turns out to be, I don't know, under a foot. So the conclusion that we may be faced with is that extraterrestrials have large and small craft.

Underground Video: What about it's just a model?

Dilettoso: Well, it could be a model, you know. I did not have a quality enough image of the Paul pictures to test.

COMMENT:
This quote from Dilettoso is yet another example of how *unscientific* his approach is. In addition to contradicting himself (first he says he tested Villa's pictures, then he says he didn't

have a good enough quality image to test), the idea that the Villa pictures are obviously of a small, fake "UFO" model seems to have never occurred to him. Indeed, the very idea that "ETs" have spaceships under a foot in diameter is probably even more incredible than the notion that Villa's pictures might be real.

Since Villa's "UFO" pictures are supposed to show the *same object*, the size discrepancies of the "UFO" image in his photographs are strong evidence *against* their authenticity. This is a fact that Dilettoso fails to consider, which is further evidence of his lack of expertise in basic photo analysis techniques.

Not surprisingly, on a similar note, Wendelle Stevens also endorses as "authentic," the Paul Villa series of "UFO" photographs.[10]

Notes

1. Kal K. Korff, remarks made during debate on the cable-radio show "UFOs Tonight," taking Jim Dilettoso to task over his untruthful statements concerning his "honorary doctorate" he claims to have received from McGill University. March 12, 1994, Los Angeles, California.

2. Ibid.

3. Karen J'bari, Secretary to the Registrar, McGill University, FAXed letter to the author written for the public record and TotalResearch's files, November 17, 1994.

4. Jim Dilettoso, tape-recorded personal interview for the record with Kal K. Korff, Al Reed, and Barbara Reed, at the offices of Publication Professionals, Sunnyvale, California, September 6, 1980.

5. Wendelle Stevens, *UFO . . . Contact from the Pleiades—A Supplementary Investigation Report—The Report of an Ongoing Contact* (Tucson, Ariz.: Wendelle Stevens, 1989), p. 10.

6. Kal Korff, *The Meier Incident—The Most Infamous Hoax in UFOlogy* (Prescott, Ariz.: Townescribe Press, 1981), pp. 112–14.

7. Eduard "Billy" Meier, interview for NIPPON TV and the video documentary *Contact*, with Japanese TV producer Jun-Ichi Yaoi, 1981.

8. Wendelle Stevens, *UFO . . . Contact from the Pleiades—A Preliminary Investigation Report—The Report of an Ongoing Contact* (Tucson, Ariz.: Wendelle Stevens, 1983), pp. 380–99.

9. Kal Korff, personal interviews with the staff of Underground Video, San Mateo, Modesto, and Los Angeles, California, October 1993 to present.

10. Wendelle C. Stevens, illustrated lecture on alleged UFO "contact" cases, UFO '80 Symposium, Oakland, California, August 23, 1980.

9

The CIA and Wendelle Stevens's Prison Sentence

Wendelle Stevens was framed by the CIA because he was getting too close to the answer of what UFOs are. Didn't you know that?
Phoenix-based UFO bookseller at the
UFO West '94 Conference[1]

Have you ever seen the court documents from Wendelle's case where Wendelle voluntarily pleaded guilty?
Kal K. Korff, in response to the vendor

No, this is just a rumor I heard. You know how the UFO field is.

In the early part of 1983, I received an invitation from James W. Moseley, Chairman of the Board of the National UFO Conference (NUFOC), to present a paper at their annual symposium, which was to be held that year in the city of Tucson, Arizona. Moseley is also editor and publisher of the journal *Saucer Smear*, which most prominent UFO researchers receive.

Hosted by UFOlogist Ed Biebel, the appearance meant that for the first time since the publication of my 1981 book, I would be able to express my views on the Meier case and UFOs in general in Wendelle Stevens's own backyard. Natu-

357

rally, I looked forward to this opportunity, especially after Stevens announced his plans to also attend.

In the time between the invitation and the actual date of the conference, Stevens had released the book *UFO . . . Contact from the Pleiades—A Preliminary Investigation Report*. Upon learning this, I looked forward even more to our face-to-face meeting. However, by the time the date of the conference arrived, my whole attitude had changed. Instead of giving a speech about the Meier case (which everyone expected), I decided to use the platform of the convention to encourage people to be more *critical* in their thinking, stressing the need for always maintaining a scientific approach when investigating alleged UFO evidence.

The number of conversations I had concerning the Meier case totalled an even dozen during the days of the conference. The number of discussions I had with Wendelle Stevens totalled three, two in private and one in public. To my relief, Stevens was extremely courteous (though cautious) in his interactions with me.

While our private discussions were very brief, touching on nothing either of us didn't already know about the other, Stevens tried to convince me that the claims of Meier were genuine, and I would have none of it.

The one public discussion Stevens and I held concerning the Meier case took place during the question-and-answer session I always allow after my lectures. When UFO researcher Greg Long asked me about the Meier case, I had my slides ready. In all, I took about five minutes to explain my side of the controversy and to quickly present some facts to prove it was a hoax.

Stevens, who was present in the audience, immediately responded and, as expected, failed to address a single criticism I raised about the case! As an example, it was obvious when I pointed out the optical problems inherent in Meier's "cosmonaut" photos (see chapter 5) that Stevens was unprepared. Based on the surprised look on his face, he apparently had never thought of basic optical physics before and was dumbfounded. After all, what could he possibly say? Facts are facts and optical physics have to be accounted for even in Billy Meier's "UFO" photographs.

After the conference concluded, all of the speakers went out to dinner, accompanied by local UFO researchers from the area. In all there were about twenty-five of us, including Stevens.

Holding true to form, Stevens continued to spin yarn after yarn about all kinds of assorted things, from Billy Meier to stories of primitive tribesmen being in regular contact with extraterrestrials. Wendelle had a tale for anyone who would listen.

UFOlogists Jim Moseley and J. Richard Greenwell took Stevens to task. Moseley had been to the area Stevens referred to and simply knew Stevens was wrong.

Stevens finally stopped when Greenwell said, with his usual good charm, "Oh, come on now Steve, that's enough, we know better." Stevens then laughed and stopped playing the role of storyteller.

In retrospect, the convention, in my opinion, was a success. Mr. Biebel was a superb host, and the number of leads I received on a wide variety of other UFO cases proved most fruitful.

When I finally returned home about a week later, waiting for me was a letter from Wendelle Stevens. In this letter he wrote:

Dear Mr. Korf [sic],

Though I had no official part in Jim Moseley's National UFO Conference I want to thank you from the standpoint of a delegate to the convention for your participation and for its success. I offer you my apology for what I considered some degree of hostility toward you and your views on the part of some of the other delegates during the two closed sessions. The point that you advocate concerning proper scientific investigation of everything that can be investigated in these matters is certainly well taken and should always be kept in mind.

I know that Jim Moseley never stages a conference like this without a good counter advocate to keep the whole thing in balance. You represented that stability factor in this one, and you did well. Most of the delegates agreed on this. I hope you did not get stuck with any of your expenses overall.

No hard feelings, OK?

Best regards,

Wendelle C. Stevens

No hard feelings!? While I certainly did not harbor any, was Wendelle suddenly *apologizing* for all of the *ad hominem* attacks,* the distortions, and his general behavior regarding the Meier case? Was he for the first time being honest regarding the case?

---

*One example of some of the ridiculous *ad hominem* attacks Wendelle Stevens has launched against me in the various media dating back to 1981 includes inferences that because my initials just happen to consist of the three letters "KKK," that I must be a member of the infamous racial hatred group, the Klu Klux Klan! (Stevens, "Billy Meier Is No Hoaxer!" *Frontiers of Science*, March–April 1981, p. 44) Of course, this isn't true. Other *ad hominem* attacks made by Stevens over the years have had to do with my age because I was only fifteen years young when I first started researching the Meier case in March of 1977. Although I was eighteen by the time I later wrote my original exposé, Stevens still had a hard time accepting the fact that someone "relatively immature" (Stevens, "Kal Korff and the 'Meier Hoax'—A Response Part 1," *MUFON UFO Journal*, October 1981, p. 4) could possibly write a book, let alone disprove his research. Thus, Stevens later "concluded" (incorrectly) that Bill Moore was the "real author" of my original exposé book. Stevens then told his cohorts at Genesis III this "fact." This is why Dilettoso made the remark "Kal Korff, that eighteen-year-old kid that Bill Moore had . . ." mentioned earlier in chapter 8. Obviously, for the Genesis people, myths die hard!

Was Stevens serious? While part of me wanted to believe him, I could not help but feel that Stevens's advocating the use of "proper scientific investigation of everything that can be investigated" smacked of extreme hypocrisy on his part, especially considering his poor track record in the Meier and other UFO cases.

In spite of my mixed reactions, the letter renewed the hope, in my mind at least, that we could perhaps begin to exchange UFO data again in a constructive manner. But the question still burned in my mind, *why* the sudden apparent change of heart in Wendelle Stevens?

A few days later I discovered what I believe to be the reason: Stevens was now locked up *in prison!* On November 16, 1982, the state of Arizona had filed a Direct Indictment against Wendelle Castyle Stevens, charging him with ten felony counts of child molestation; four felony counts of furnishing obscene or harmful items to minors; and two felony counts of filming or photographing minors engaged in sexual conduct which is obscene.[2]

According to the court documents, after Stevens was formally served he was later booked and fingerprinted on Tuesday, November 24, 1982. He was then released after signing a Conditions of Release Order the same day, which stipulated that Stevens "have no contact of any kind with the victims or any minor children."[3]

On December 29, 1982, Stevens and his attorney, Mr. Howard Kashman, filed papers to have the indictment dismissed.[4] On February 11, 1983, Stevens and Kashman filed a Plea Stipulation (change of plea) after their attempt to get the charges thrown out had failed.[5]

On February 16, 1983, Wendelle Stevens *voluntarily pleaded guilty,** and in exchange for doing so was able to "plea bar-

---

*I stress the words "voluntarily pleaded guilty" because some misinformation on this issue exists. It has been reported by some, for example, that Stevens simply pleaded *nolo contendere* or "no contest" to the charges, thus never admitting his guilt. This is not true, Pima County Court documents prove.

gain" his charges down so that he was convicted of only three of the sixteen felony counts originally filed against him. All of the other charges were dropped in exchange for his guilty plea.[6]

On March 15, 1983, Wendelle Stevens was sentenced to seven years in prison for each of the three felony counts, with each sentence to be served concurrently.[7]

On June 1, 1983, barely two weeks after I saw him, Stevens formally began serving of his sentence at the Santa Rita Correctional Facility outside of Tucson, where he remained incarcerated until 1990.[8]

The news of Stevens's arrest spread rapidly throughout the UFO community. While some of his critics were delighted, Stevens's followers and Billy Meier's supporters were stunned. With Stevens now behind bars, both the Genesis group and the Meier faithful had lost their "supreme commander." Did this turn of events put an end to the Meier charade?

The answer is no. Shortly thereafter, the faithful would portray Stevens as a "martyr" that the CIA had "framed" because he was getting "too close to the UFO truth," and that Stevens's investigation of the Meier case had caused the U.S. government to "come down hard" on him. Stevens himself would mail strange letters to various people around the world proclaiming not only his innocence, but charging that he was framed as well.[9]

Because I was literally the first UFOlogist outside Stevens's close-knit group of friends to hear of his dilemma (I had been told by one of my many law enforcement sources about Stevens's situation), I immediately arranged to receive copies of all relevant court documents pertaining to his case. The next thing I did was make six complete photo-static copy sets, and then mailed them to various UFO associates of mine who I felt needed to know this information before various "incarnations" of it began to creep into the UFO rumor mill. I sent these documents to Bill Moore, Colman VonKeviczky, Walt

Andrus (Director of MUFON), Coral and Jim Lorenzen of APRO, and James Moseley.

Before sending the material to Moseley, however, I discussed with him the issue of publishing the news in his magazine first, thereby giving him the exclusive story, on the condition that he *not* name his source. Moseley, true to his word, not only published the story on Stevens, but never named me as his source of information.

Because I felt it was predictable that the "lore" and myths regarding Wendelle Stevens would try to paint him as the ever-so-innocent "victim" of what had happened, I fired off a letter to Stevens mentioning this and tried to solicit a reply from him for the record. These are excerpts from the letter I wrote Wendelle Stevens, to which he *never* responded:

April 23, 1983

Dear Wendelle,

I am in receipt of your letter dated April 17th, for which I thank you.

Frankly, I was surprised that I even received such a response, especially after such a long period of time. Now I understand the reason for the delay. . . .

I am pleased, too, that you have decided to resume trading slides. Within the next few months I shall begin the long process of duplicating those slides I mentioned.

Speaking of trading slides, you mentioned that you would be willing to do so after you got back to your files. Do you have any idea how long this will be?

The reason as to why I ask, Wendelle, is because I have heard an unbelievably (but predictable) assortment of rumors regarding your unfortunate predicament.

I have heard, for instance, that you have claimed that the CIA framed you because you got "too close" to the UFO "truth." Is this so? If you honestly think so, what proof do you have?

If you are ever fortunate enough to get to the real UFO "truth," and the government finds out about it, why merely frame you? Wouldn't it be to their advantage to simply arrange your "accidental" death, similar to what supposedly happened to Morris Jessup and Jim McDonald?* I think so.

A "frame," in my mind, is not logical.

At any rate, I would appreciate a clarification.

One final note on this matter: If you can prove that you have been framed, especially by the CIA or some other govt. agency, I would think that it would be in your best interest to lay your proof out on the table per se, for the world to see. It should be obvious that if you can prove such a charge, you have one heck of an ace in your hands. So, why not use it? . . .

Well, that should do it for me this time around. If time permits, I am very busy winding down my new book, I hope to drop you a letter of greater length and substance.

Thank you again for writing, and I look forward (seriously!) to hearing from you in the near future. I have some semi-serious questions that I am contemplating asking you for your input.

Unfortunately, I would never hear from Stevens again. While Stevens refused to answer my inquiries concerning the alleged "framing" by the CIA, instead he would write letters "in confidence" to other UFO researchers such as A. J. Gevaerd in

---

*Many UFOlogists believe that UFO researchers James McDonald and Morris Jessup were murdered by sinister elements of the U.S. government for their involvement in the study of UFO reports. Despite such conspiracy notions, there is no credible evidence to date that this is true.

Brazil, claiming he was indeed innocent and had been framed.[10] Here are some excerpts from Stevens's letter to Gevaerd dated November 8, 1985, which he wrote in response to a negative article on Billy Meier which Gevaerd had published, written by UFO researcher Irene Granchi. Strangely, Stevens refers to himself in the third person in his letter, and asked Gevaerd to keep the fact that he was the author of this letter a "secret."[11] Included after Stevens's remarks are my comments.

Stevens: William L. Moore is not the famous author of *The Philadelphia Experiment*. Charles Berlitz is the author. Moore was Berlitz's paid ghost writer, who tried to get in the act. The same with *The Roswell Incident*. If Moore said he wrote those books he lied and if he insists that no credible UFO investigators in the U.S.A. have looked into the Swiss [Meier] case he also lied, and you will notice that he has not mentioned them because he would then have to back down on his statement.

COMMENT:
Stevens is wrong. When I checked with Bill Moore he confirmed that it was he, and not Charles Berlitz, who wrote the bulk of the text for their two collaborative works, both of which became bestsellers. In addition, when I checked with UFO researcher Stanton Friedman, who was an advisor to Moore on the Roswell book, he confirmed that Moore had done most of the writing. Friedman and Moore have known each other for over twenty years, and for a long time were best friends.

Stevens: Moore then proceeds with highly defamatory remarks [about Stevens being a convicted child molester] entirely out of keeping with his claimed status as an investigator and public lecturer, and certainly as a gentleman because he is making those statements without the benefit of the least investigation. If he had investigated he would have found that the Grand Jury issued an indictment with no presentation of evidence, and that the Court threw it out as insufficient. Another was issued with no presentation of evidence, and that the Court again threw it out as insufficient. That Stevens was advised to flee, making himself a fugitive and subjecting his property and files to confiscation. He stayed and a third indictment was handed down obtained by splitting the first 3 charges into first 9 elements and then by splitting again to double them, thus creating 18 charges out of the first three. This is an intimidation tactic that worked. The Court would have thrown this out for insufficiency also, but Stevens declined, having been warned what the alternative would be.

COMMENT:
Wendelle Stevens has his "facts" mixed-up. Stevens was charged with *sixteen* felony counts, not eighteen, contrary to what he claims. In addition, as the court documents prove, Stevens was charged with one count of molestation for *each time* he became sexual with the three girls, having committed the offenses with each victim repeatedly, according to the court documents.[12] Moreover, the court files pertaining to his case also disprove Stevens's claim that he was somehow "intimidated" into confessing, and that the grand jury "dismissed" the charges brought against him.

In truth, Stevens opted at first for a *jury trial,* which was scheduled to have begun at 9:00 A.M. on February 9, 1983.[13] A trial by jury, of course, would have meant that the evidence against Stevens would have been made public, unless ordered "under seal" by the court.

However, rather than face a trial by jury and risk public disclosure of the evidence against him, Stevens voluntarily pled guilty instead, as previously noted.

Stevens: Another tactic was for the prosecutor to go up to the court and *secretly obtain a ruling* [emphasis added] that each charge be considered a prior offense for the next, thus by the third charge making the respondent [Stevens] a habitual criminal, a man who had never been arrested in his life for anything before. Having been advised of the alternatives, Stevens elected to accept a plea bargain, going back to the first three charges, if he accepted them and he would be allowed to choose the Judge to do the sentencing. This was a simple ploy because the charges he would have to accept carried a statutory sentence of 7 full years "with no discretion," meaning that the judge could not nullify the sentence. There was never any allegation of "producing pornographic films," nor was "molesting" defined. Any investigation would have shown all this. What investigating did Moore do?

COMMENT:
Stevens is mistaken again. In reality, there were no "conspiratorial" moves to "secretly obtain a ruling" by the prosecution so that each charge against Wendelle Stevens would be considered a prior offense. Indeed, the prosecution's precise actions, specifically those of Pima County Attorney Stephen D. Neely, are clearly explained in the court document "Allegation of Prior Conviction" (*State of Arizona* v. *Wendelle Castyle Stevens* CR–09514), which cites the following facts on page one:

> The Defendant [Wendelle Stevens] is charged with more than one offense and that while those offenses were not committed on the same occasion they have been *consolidated for trial purposes.* The State hereby elects to treat each offense for which the Defendant is convicted as a prior conviction for the *purpose of determining the sentence to be imposed for every other offense for which he is also convicted.* [Emphasis added]

In addition, the duration of the sentencing for each felony count of child molestation for which Stevens was convicted is defined very clearly in Arizona Statute §13–1410 as "not less than five years."[14] The fact that Stevens was sentenced to seven years was due to his plea bargain agreement with the

district attorney's office. Under such plea bargaining arrangements, a judge cannot normally change or shorten the
requested time that a defendant spends behind bars, since
both parties have to agree to the terms in order for the "deal"
to be accepted. If Stevens had chosen not to opt for the plea
bargain, he faced the prosecution's full wrath of being charged
with all sixteen counts of the indictment against him, plus the
potential humiliation of a trial by jury and all the unwanted
visibility that goes with it.

Stevens is also wrong when he claims that "there was
never any allegation of 'producing pornographic films,' nor
was 'molesting' defined." Indeed, a simple examination of his
original sixteen-count indictment clearly proves that in addition to the ten felony child molestation counts filed against
him, Stevens was also charged with *four felony counts of furnishing obscene or harmful items to minors; and two felony counts
of filming or photographing minors engaged in sexual conduct
which is obscene*[15] (emphasis added).

Stevens: The documents [from Stevens's court case] Moore
carries around to do his dirty work are from a package offered
for sale to Coral Lorenzen by somebody in the County Court
system, for which she paid $200 U.S. Dollars, delivered by
the same "honorable" William L. Moore. Those documents
are not even the court records. They are a package put
together especially for sale to APRO and Bill Moore. The fact
that he carries this confirms part of this evidence. The court
records are sealed. Both the purchase of and exhibition of such
documents constitute felony crimes in several different categories in Arizona, and they were obtained by felony means,
punishable by heavy fines and long terms in prison. Is this a
gentleman, and an honorable and respectable source? They
could very easily end up neighbors of Stevens in his cell!

COMMENT:

Since it was *me* (Kal Korff) who obtained the original court documents from a law enforcement source, Bill Moore is *not* to blame here. As mentioned earlier, I made six copy sets of Stevens's court case files, and sent them *free of charge* to Coral and Jim Lorenzen of APRO, Bill Moore, Jim Moseley of *Saucer Smear* (to whom I deliberately leaked the story for publica-tion), Bill Spaulding of Ground Saucer Watch, and Colman VonKeviczky. No one ever paid "$200.00" for these docu-ments, and all I paid for was the cost of photocopying.

Wendelle Stevens is wrong when he says that these docu-ments "are not even the court records" and that they are sealed. As proof, readers who wish to research this matter for themselves should feel free to write or visit the Pima County Courthouse and request copies of Wendelle Castyle Stevens's criminal case files, CR–09514. Stevens's court records are pub-lic documents, and anyone can obtain copies. In addition, the relevant court documents from Stevens's trial are also avail-able through both Underground Video and TotalResearch, in a fifty-page public service publication titled *The Incredible Wen-delle C. Stevens,* which has been released to set the record straight. Included in this report are also copies of some of the letters which originated out of Tucson shortly after Stevens began serving out his sentence. These letters, some of which are "anonymous," perpetuate the various myths and allega-tions about the "$200.00 bribe"and how Stevens was suppos-edly "framed."

In summation, the statement, whether made by Wendelle Stevens or not, that he was "framed" by the CIA or other sup-posedly "sinister" U.S. government agencies, is simply *not true.* As the statutes and court documents Wendelle Stevens freely signed prove, Stevens *voluntarily pleaded guilty* and "plea bargained" his way toward a lighter sentence. For rea-sons only Wendelle Stevens can explain, he repeatedly molested three teenage girls while they were visiting his home. The claim that he was "set-up" or "framed" has no credible evidence whatsoever, and has absolutely nothing to do with his "getting too close to the UFO truth," or his involvement and "investigation" of the Billy Meier case in Switzerland.

Notes

1. Phoenix-based UFO bookseller at the UFO West '94 Conference, San Mateo, California, November 5, 1994.

2. Direct Indictment, *State of Arizona* v. *Wendelle Castyle Stevens* (Pima County Court Records, CR–09514), November 16, 1982, pp. 1–5.

3. Conditions of Release Order, *State of Arizona* v. *Wendelle Castyle Stevens* (Pima County Court Records, CR–09514), November 24, 1982, p. 1.

4. Motion for New Finding of Probable Cause, *State of Arizona* v. *Wendelle Castyle Stevens* (Pima County Court Records, CR–09514), December 29, 1982, pp. 1–3.

5. Plea Stipulation, *State of Arizona* v. *Wendelle Castyle Stevens* (Pima County Court Records, CR–09514), February 16, 1983, pp. 1–2.

6. Plea Agreement, *State of Arizona* v. *Wendelle Castyle Stevens* (Pima County Court Records, CR–09514), February 16, 1983, pp. 1–5.

7. Sentencing Notification Form, *State of Arizona* v. *Wendelle Castyle Stevens* (Pima County Court Records, CR–09514), February 16, 1983.

8. Commitment Order, *State of Arizona* v. *Wendelle Castyle Stevens* (Pima County Court Records, CR–09514), March 15, 1983.

9. Wendelle Stevens, confidential letter to A. J. Gevaerd, November 8, 1985, pp. 2–3.

10. Ibid.

11. Ibid., p. 1.

12. Direct Indictment, *State of Arizona* v. *Wendelle Castyle Stevens* (Pima County Court Records, CR–09514), November 16, 1982, pp. 1–5.

13. Minute Entry, *State of Arizona* v. *Wendelle Castyle Stevens* (Pima County Court Records, CR–09514), November 24, 1982, p. 1.

14. Arizona Statute §13–1410 defined, Arizona State Statute Directory, State of Arizona, 1984.

15. Direct Indictment, *State of Arizona* v. *Wendelle Castyle Stevens* (Pima County Court Records, CR–09514), November 16, 1982, pp. 1–5.

10

Light Yarns: Gary Kinder's
Travesty of Truth

Gary Kinder was originally a skeptic when he studied that [the
Meier] case.

Morgan Entrekin, Gary Kinder's editor[1]

If so, then how do you explain the fact that Kinder never included
any of the evidence proving that Meier is a fraud? Also, are you
aware that someone went over to Switzerland undercover and
found conclusive evidence of fraud and that there's a book coming out exposing the case as a hoax?

Kal Korff, responding to Entrekin

I don't want to talk about it anymore.

Morgan Entrekin, before turning his back and walking away

Gary Kinder received widespread praise from both the mainstream press and even in UFO circles for conducting what
many believed was an honest, impartial reporting and investigation of the Billy Meier case. Many people, after reading his
book *Light Years: The Extraterrestrial Experiences of Eduard Meier*,
became convinced that at least some, if not all, of Billy Meier's
UFO "contacts" were genuine. If Gary Kinder is to be com-

mended for his skill in gathering facts, then he deserves an even greater award for being excellent at *hiding* them as well.

What many of those who were fooled by *Light Years* failed to grasp is the fact that Gary Kinder worked very closely with Lee and Brit Elders during the writing and research of his book on Meier. In fact, Kinder even went so far as to share not only the *copyright* with the Elders, but gave them a percentage of the book's royalties as well![2]

Contrary to popular opinion, Gary Kinder's "investigation" into the Meier case was not unbiased, nor was it even scientific. While *Light Years* was disguised as an objective treatise, it in fact is not. The reason I can state this with absolute certainty is due to my own personal involvement with Gary Kinder and the input that I gave him for what would later become his published work.

In late March 1985, Gary Kinder wrote to me inquiring about what information I had on the Billy Meier case.[3] Kinder later disclosed to me that he had just been given a $100,000 advance from his new editor, Morgan Entrekin[4] of the Atlantic Monthly Press, and was hot in pursuit of delivering his project, a book on UFOs which specifically focused on the Billy Meier case.

Before I recount how my meeting with Gary Kinder went and what we discussed, here are highlights from the letter he wrote me on March 28, 1985, requesting my help with his research for his book *Light Years*:

Dear Kal:

I have tried to find a phone number for you so I could call, but after speaking with Dick Haines and with the Lorenzens, the best they could come up with was a post office box. Then I met with Bill Moore this past week in L.A., and though he has your phone and home address, he honored your request not to give it out. Hence this letter sent to him for mailing to you.

I am researching a book about the UFO community, what it does, who it is, where it is (in more ways than one). I'm particularly interested in the Swiss Case or the Meier Case, which seems to have generated a fair amount of emotion within the community. I know you have referred to it as the most infamous hoax in the history of ufology. I will be in the San Francisco area and I would like to talk with you about ufology and about your involvement with the Meier case, at your convenience of course. . . .

You are the first one I am contacting in the area, because I feel my interview with you is the most important. The others I will arrange accordingly.

I have published a book titled *VICTIM: The Other Side of Murder*, which you may have seen reviewed in the *San Francisco Chronicle* or the *L.A. Times.* I will bring a copy of the most recent paperback edition of *VICTIM* for you to keep.

I look forward to meeting you.

Best regards,

Gary Kinder

While I appreciated the flattery, I was intrigued by this letter from Gary Kinder, even though I had never heard of him until I received his letter. After considering his request for an interview, I decided to give Gary Kinder a call at his (then) home in Sun Valley, Idaho. Kinder and I spoke on the phone for perhaps ten minutes. During our conversation, I questioned Kinder about what the "angle" of his book was, and asked him why he wished to speak with me, of all people, about the Meier case.

Since my own book exposing Billy Meier had been on the market for three years by that time and had long ago sold out, the Meier case seemed pretty much a "dead" issue as far as I was concerned.

After feeling comfortable with Kinder over the telephone, and being given his repeated assurance that he was going to conduct a *fair* and *impartial* investigation and reporting on the Billy Meier case, I agreed to meet with him in person on Saturday, April 13, 1985.

Gary Kinder arrived mid-morning and we spent most of the day in my office. I had much of my Meier files and other material with me, and shared everything I knew with him about the case up to that point.

One of the very first things I mentioned to Kinder was that the Meier case was certainly a hoax. I then recounted for hours on end the numerous pieces of evidence which proved this. While Gary Kinder listened very patiently and attentively, he seemed to be genuinely interested in my material.

Other pieces of evidence I shared with Kinder were many of the numerous "smoking guns" I had discovered up to that time. While they now pale (admittedly) in comparison to what Tina and I would discover during our trip to Switzerland some six years later, nonetheless, the facts I disclosed to Kinder were sufficient at that time to more than establish that the Meier case was a hoax. However, no matter what I said, or how hard I tried, Kinder still kept trying to wring from me some sort of statement conceding that maybe *some portion* of the Meier "evidence" might be genuine. This concerned me.

For someone who professed to be interested in writing a book about the "UFO community" and "what it does," Kinder didn't seem to ask many questions about any subject other than Billy Meier. Indeed, apart from the usual "politically correct" small talk, I do not recall discussing with Kinder much of anything about the other areas he had indicated in his letter to me that were of "interest" to him. This started to make me suspicious of his motives.

In the early evening, Gary Kinder left and I never heard from him again. Curiously, Kinder never tried to contact me to help him answer any further questions he might have, nor did he include me in any sort of "peer review" process before his Meier book was published. This fact also made me suspicious about Kinder's true intentions, since I was universally regarded at that time (and still am today) as Meier's "chief critic." It made no sense that Kinder would speak with me only once.

Obviously, my conclusions and Wendelle Stevens's opinions about the Meier case can't both be right. The fact that Kinder spent most of his time in the pro-Meier camp revealed not only his true bias, but was a good indicator of where his book was heading.

Because I know pretty much every "name" in the UFO field personally, it was easy for me to follow Kinder's tracks (unbeknownst to him) and learn who he was talking to without really trying. Often, my phone would ring and it would be a call from UFO researchers such as Hal Starr, the Lorenzens, Bill Moore, Stanton Friedman, and others, all telling me what Gary Kinder had done and what he was up to.

Although it was obvious to many of my UFOlogist colleagues that Kinder clearly preferred the company of the pro-Meier crowd, many in the UFO field were utterly shocked when his much-vaunted *Light Years* finally hit the market in the first half of 1987. Almost immediately after its release, most of the prominent or "name" UFOlogists cried "foul" and were horrified to see that Gary Kinder's book was a distinctly "pro-Meier" work which seemed to present basic, scientifically credible "evidence" that Meier and his claims were true.

Since a good number of these same UFO researchers who were outraged were also friends of mine, several of whom owned copies of my original 1981 Meier exposé book, this caused a dilemma for many in the UFO field, and several turned to me for answers and counterarguments to Kinder's "evidence."

While the UFO community was generally outraged by Kinder's book, on the other hand the general public, which had either heard, read, or seen something about the Meier case sporadically since late 1979, swallowed the claims in *Light Years* hook, line, and sinker.

Indeed, Morgan Entrekin, with the full marketing and budgetary resources of the Atlantic Monthly Press to back him, pulled out all the necessary stops in order to ensure that *Light Years* (which bore his new imprint "A Morgan Entrekin Book" on the inside title page) was a commercial success. Entrekin succeeded.

Although *Light Years* was a hit with the general public, and would eventually become the bestselling book of all time ever written on the Meier case, as mentioned previously Kinder's tome received a cool reception initially within the ranks of the UFO field. Gary Kinder, in an attempt to justify his behavior, released a ten-page "Open Letter to the UFO Community" which he made sure was circulated widely.

What follows now are the entire contents of Gary Kinder's "Open Letter," a copy of which he sent directly to me. Although Kinder signed the photocopied version I received with the notation "Best," this was only the *second time* I had ever heard from him! It would also be the last time, as of this writing.

As will be demonstrated, when viewed objectively and subjected to the standards of scientific evidence and critical review, Gary Kinder's widely distributed "Open Letter to the UFO Community" proves to be nothing more than a master-piece of propaganda, carefully crafted by a skilled writer who excels in the art of selective choice of data, and the omission of significant facts.

Included are my comments and responses to specific claims made by Gary Kinder as they appear in his "Open Letter."

An Open Letter to the UFO Community:

March 6, 1987

I have received so many phone calls and letters (and copies of letters sent to others) about the forthcoming LIGHT YEARS, it seems appropriate for me to write a letter of explanation. Had I not been involved with the arrival of a new daughter two weeks ago, I would have written this letter much sooner. I know that many of you were confused to hear I was writing a book on Meier; I also know that most of you will understand when I offer a proper explanation. Here it is.

Though no one in the UFO community has seen the manuscript for LIGHT YEARS, much of the vehemence over its publication seems to arise from a feeling that I betrayed the UFO community, that I pretended to be interested in ufology, its history, and its people, when my only intention was to write about Meier. Some of you may have felt used.

COMMENT:
I certainly felt "used" by Gary Kinder, as did several of my colleagues. If Kinder had only bothered to include in his book *any* of the negative evidence that I spent nearly a full day showing him, then things might have been different. Instead, Kinder ignored this material outright, and makes no mention of it at all in his book.

I have been researching the Meier case since the fall of 1983. In 1984 and the first half of 1985 I made three trips to Switzerland totaling about thirteen weeks in [the] country visiting the alleged contact sites, speaking with Meier, interviewing witnesses (some of whom are detractors), and talking to neighbors, town administrators, etc. I also made side trips to Munich and London. In the States I traveled several times to Phoenix, Tucson, Flagstaff, San Jose, and the Los Angeles area to speak with the people who had investigated the case, the ufologists who had called it a hoax (Korff, Lorenzen, Moore, Spaulding), and the scientists who had analyzed the Meier evidence.

COMMENT:

Kinder's boasting about having journeyed around the globe during the course of his "research" into the Meier case is nothing more than "window dressing" designed to make his "investigation" appear more credible than it really was.

The relevant issues are what Gary Kinder specifically discovered (if anything), how he approached his "investigation," what methodologies he used, and what it was he subsequently did with the data he acquired.

Kinder's bravado about having spoken with "the UFOlogists who called it [the Meier case] a hoax," such as myself, is a fine example of what is known as a "half-truth." While Kinder brags about the *number* of UFO researchers he interviewed, what he *fails* to mention is that he *ignored* much of the evidence that was presented to him that indicates the Meier case is a hoax.

> Yes, qualified scientists, engineers, and a special effects expert did analyze the Meier evidence, and yes they were intrigued by what they found. More on that later. Everyone I talked to in the UFO community, except Lou Farrish, warned me that the Meier case was poison. They said that Meier made preposterous claims about traveling back and forth in time to speak with Jesus and to photograph the future destruction of San Francisco. Some pointed to Bill Spaulding and said that he had found ten of the Meier photos to be patently fraudulent.
>
> Others pointed to Kal Korff, who, they claimed, had conducted an exemplary investigation of the case. After two years of research and over 120 interviews in Switzerland and the U.S., I finally told my editor I simply could not make sense of the Meier case; it all was too confusing, and I had no idea how to begin laying out the story. If everything I had uncovered concerning the case had proved to be negative, I would have found it easy to abandon the project—my editor had given me that option from the beginning; the problem was that I discovered many aspects of the case that truly were intriguing and difficult to explain.

COMMENT:

While the Meier case is hardly "poison," as chapters 1, 2, 4, and 5 of this treatise have shown, Billy Meier's fictional claims of "time-travel," of meeting Jesus Christ, of even being Jesus Christ reincarnated are simply not true.

On the other hand, Gary Kinder's "treatment" of these fraudulent claims by Meier in his book is inexcusable, since he all but ignores them entirely! While Kinder does concede that *one* of Meier's "time-travel" photos is a hoax,[5] a careful reading of *Light Years* reveals that Kinder mentions Meier's outlandish claims only in passing, devoting a total of just *seven sentences* to the general topic![6]

If Gary Kinder had truly conducted a thorough and objective examination of the Meier "evidence" as he professes, he would not have ignored yet again these questionable claims by Billy Meier.

Finally, Kinder's statement that he "simply could not make sense of the Meier case; it all was too confusing" is hard to accept. Indeed, Gary Kinder's decision to ignore almost entirely any and all of the negative evidence in the Meier case to which he was privy is a calculated one on his part. The only other logical explanation for Kinder's professed state of "confusion" is that he is incapable of conducting objective study and analysis of Meier's UFO case material.

> In the meantime I had read many books on ufology to become familiar with the field, and I found the UFO community and the history of UFOs fascinating. I felt there was a book in it, and during the fall of 1985 I began to focus my research on the broader picture, traveling first to Washington, D.C., to spend a week with Dick Hall, Bruce Maccabee, Larry Bryant, et al., though I still was under contract for a book on Meier. (When Maccabee asked me how I became interested in the field, I told him and several others present at a Fund meeting that my first exposure was through the Meier case.) My editor agreed that a bigger UFO book would be a good one. I began to concentrate on this book, quitting work on

Meier, packing up all of my research on him in big boxes, and throwing them into the basement. When I spoke with the Washington, D.C. group, and later in the spring/summer of 1986 attended Hal Starr's conference in Phoenix, the MUFON symposium in Lansing, and Sprinkle's contactee convention in Laramie, I myself was under the impression my research was for a book on ufology, not the Meier case. At the same time I began traveling to attend the various UFO symposia to acquaint myself with more of the community, my editor met with me in Phoenix at Starr's conference and encouraged me at least to give the Meier story a try, just to write it simply and as it happened. Continue to research the other book, he said, but get something on paper about Meier. With that completed, I could go on to the bigger book on ufology. So I pulled my Meier research out of the basement and forced myself to sit down and wade through all of it to try to piece something together. Once I did that, though, all of a sudden LIGHT YEARS came pouring out of me. A 15-page treatment grew in three weeks to a 100-page outline, and in three months I had a 300-page manuscript. Then I rewrote and rewrote and rewrote. Once it began to fall together I liked it more, and when I assembled all of the quotes from the scientists the story began to feel far more solid than it had while I was researching. I also finally located the two sound engineers who had analyzed Meier's audio tapes, and the special effects expert who had studied the Meier 8mm footage and some of the photos back in 1980. The two engineers told me the sounds were unlike anything they had ever heard, or seen, on a spectrum analyzer. The special effects expert informed me that Meier could have created the films and photographs only with a team of experts and tens of thousands of dollars worth of sophisticated equipment. (From my own experiences in Switzerland I knew that neither of these existed.) I had heard so many negative references to Meier for so long I had nearly forgotten similar intriguing things that the scientists had told me two years earlier.

COMMENT:

No amount of rationalizing will ever change the fact that Gary Kinder deceived both me and my fellow UFO colleagues. As Kinder admits in the above paragraph, he was "under contract for a book on Billy Meier" all along. Thus, Kinder's professed interest in the "UFO community" and "what it does" as stated in his original letter to me which he used to secure an interview, is further evidence that his intentions were not sincere from the beginning, or at least during our one and only meeting.

As Kinder also admits, it was his editor, Morgan Entrekin, who kept pushing him to focus on writing a book about Billy Meier. Entrekin probably realized that if a book could be written implying that the claims of Meier were genuine, it would be commercially profitable. Once again, Entrekin was right.

Kinder's listing of the numerous UFOlogists he met with and the UFO-related symposia he attended are more "window dressing" designed to boost his credibility. In fact, what is obvious (and tragic) is that while Gary Kinder did indeed meet with all of these individuals, he obviously ignored what most of them had told him, that the Meier case was "poison" to quote his own term.

Kinder is either ignorant or deliberately ignores the fact that tape recordings (no matter how clear they may sound) are not scientific proof of anything unless they are made under controlled conditions or the original source object is made available for quantifiable comparison and analysis. Thus, regardless of what the two sound engineers allegedly told Kinder, the truth is that Billy Meier's recordings of the weird noises he claims are the "sounds" of the "Pleiadian beamships" are scientifically worthless.

As was established in chapter 3, the comments and "analyses" of Meier's UFO photos by Wally Gentleman are hardly scientific. As noted in chapter 3, Gentleman does not have the background to properly conduct such a study, nor was he provided with adequate materials and equipment with which to do so even if he possessed the appropriate skills.

Finally, if Kinder's "investigation" had been as objective and thorough as he would like everyone to believe, he would not have cited uncritically the mythology of Gentleman's "involvement" in the production of Stanley Kubrick's *2001*, or the ridiculous claim allegedly made about Meier needing "a crew of at least fifteen people" in order to fake his UFO pictures and motion picture films.

My editor liked what I was writing. He showed it to the people at Atlantic Monthly Press, where he has his new imprint, and everyone there liked it, too. Last October they took the first half of the manuscript to the Frankfurt Book Fair as their lead title, while I continued to work on the manuscript, as it was far from being finished. I honestly don't know how many drafts I finally completed, but the figure is somewhere between five and seven. Then last fall two things happened: My editor felt that the Meier story needed to be set in historical context, that I needed to provide the reader with background on the UFO phenomenon itself. Not only did I already have a tremendous amount of research in that area, I had also completed 35 pages of a proposal on the bigger UFO book. I expanded that work, pulled in more detail, and weaved it into the Meier story. You will find about one-half of the second half of LIGHT YEARS is all Arnold, Robertson, Condon, Hynek, Blue Book, Hill, etc. The second thing that happened was that when my editor took the manuscript to Frankfurt he discovered that even in Europe books on UFOs are difficult to sell, too difficult. After that experience he and his publisher both told me they felt it would be unwise for me to follow a book on Meier with another book on UFOs. So we decided to utilize all of my research into the history of ufology for the Meier book and go on to something new for my next project, a decision that frankly left me not too unhappy. Ufology is a frustrating field to research and more frustrating to try to make sense of and put down on paper in a readable fashion. Emotions run so high and name-calling among the ufologists (even without the Meier case) is so rampant, a writer finds himself wallowing in explanations and counterexplanations until every sentence dissolves into battle and nothing is decided. Anyhow, the foregoing is why many of you (and I) thought I was researching a book on ufology when we met in Michigan, or Washington, D.C., or Phoenix, or Laramie. Prior to beginning that general research, I always informed those I interviewed that while I wished to know more about the entire field, I was particularly interested in the Meier case. Spaulding, Moore, Lorenzen, Korff, Starr, all knew back in 1984–85 that I was looking primarily at the Meier case during the early part of my research. This sentence from my letter to Kal Korff on March 28, 1985, is indicative:

> "I am researching a book about the UFO community, what it does, who it is, where it is (in more ways than one). I'm particularly interested in the Swiss Case or the Meier case, which seems to have generated a fair amount of emotion within the community. I know you have referred to it as the most infamous hoax in the history of ufology."

The next quote comes from a letter written by Bill Spaulding the day after I interviewed him.

> "It was a pleasure talking to you on January 6, 1985, regarding the subject of unidentified flying objects and the Billy Meier hoaxed UFO photographs. Because the Meier incident is such an obvious hoax, any further publicity extended to this incident . . . will only provide additional exposure to this case. We cannot involve ourselves to any extent which could further generate favorable publicity for the conspirators of the Pleiades book."

In a small community whose members correspond regularly, it was no secret that I was researching the Meier case.

COMMENT:

It is a fabrication by Kinder to claim that "everyone" at the Atlantic Monthly Press "liked" his book. In reality, several senior members of the editorial staff resigned their positions at Atlantic Monthly in part over the publication of *Light Years*, citing reasons of integrity problems both with the book and Mr. Entrekin himself![7] The *New York Post* exposed these facts in a story they did which appeared in their January 12, 1987 issue. In fact, one of these senior staff members who resigned, as the *New York Post* correctly noted, specifically labeled *Light Years* as "absolutely ridiculous."[8]

Kinder's inclusion of an excerpt from his letter to me, citing it as "evidence" of his supposedly "innocent" intentions, is especially insulting since the *only reason* I agreed to meet with Kinder was because of his assurances to me that his "investigation" of the Meier case would be objective, a promise he made to me that he now conveniently fails to mention. I do not appreciate having my reputation misused by Kinder to bolster his perceived credibility among my peers.

Finally, Kinder's use as "evidence" of this excerpt in his letter to me is hypocrisy at its finest, since he and I never really discussed anything other than Billy Meier. As stated previously, although Kinder *professed* to be interested in the "UFO community" and "what it does," he never asked any significant questions or raised any issues about these topics.

> Now on to the substance of LIGHT YEARS. Many of the witnesses I interviewed in Switzerland, none of whom had ever been contacted by anyone in ufology, had seen things happen to Meier that no one could explain: Standing next to another man, he once disappeared instantly from the roof of a barn twelve feet off the ground; in a separate incident he suddenly reappeared, warm and dry, in a group of men standing in a dark and secluded forest in a freezing rainstorm. These scenes, associated with alleged contact experiences, appear in much greater detail in the book. They may be tricks, but if so they were performed by a master illusionist. When Meier claimed to have had a contact, sets of three six-foot diameter circles would appear in a meadow surrounded by thick woods. I did not see these myself, but I talked to several people who had seen them and who had photographed them while still fresh. Swirled counterclockwise and perfectly delineated in tall grass, one set remained for nine weeks, until a farmer came and mowed the grass. Here is the mystery of the landing tracks: Grass that is green rises even after being mashed down; grass that dies turns brown and lies flat. This grass remained green but never rose; it continued to grow in a flat circle. The landing tracks puzzled everyone I spoke to who had viewed them, including Meier's most ardent detractor, Hans Schutzbach. Schutzbach told me that other people had tried to duplicate the landing tracks, but that

their efforts were "a bad copy." Meier's were "perfect." I listened to dozens of such stories, so many I could not include all of them in the book, including nighttime sightings of strange lights reported by a variety of people, many of whom witnessed the same incidents and corroborated each other's accounts. One nighttime photograph, taken by a school principal from Austria during an alleged contact, will appear in the book. On the other side, I know that Meier's photos of the alleged future destruction of San Francisco, for instance, came right out of the September 1977 issue of *GEO* Magazine. After one of the witnesses reported this to me, I found the magazine myself and compared the photographs. They were identical. All of this is in the book—the crazy claims, the apparent lies, the unexplained disappearances, the mysterious landing tracks, all weaved into the narrative.

COMMENT:

This paragraph by Kinder is a shining example of pro-Meier propaganda and, once again, selective omission of data. What Kinder fails to disclose is that most of the "witnesses" he interviewed in Switzerland are, in fact, either current or former members of Meier's cult! Furthermore, Kinder's statement that none of these "witnesses" had ever been contacted by anyone in UFOlogy before is patently false!

Ironically, the Meier "witnesses" were first interviewed in detail by Wendelle C. Stevens. In fact, their "testimonies" appeared in Stevens's 1983 *Preliminary Investigation Report* treatise, as mentioned earlier in chapter 7. It should be noted that Stevens's book *predates* Kinder's *Light Years* by some four years, and was released several months before Kinder even began his "research" into the Meier case in late 1983, according to the text of his very own "Open Letter"!

Gary Kinder's comments about the alleged Pleiadian landing-tracks have already been addressed in chapter 7. In short, since no scientific tests were ever conducted on them until *my* investigation in 1991, Kinder's claim that they are somehow "mysterious" is groundless. In addition, it is doubtful that Kinder is being completely truthful when he claims he "never saw" any of these tracks, for the reasons previously stated in chapter 2 and shown in figure 10.

Finally, Gary Kinder's remark that "[a]ll of this is in the book—the crazy claims, the apparent lies, the unexplained disappearances, the mysterious landing tracks" is a blatant exaggeration.

As a simple reading of *Light Years* easily proves, as well as the facts contained in this book, Kinder presents a very *one-sided* and overtly *biased* account of the Meier "evidence." Indeed, Kinder's omissions of relevant data in the Meier case, coupled with his failure to conduct his "investigation" via long-established standards of objective methodologies, relegates his work to the arena of pseudoscientific puffery.

In London, Timothy Good provided me with many lengthy letters from Lou Zinsstag (who often had been pointed out by ufologists in the States as one who thought that Meier was a fraud and "crazy"). Zinsstag had written the letters between June 1976 and October 1977, as she investigated Meier and reported back to Good. In one letter she calls Meier "the most intriguing man I have ever met." She goes into great detail in her observations, including a description of "this feeling of discomfort" she experiences in Meier's presence. In another letter she writes, "If Meier turns out to be a fake, I shall take my whole collection of photographs to the ferry boat and drown it in the old man river of Basle."

Back in the States I interviewed nine scientists/engineers/special effects experts who had analyzed or otherwise studied the Meier evidence. (One, Bob Post, is none of the three, but heads the photo lab at JPL.) Following is a sampling of what they had to say. Realize that where the photos are concerned an original transparency was never available for analysis, so none of the work done on those was definitive (Spaulding himself told me he had no idea the generation of the photographs he analyzed); however, knowing this limitation, the scientists who did agree to examine them told me they would have been able to detect all but a very sophisticated hoax.

Dr. Michael Malin is an associate professor of planetary sciences at Arizona State University; he wrote his doctoral thesis on the computer analysis of spacecraft images beamed back from Mars. He was at JPL for four years and he's worked with the special effects people at LucasFilm. He works under various government grants at ASU, and a recent experiment he devised has just been accepted for a future Shuttle launch. A friend of mine who is the science editor at *National Geographic* and who has researched and written many cover stories on the Universe, the Space Shuttle, etc., had spoken to Malin before and once told me, "If Malin says it, you can believe it." Here is one thing Malin said concerning the Meier photographs which he analyzed in 1981: "I find the photographs themselves credible, they're good photographs. They appear to represent a real phenomenon. The story that some farmer in Switzerland is on a first name basis with dozens of aliens who come and visit him . . . I find that incredible. But I find the photographs more credible. They're reasonable evidence of something. What that something is I don't know." Malin also told me, "If the photographs are hoaxes then I am intrigued by the quality of the hoax. How did he do it? I'm always interested in seeing a master at work." These quotes, and all of the rest of the quotes I attribute to the scientists here, appear verbatim in the book.

COMMENT:
As was proven in chapter 3, without original negatives available for scientific study, the remarks by these analysts are not evidence for the authenticity of Billy Meier's UFO photographs. Indeed, in a pattern that has become all too familiar by now in his "Open Letter," Kinder omits Malin's significant comment, "The important thing would have been the original film. Without the very detailed information about the originals, there's almost nothing you can say."[9]

In addition to these selective omissions, there is also the possibility that the quote from Malin cited by Kinder is additionally misleading. Since the quote Kinder cites from Malin has ellipses in it, there's no way of knowing what other words were selectively edited out.

Steve Ambrose, sound engineer for Stevie Wonder and inventor of the Micro Monitor, a radio set complete with speaker that fits inside Wonder's ear, analyzed the Meier sound recordings. "The sound recording's got some surprising things in it," he told me. "How would you duplicate it? I'm not just talking about how to duplicate it audio-wise, but how do you show those various things on a spectrum analyzer and on the scope that it was doing? It's one thing to make something that sounds like it, it's another thing to make something that sounds like it and has those consistent and random oscillations in it. The sound of the spacecraft," he added, "was a single sound source recording that had an amazing frequency response. If it is a hoax I'd like to meet the guy that did it, because he could probably make a lot of money in special effects." His findings were corroborated by another sound engineer named Nils Rognerud.

COMMENT:

As stated earlier, tape recordings, regardless of what they purport to contain, are not scientific proof of anything unless they are obtained under scientifically controlled conditions. Moreover, what Kinder conveniently fails to mention is that the tape recordings of Meier's alleged Pleiadian beamships that were analyzed were not the originals, but rather a third-generation copy![10] This makes Kinder's "argument" that Meier's tapes constitute any sort of significant evidence even more tenuous.

Finally, also omitted by Gary Kinder, both in his "Open Letter" and in *Light Years*, is the fact that the distinctive sound of a switch being thrown was detected twice![11] Since Meier was holding only his camera and tape recorder at the time (the latter of which was already turned on), the detection of a switch being thrown is very suspicious. While sounds of switches clicking are *not* consistent with Meier's account of his alleged incident, they are consistent with a hoax being created by turning off and on certain sounds in order to fabricate a tape recording of the professed event.

In 1979 Dr. Robert Nathan at JPL was sufficiently impressed with the Meier photographs to have copies made of Meier transparencies at the JPL photo lab. After the transfer he refused to analyze the photographs, however, because his developer discovered they were several generations away from the originals. Nathan felt that the transparencies were so far away in generation from the photographs he had seen that Wendelle Stevens had attempted to trick him. Later, I showed the Meier films to Nathan, and he laughed at some of them, but he couldn't figure out how Meier flew the ship into a scene and had it come to a sudden halt; or how it could hover motionless while a pine branch in the lower right corner blows in a stiff wind. Nathan said, "He would have to be awfully clever, because that's a very steady holding. It would have to be a very, very good tethering." Then he said, "Apparently he's a sharp guy, very clever. So he should be given some points for effort." Nathan concluded about the films, "If this is a hoax, and it looks like it is to me but I have no proof, this is very carefully done. Tremendous amount of effort. An awful lot of work for one guy." From all of the scientists, these were the most negative comments I received.

With Nathan saying that in theory the films could be hoaxed, I was curious about the logistics involved. Then I discovered that a special effects expert, Wally Gentleman, who for ten years had served as Director of Special Effects on the Canadian Film Board and who, for a year and a half, was director of special photographic effects for Stanley Kubrick's film *2001*, had viewed these same films. This is what he told me: "To produce the films, Meier really had to have a fleet of clever assistants, at least 15 people. And the equipment would be totally out of [Meier's] means. If somebody wanted me to cheat one of the films, $30,000 would probably do it, but this is in studio where the equipment exists. The equipment would cost another $50,000." That's for each of the seven Meier films. Gentleman also had examined the photographs. "My greatest problem is that for anybody faking this" [he pointed to one of the photographs] "the shadow that is thrown onto that tree is correct. Therefore, if somebody is faking it they have an expert there. And being an expert myself, I know that that expert knowledge is very hard to come by. So I say, 'Well, is that expert knowledge there or isn't it there?' Because if the expert knowledge isn't there, this has got to be real."

Then there is Robert Post, who had been at the JPL photo laboratory for 22 years and was the head of that lab in 1979, when Nathan brought the Meier photos to him to have copies made. Post oversees the developing and printing of every photograph that comes out of JPL. Though he analyzed nothing, his eye for spotting fabrications far surpasses a lay-person's. Post told me: "From a photography standpoint, you couldn't see anything that was fake about the Meier photos. That's what struck me. They looked like legitimate photographs. I thought, 'God, if this is real, this is going to be really something.'"

COMMENT:

As chapter 3 has already shown, once again Kinder's account of Nathan's involvement is a watered down one. He omits the fact that Stevens refused to give Nathan the clear copies of Meier's pictures that he had used to entice the JPL analyst. Such behavior, of course, is both curious and suspicious.

Kinder's quotation from Bob Post is more "window dressing" than anything else. It's obvious that if the Meier UFO photographs were proven to be authentic, that it would be "really something" as Post noted. But what does Bob Post's casual comment have to do with the issue of the integrity of Meier's alleged UFO pictures? Absolutely nothing.

Finally, as was established in chapter 3, Wally Gentleman's "analyses" of Meier's UFO pictures are irrelevant, since he is not qualified to conduct such studies properly. In addition, my experiments conducted with Tina Layton have shown that "at least 15 people" are not needed to duplicate Meier's UFO movies.

A glaring example of Gentleman's lack of expertise in photo analysis is his comment regarding the alleged "shadow" purportedly cast by one of the "UFOs" that Kinder claims he observed in Meier's pictures. The relevant issue is not the existence of this apparent shadow, but how *large* this shadow was! Objects which are 22.75 feet in diameter (the supposed dimensions of Meier's Pleiadian craft) cast bigger shadows than do small models, depending of course on how high the objects are suspended in the air. Instead of merely commenting on the existence of this shadow (if indeed it exists), why didn't Gentleman determine its true size? Gentleman didn't do this because he is not and never has been a trained, qualified photo analyst.

As chapter 3 also proves, Kinder's account of Gentleman's true role in Kubrick's *2001* is also distorted. As a simple viewing of the video release of this movie establishes, Gentleman's name is listed nowhere in the credits.

> Besides working in the highly classified field of military defense, David Froning, an astronautical engineer with McDonnell Douglas for 25 years, has done exploratory research to develop ideas and technology for advanced spacecraft design. As a longtime member of the British Interplanetary Society and the American Institute of Aeronautics and Astronautics, he has presented many papers on interstellar flight at technical conferences in Europe and the United States. In October 1985, he addressed the XXXVI International Astronautical Congress in Stockholm. Froning's wife discovered at a friend's house the photo journal published by the Elders in fall, 1979, and took it home to her husband because of one word in the text—tachyon. In Meier's notes from 1975, he spoke of the tachyon propulsion system utilized by the Pleiadians. For over a year Froning had been spending most of his spare time working to design just such a theoretical system. When he read more of Meier's notes on faster-than-light travel (he had contacted the Elders and Stevens for more information), he found that Meier's figures for the time required to achieve the speed of light (at which point, according to Meier, the tachyon system would kick in to make the hyper leap), and the distance a ship would have traveled at that point, were within 20 percent of his own calculations determined through the use of complex acceleration formulas. Froning told me, "If what this Meier is saying is just a hoax, he's being cued by some very knowledgeable scientists. I've only discussed this Meier case with scientists who are fairly open-minded about interstellar flight, but I'll tell you, the majority of them think it's credible and agree with at least part, or sometimes all, of the things talked about by the Pleiadians."

COMMENT:
As the information presented in the various chapters of this book indicates, Kinder misquoted and/or quoted out-of-context the full story of what all of these scientists have reported. Indeed, much of the comments Kinder cites are of no real scientific or analytical value, nor do they establish the credibility of the Meier case. In truth, many of these statements are pure "window dressing," designed to prop up the objectivity of both Kinder's investigative efforts and the so-called Meier evidence.

As shown earlier in chapter 2, Billy Meier gets much of his "Pleiadian information" from the many publications he regularly purchases at Schnarwiler Books in the town of Wetzikon.

Finally, unlike Gary Kinder, during the past sixteen years I have read several thousand pages of Billy Meier's "Pleiadian contact notes" and his other "alien wisdom" writings in their original German language. It is intriguing to note that *none* of the Meier/Pleiadian writings contains the slightest detailed scientific data or other technical information which transcends what is already known to modern day science. In reality, many of Meier's writings, contrary to what Kinder implies, contain blatant errors in the "facts" they present. As mentioned in chapter 2, several German scientists revealed that the Meier manuscripts "abound with scientific nonsense."

During my research I read an article from a British publication called *The Unexplained*, in which the author, referring to the alleged Meier metal analysis by Marcel Vogel at IBM, wrote, "Jim Dilettoso characteristically failed to further the cause by claiming that [the Elders] hold a 10-hour videotape of 'the entire lab proceedings' (which Dr. Vogel denies having made). 'And,' Dilettoso incautiously persisted, 'we have about an hour of him discussing why the metal samples are not possible in earth technology, going into intrinsic detail of why it is not done anywhere on earth.'" The author, of course, is poking fun at such a claim. I have seen that video. I have also seen another video in which Vogel states, "I cannot explain the metal sample. By any known combination of materials I could not put it together myself, as a scientist. With any technology that I know of, we could not achieve this on this planet." I've interviewed Vogel twice and he insists that the metal sample he spent so much time analyzing is unique. I spoke with him again three weeks ago and to this day he remains fascinated with the specimen. He said that if the metal sample had not disappeared while in his possession, he would now be continuing research on it with a number of other scientists from IBM and Ames Research. A reporter from the *Washington Post* also called Vogel two days ago and Vogel again verified the above quote.

COMMENT

As chapter 6 has proven, Marcel Vogel's credibility in his "analysis" of the Meier metal samples is nonexistent. The fact that Gary Kinder does not disclose that Vogel had bogus credentials, and was not qualified to conduct the analysis he claims he did, is further evidence of how unobjective and incomplete Kinder's "investigation" is.

With the exception of Vogel, and possibly Nathan, though he doesn't remember, none of these men had ever been interviewed by anyone in the UFO community. And Vogel even said to me on tape regarding one of the ufologists who did interview him about Meier: "Treat him with caution. He'll ramble on and he'll quote you out of context. So watch it." He also told me this same person "has taken my statements completely out of context and published them. This case has been badly mangled."

In the book, I go into much greater detail with each of the scientists and engineers. I mention each by his real name (as I do everyone else in the story) and I include his place of employment. After completing the final draft of the manuscript I mailed to each of the scientists a packet which included everything in the manuscript pertaining to him. I asked that each make any corrections, technical or otherwise, he cared to make. I have heard back now from all of them either by mail or by phone during the past six weeks. Some had nothing to change, others made minor changes. Everything concerning their analyses of the evidence will appear in the book exactly as they have authorized it to appear. (Two weeks before sending his letter to my publisher attempting to persuade him not to publish LIGHT YEARS, Walt Andrus called me and we talked for forty-five minutes. During that conversation, I told Andrus of the comments made by the scientists. I gave him their names, I spelled the names for him, I gave him their places of employment, and I encouraged him to contact them for verification of their statements, three of which appeared in an ad for the book in *Publishers Weekly*. Apparently, he never did so.) In his letter to me Michael Malin opened with this: "Thanks for letting me see what you have written. It's a credit to your writing that I cannot tell whether you are a supporter or a detractor of Dilettoso, and of the claims of the people who supplied the UFO images."

Eric Eliason of the U.S. Geological Survey in Flagstaff, Arizona, is the ninth of the experts I spoke with. After receiving his packet, he wrote to me, "Thank you for the accurate representation of my views on the Meier UFO photographs. If your LIGHT YEARS publication remains as objective as the pages you provided, I will look forward to reading what you have to say." Eliason creates image processing software so astrogeologists can analyze photographs of the planets beamed back from space. He spent two years producing the intricate radar map of cloud-covered Venus acquired by Pioneer 10, and his software has been applied in processing space photography beamed back by both Viking and Voyager. He was sent to France and to China as a representative of the U.S. space program and an expert in image processing. He had analyzed the Meier photos on his equipment in 1981. He told me in an interview in August 1984: "In the photographs there were no sharp breaks where you could see it had been somehow artificially dubbed. And if that dubbing was registered in the film, the computer would have seen it. We didn't see anything."

COMMENT:

Kinder's selective comments by Eliason are yet more "window dressing." Once again, as previously shown in chapter 3, Gary Kinder omits in his "Open Letter" the most important statement Eliason made, which was: "You need to start with the original [negatives] if you're going to play games like this.

So in a sense this [his other comments cited by Kinder] is not really a scientifically valid statement."[12]

> What would you do with evidence like this? Would you disregard it because Meier makes outlandish claims? Or because a ufologist reports that a colleague in Germany has a friend who saw ropes and pulleys hanging in Meier's barn? Or because Wendelle Stevens is a believer anyhow? Or because Wendelle Stevens is now in prison? Or because Meier has an 18-inch model of one of the Pleiadian beamships sitting in his office? Or because a group of believers has formed around the man? And if you had a choice between the analyses performed by the scientists Malin at ASU and Eliason at USGS and those performed by Bill Spaulding at Ground Saucer Watch, on which would you stake your reputation? After all of the bad-mouthing given the Meier case, I was surprised to learn that ufologists like Walt Andrus had never heard of Malin, or Eliason, or Gentleman, or Froning, or Ambrose, or even the alleged detractors in Switzerland Hans Schutzbach and Martin Sorge. Schutzbach was Meier's right-hand man for two years, with him night and day, driving him to contacts, organizing and cataloguing all of the photographs, measuring and photographing the landing tracks. Then they had a falling out, and Schutzbach left. He hates Meier and is certain Meier is a fraud; if anyone would know Meier's "technique" and be ready to divulge it, Schutzbach would be the man, yet to this day he has no clue how Meier could have made the tracks, or the photos, or the sound recordings, or the films. Nor does he have even one suggestion for an accomplice. Sorge, a cultured man with a university degree in chemistry and author of two books, had been mentioned frequently by ufologists as the one who discovered charred photographs and thereby exposed Meier as a fraud. He told me in the summer of 1985 that he is "certain" the contacts took place, though in a different fashion than Meier describes. He also told me the real story of how he obtained the burned slides. That, too, is much different than the version I got from ufologists here in the States. Again, all of this is in the book.

COMMENT:

If Kinder's investigation and reporting of the Meier case had been as thorough as he implies, he would have interviewed the Jacob and Wyss families instead of ignoring them. There is no doubt that Kinder knew about their existence because he told me that he had a copy of my original Meier exposé book (where Hans Jacob and the Wyss family property are shown) and had read it.

> One of the more interesting ironies in the current uprising of the UFO community against the publication of LIGHT YEARS is that every time someone slams the book (before it has been read) he points to Bill Spaulding and Kal Korff as the two authorities in whose skills the community places great faith. After all of the negative comments I have heard about Bill Spaulding's work from various members of the UFO community, why would anyone rely on his analysis of anything? Bill Moore, who is not known for his kind feelings toward the Meier case or the people who investigated it, had this to say about Spaulding in an interview on March 25, 1985: "He's generally regarded by anybody in the field as somebody to ignore. It's all puffery. He wrote a paper on the analysis of photographs, and I have a critique of that paper by a scientist who knows what he's talking about, and he just rips it to shreds. It sounds good unless you know what the system is and then you realize that the guy's a phony."
>
> While Korff was young and inexperienced, these factors do not necessarily discredit his work. But I am certain that few ufologists have heard him say what he told me in an interview on April 13, 1985:
>
>> "I'm even open to the possibility that Meier had some genuine experience somewhere in there," he said, "but there's so much noise around his signal that I don't even know how to sift it. I've always maintained that, yeah, maybe there's something to it. Most of the people who have read my work say, 'Ah, the Meier case is totally a hoax, there's nothing to it.' I say, 'The claims [Stevens and the Elders] have made don't hold up; but it's possible the guy may have something somewhere.'"

COMMENT:

Kinder's *omission* once again of all the evidence I shared with him proving the Meier case is a hoax is inexcusable. The fact that he chose to use just *one quote* from me, ignoring everything else I said, is proof again of his deliberate selective choice of data.

The comment that "while Korff was young and inexperienced, these factors do not necessarily discredit his work" is designed to "relieve" Kinder of the burden of addressing my work and disproving it. If my work was not "discredited" when he wrote *Light Years*, then this means that Kinder's book is wrong, since both of our works cannot be correct.

> After three years of researching and thinking about this story it finally came clear to me that two things kept the UFO community from taking a far more serious look at the Meier case: One, of course, is Meier's preposterous claims, and (in an ongoing effort to insulate itself from the fringe) the general reluctance of the community to accept any claim of contact, especially repeated contact; the other is that Lee Elders grabbed all of the evidence and sat on it. George Earley, after reviewing the Elderses' *UFO . . . Contact from the Pleiades*, wrote in *Saucer Smear* that until the Intercep group produced some of the evidence they claimed to have, they deserved to be castigated by the UFO community. And Earley was right. So was Korff. The claims by themselves don't hold up. But the evidence in fact existed; I've talked to the people who examined it.

COMMENT:
Yes, Kinder did talk with some of the people, not all of them by any means, who examined the Meier evidence. Unfortunately, he either quotes them out of context, or only recounts certain portions of their testimonies. Again, Kinder masterfully uses the technique of selective choice of data. The fact that Kinder uses just *one quote* from me, ignoring virtually everything else I said, is proof again that he has not been straightforward in his reporting of this case.

None of the foregoing is offered as proof that Meier sat in a Swiss meadow and conversed with Pleiadians, but only to demonstrate that people intrigued by the Meier case, who see a fascinating story in the man, are not simplistic in their thinking. No one, including Stevens and the Elders, has ever claimed he possesses irrefutable evidence of the Meier contacts, and I do not make that claim now. No one in ufology can make that statement about any case. After I sent a letter similar to this one to Jerry Clark, he responded that while he continued to have serious reservations about Meier's claims to meet with extraterrestrials, he, too, found the Meier story "fascinating." "My colleagues are going to be astounded and confused," he wrote. "It really has been an article of faith among us (me included) that this whole business was just an exercise in heavy-handed fraud. But apparently you have shown it is rather more interesting than that. It's ironic. Ufologists forever complain that scientists and debunkers won't take an objective look at the UFO evidence. You have demonstrated, I think, that in this case the ufologists acted just like the people they criticize."

You will find the book a balanced report that holds many surprises for you and other ufologists, and in no way degrades the stature of the UFO community or impedes its progress. Due to cooperation from many of you, the historical sections in LIGHT YEARS will provide readers with a true appreciation of the UFO phenomenon and those who study it. Like Jerry Clark, I myself remain fascinated with Meier, but uncertain about the truth behind the actual contacts. I end LIGHT YEARS with this: "I would not call him a prophet, though he may be. I would not rule out impostor, though I have no proof. I know that if you boiled the story in a kettle you would find a hard residue composed of two things: One would be Meier's ravings about time travel, space travel, philosophy, and religion; the other would be the comments by the scientists and engineers impressed with the evidence he has produced. I can't believe the former, nor can I dismiss the latter. He may simply be one of the finest illusionists the world has ever known, possessing not the power but the skill to persuade others to see things that did not happen and do not exist. Perhaps he has no such ability; perhaps beings on a much higher plane have selected him and controlled him and used him for reasons far beyond our comprehension. I do know this: Trying to make sense

of it all has been the most difficult thing I will ever do. Finally I
realized, as the Elders had years before, that the truth of the Meier
contacts will never be known."

COMMENT:

The *truth* to the Meier "contacts" is known, and I shared this
information with Gary Kinder. The verdict on the case is the
same now as it was back when Kinder interviewed me: the
case is a hoax. Instead of including this data in his book,
Kinder ignored it completely.

What is truly sad about Kinder's book is that the Atlantic
Monthly Press chose to publish such a book in the interests of
corporate profit, as the *New York Post* astutely noted in their article of January 12, 1987. The truth is the Atlantic Monthly Press
was reportedly experiencing financial difficulty at the time and
its new owners and publisher, Morgan Entrekin, were determined to turn its fortunes around.[13]

Was the *New York Post* correct in its story about Entrekin
not really caring whether or not *Light Years* was factual or not?
Was *Light Years*, as the *Post* claimed, the product of "Schlock-
meister" marketing?

Only you can decide.*

UFO researcher Jerry Clark no longer feels that Kinder's
book is the "definitive work" on the Billy Meier case. Instead,
Clark (who I have known since 1981) feels that *this* book
deserves that honor.[14]

Finally, Kinder makes no mention whatsoever in his sup-

---

*For those who wish to know all of the facts against the Meier case
which were shared with Gary Kinder but later omitted, feel free to write
Kinder in care of Grove-Atlantic Monthly Press in New York City and ask
him for a copy of the cassette tape recording that was made during our
interview. Assuming Gary Kinder's tape recording of our meeting hasn't
somehow "disappeared," it should prove most interesting. Rather than
take my word for things, feel free to ask Kinder yourself for a copy of the
tape so that you may decide.

posed "Open Letter" of the close working partnership he formed with Brit and Lee Elders of Genesis III in order to complete *Light Years.*

As previously noted, Brit and Lee Elders jointly own the legal copyright to *Light Years* along with Gary Kinder, and also receive a percentage of the book's royalties! By omitting key facts like these, Kinder creates the misleading impression that his book is an objective treatise of the "facts" in the Billy Meier case.

Notes

1. Morgan Entrekin, Publisher, Atlantic Monthly Press, personal conversation with Kal K. Korff, American Booksellers Association convention, May 1993, Miami, Florida.

2. Gary Kinder, *Light Years: An Investigation into the Extraterrestrial Experiences of Eduard Meier* (New York: Atlantic Monthly Press, 1987), p. v.

3. Gary Kinder, personal letter to Kal K. Korff, dated March 10, 1984.

4. Gary Kinder, personal conversation with Kal K. Korff, Fremont, California, May 21, 1984.

5. Kinder, *Light Years,* p. 218.

6. Ibid., pp. 218, 265.

7. *New York Post,* Monday, January 12, 1987.

8. Ibid.

9. Kinder, *Light Years,* pp 237–38.

10. Wendelle Stevens, *UFO . . . Contact from the Pleiades—A Preliminary Investigation Report—The Report of an Ongoing Contact* (Tucson, Ariz.: Wendelle Stevens, 1983), p. 439.

11. Ibid., p. 444.

12. Kinder, *Light Years,* p. 218.

13. *New York Post,* Monday, January 12, 1987.

14. Jerome Clark, personal phone conversation with Kal K. Korff, March 25, 1995.

11

The Meier Case:
Setting the Record Straight

> The unfortunate thing about this field [UFOlogy] is that if you
> have half a brain, you're automatically labeled "CIA."
> UFO researcher Russ Estes

Over the past fifteen years I have fielded thousands of questions concerning the Meier case from people all over the world. While the answers to almost all of these questions have been presented throughout this book, some could not be fitted within the general framework of this work. Therefore, this chapter has been included to specifically address these miscellaneous issues and questions.

Question #1

You and Mr. Al Reed so obviously set Jim Dilettoso up with your "C-Band" radar-frequencies question. Do you think that this was fair?

The "C-Band" question recounted in chapter 8 was designed as a "yardstick" to see just how far Dilettoso would go to fabricate his "facts." It was a fair thing to do, and if Dilettoso had nothing to hide, he would not have fallen for it.

One must remember that *prior* to the lengthy interview with Mr. Dilettoso, Al and Barbara Reed and I possessed irrefutable evidence that Dilettoso had repeatedly misrepresented various aspects of the Meier case. Those who cry "foul" over the tactic we used are not addressing the only relevant issue here: the fact that Jim Dilettoso was not being completely honest during this part of his interview.

Question #2

Are you saying that all of Mr. Meier's claims and UFO photographs are bogus?

No, I am not, and I have never made this claim. I can only comment on the evidence I have studied firsthand, which has been presented here.

I am certainly open to the *possibility* that somewhere in his past Billy Meier may have had what *he believes* is a genuine UFO experience, for lack of a better term. However, if this is the case, there is absolutely *no credible evidence to prove it*. Indeed, all of the "evidence" Meier and his proponents have put forth is sadly wanting. Since there is no way to separate the "signal from the noise" in this case, the issue as to whether *any* of Meier's UFO claims are true cannot be resolved.

Question #3

Wendelle Stevens and Jim Dilettoso keep claiming that you did not write the original exposé on Billy Meier that was published with your name on it in 1981. They keep insisting that UFO researcher Bill Moore did most of the work on the book and only "used" you because you were under age eighteen at the time and therefore exempt from the laws of libel and slander.[1]

This is another ridiculous claim by both Dilettoso and Stevens. The truth of the matter is that I wrote *all* of the book that was published in 1981. Bill Moore simply arranged for the publishing contract and helped edit the final text that made it into the book that was eventually released.

The entire 127-page volume was written in only two weeks and to be honest, I was never happy with it for that reason. I wanted more time to do a better job at writing it, but it was either get it done in that two-week period of time or lose the "publishing window" that Moore had opened for me.

The text for the book was word processed at Pamela Ezra and Roma Donovan's house in Millbrae, California, and the halftones and typesetting were done by Al and Barbara Reed of Publication Professionals. Garret Moore (no relation to Bill Moore) of Gravity Graphics supplied the drawings of Meier's photos, and Al Reed and I did the final paste-up and layout for the publisher in Arizona because of the tight deadline.

The notion that Bill Moore "used" me to get around issues of potential libel and slander are ridiculous. In fact, I invite Dilettoso and Stevens to *prove* this allegation.

Finally, since I was born in March of 1962, and the book was published in May 1981, I was *nineteen years old* when it was finally released, and *eighteen years of age* when it was written. This means that I was not exempt from any libel or slander laws.

Question #4

Wendelle Stevens says that since age fourteen, you were a mischievous teenager who doctored UFO photos on your personal computer and sold them to Wendelle trying to pass them off as authentic.

This is simply *not true*. Wendelle Stevens, for reasons only he knows, recently repeated this distortion once again to UFO researcher and Billy Meier supporter Dave Hurlburt, who then told it to an audience of roughly 150 people at the UFO Experience symposium in North Haven, Connecticut, on October 8–9, 1994.

When Hurlburt later sent Underground Video a tape recording of his talk where he repeats Stevens's claims about me, I listened to the tape and called Hurlburt myself to set the record straight. After a very pleasant conversation with Hurlburt, he agreed not to say such things anymore and to check with me firsthand in the future.

For the record, personal computers *did not exist* in 1976 when I was fourteen years old. Even if they did, I did not even know *how* to use a computer until 1982, when I first began working in the computer industry. By the time 1984 rolled around, I was twenty-two years old and hooked on computers.

Stevens also told Hurlburt that I had performed these supposed "digital manipulations" on my Macintosh® personal computer. This is another impossibility, since the Macintosh® PC was not even released until *January 1994!* I should know, because I was personally present during the machine's roll out and worked at Apple Computer at the time as a supervisor.

Stevens's other remarks about me charging him for photos and that I was a "mischievous teenager" are also untrue. If anything, I was what one might call a "square" in high school and I was wrapped up in my studies, article writing, media appearances, and lectures, which all began for me at a very young age.

Question #5

Wendelle Stevens has claimed that you never went to Switzerland, and so has Billy Meier.

Jim Dilettoso also made this claim when he called me in September 1994 asking me ahead of time what I would say in the debate against him on FOX TV's "Encounters." This is another erroneous statement that Stevens told Hurlburt as well.

The reason Billy Meier does not remember me being at his place is that we never formally met. However, as the photos and video footage both in this book and in Underground Video's *EXPOSED* documentary prove, I was certainly in Switzerland and at the Meier farm with Tina Layton as I claimed in chapter 2. Indeed, some of my undercover footage has been shown at various UFO West conventions since 1993 and was even featured on "Encounters."

Although Stevens claims he checked Meier's visitor's log (which Tina and I signed twice) going back to 1992 and was unable to find my name, if he had checked back to *1991* he would have seen it. Figures 118 and 119 show some of these written denials by Meier and Stevens.

Question #6

How can you say that Colonel Stevens has masterminded the whole Meier case and is behind it all?

I have never made this claim, though Wendelle Stevens continues to say that I have, repeating it recently to Dave Hurlburt.

It is obvious by reading this book that Stevens is *not* the driving force behind the Meier case. *Billy Meier* is the primary culprit who fabricates the basic "evidence." Wendelle Stevens and his associates then embellish it and promote it.

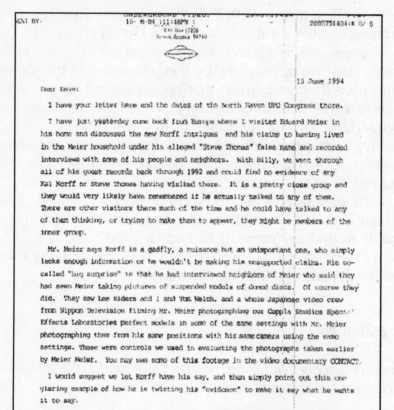

15 June 1994

Dear Dave:

I have your letter here and the dates of the North Haven UFO Congress there.

I have just yesterday come back from Europe where I visited Eduard Meier in his home and discussed the new Korff intrigues and his claims to having lived in the Meier household under his alleged "Steve Thomas" false name and recorded interviews with some of his people and neighbors. With Billy, we went through all of his guest records back through 1992 and could find no evidence of any Kal Korff or Steve Thomas having visited there. It is a pretty close group and they would very likely have remembered if he actually talked to any of them. There are other visitors there much of the time and he could have talked to any of them thinking, or trying to make them to appear, they might be members of the inner group.

Mr. Meier says Korff is a gadfly, a nuisance but an unimportant one, who simply lacks enough information or he wouldn't be making his unsupported claims. His so-called "big surprise" is that he had interviewed neighbors of Meier who said they had seen Meier taking pictures of suspended models of domed discs. Of course they did. They saw Lee Elders and I and Tom Welch, and a whole Japanese video crew from Nippon Television filming Mr. Meier photographing our Coppla Studios Special Effects Laboratories perfect models in some of the same settings with Mr. Meier photographing them from his same positions with his same camera using the same settings. These were controls we used in evaluating the photographs taken earlier by Meier Meier. You may see some of this footage in the video documentary CONTACT.

I would suggest we let Korff have his say, and then simply point out this one glaring example of how he is twisting his "evidence" to make it say what he wants it to say.

You might also mention the woman from India who we met there in New York at the Whole Life Expo a year ago, who told us she and her brother knew Eduard Meier in India when he lived in the Ashram at Ashoka, where her grandfather was the head Monk. She was 10 and her brother was 8 years old at the time. She said the local villagers regarded Meier as "strange" at the time, because he was being visited "by a celestial woman", Asket of course, and was taking pictures of their craft. Do not let anybody draw you into an argument over this because when you get into a "pissing contest with a skunk, you know who has the advantage"

All my best, Dave. I simply don't have any more Meier material available for sale. Sorry.

Wendelle C. Stevens

Fig. 118. A FAX from Wendelle C. Stevens to Connecticut UFO researcher and Billy Meier lecturer Dave Hurlburt, denying that Kal Korff has ever been to Switzerland or at the Billy Meier cult! I have never claimed that any of Meier's neighbors reported seeing him faking his "UFO" photographs. (Photo courtesy: Dave Hurlburt.)

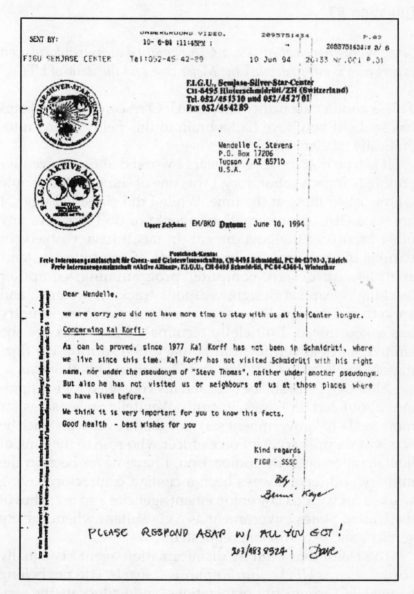

Fig. 119. A FAX from Billy Meier himself to Wendelle Stevens denying that Kal Korff has ever been to Switzerland or at the Billy Meier cult! (Photo courtesy: Dave Hurlburt.)

Question #7

Some people have called you a CIA operative or a disinformation expert who is out to debunk the Meier case and the issue of UFOs.

This is another absurdity and like UFO researcher Russ Estes has said, "If you have half a brain in this field, you're automatically labeled 'CIA' "!

It is true that for several years I worked at Lawrence Livermore National Laboratory. I was one of some 10,000 people who worked there at the time. While I did classified work, I am *not* a CIA "disinformation" agent nor do I work for any other branch of the government. In fact, I have worked for various federal agencies in the fields of computer systems analysis and design, computer programming, computer teaching, weapons design, weapons tracking systems, and antiterrorist and intelligence analysis only when my country has asked me to. I officially terminated my work for the United States government in January 1991, during the final days of the Persian Gulf War and Operation Desert Storm.

Although I will still be occasionally consulted for my opinions about certain issues, in truth, Wendelle Stevens has far more years of "government service" than I ever will, since he was a *career* military Air Force officer who rose to the rank of lieutenant colonel. By comparison, I have never been in the military and have always been a civilian contractor, having worked for various law enforcement agencies and branches of the United States government as a consultant whenever my services and expertise are requested.

The claim that I am a "disinformation agent" is equally absurd. I am a *UFO researcher pure and simple.* I do not belong to any UFO groups or organizations, and I advocate the serious, objective, and scientific study of UFO cases.

Also, as president and CEO of TotalResearch, a research

"think-tank" dedicated to the study of universal mysteries and humanitarian causes, UFOs fall within TotalResearch's Science and Technology charter. This is why both TotalResearch and I have funded in the past, and continue to provide resources for serious scientific studies of this phenomenon. Dr. Keith Harrary, an expert on cults and a psychologist, wrote a magazine article for *Omni* magazine on my endeavors and several newspapers and TV stations have also chronicled my activities.

Those who claim that "Kal's with the government" are *ignorant* of the facts and do not want to admit that the Billy Meier case and some of their other "favorites" are unfortunate hoaxes. By comparison, I am after the *truth* behind the UFO phenomena and I do not care what that "truth" is, since I take each UFO incident on its merits.

Question #8

Why study the Billy Meier case if it is a hoax?

When I started my investigation of the Billy Meier case, I did not *know* that it was a hoax. In fact, because I both knew and trusted Wendelle Stevens, I thought at first it might be real. However, when I began to study the case I quickly discovered that it was a hoax. Millions of people, unfortunately, believe that the Meier case is genuine. They have been fooled by Billy Meier and his various cohorts.

In trying to find the truth behind various UFO cases and purported experiences, the Meier case is one of thousands I have studied. This book is presented to get the full facts out to the public so that they can make an informed decision about this case. To investigate the Meier claims thoroughly and not release the data to the public in as wide a variety of media and products as possible would be a crime against humanity's understanding of this case. I cannot do this. Regardless of what conclusions are reached in my investigations, I always make the information available to the public where possible.

Question #9

Who, other than yourself, has conducted a legitimate, unbiased investigation into the Billy Meier case the results of which can be independently verified by anyone?

Underground Video has conducted the second most thorough investigation of this case, having originally started out as Billy Meier "believers." Colman VonKeviczky and Bill Moore have also done very good jobs at researching the case, but their investigations have been limited to specific areas. Hans Jacob conducted a far more extensive investigation than either Underground Video, Colman VonKeviczky, or Bill Moore, but Jacob passed away several years ago and I ended up with his Meier-related files as mentioned in chapters 2 and 4.

Question #10

What is the single most important lesson one can learn from the Billy Meier case, now that we know it is indeed the most elaborate hoax in UFO history?

Don't be so gullible! Whenever *anyone* (especially Billy Meier's supporters) makes such sweeping claims of either UFO visitations or "extraterrestrial" contact, feel free to demand hard, objective proof. Make these advocates fill in the *who, what, where, when, why,* and *how* of the details of their cases. Try to think *critically* and *demand proof,* do not accept anyone's "word" or blanket assurances.

Remember, this book has been written so that anyone can independently check the facts presented in it. Make other people do the same, and hold them *accountable* to hard, scientific, and verifiable standards of evidence and results.

Note

1. Wendelle Stevens, *UFO . . . Contact from the Pleiades: A Supplementary Investigation Report—The Report of an Ongoing Contact* (Tucson, Ariz.: Wendelle Stevens, 1989), p. 10.

12

The Meier Case:
Some Lessons Learned

Scientific credibility has high standards indeed. Why should this
burden be placed upon UFOlogy?

M. S. LaMoreaux, *MUFON Journal*, May 1994

The Billy Meier hoax is not the first to crop up in UFO history,
nor is it going to be the last. Unfortunately, UFOlogy is over-
loaded with people willing to take advantage of the gullibility of others. However, the same is true for many other areas
of study as well.

Notice that I termed UFOlogy an "area of study" and not
a science. While I define UFOlogy in my *UFO Dictionary* as
"the scientific study of UFO reports," I admit I'm being a bit
idealistic because that's what UFOlogy *should* be! Instead, the
number of researchers who employ science and its disciplined
methodologies is appallingly small. While I shall decline to list
any names, let me just say that out of the over 263 UFOlogists
with whom I currently correspond, the number of researchers
who apply the rigors of science can be counted on the fingers
of my two hands!

Though most of these people do not correctly apply the
methods of science, at least a few more employ critical think-

413

ing. But like the scientific practitioners, the critical thinkers also constitute a small tribe. If critical thinking were applied by more UFO researchers as well as the general public overall, the Dilettosos, Elderses, Meiers, and Stevenses of the world would find it far more difficult to continue to mislead people. Instead, they thrive!

For example, I am sure that most people remember a series of books written by Erich von Däniken. He is the Swiss hoteler who wrote *Chariots of the Gods?*, *Gods from Outer Space*, and *Gold of the Gods*. To date, von Däniken's numerous books have managed to generate worldwide sales of over *42 million* copies![1]

Undoubtedly, the enormous success of von Däniken's books can *in part* be attributed to widespread fascination in the *possibility* that benevolent beings from outer space once visited us as "gods" who later helped humanity build the world's greatest ancient monuments. But I would submit that the main, underlying reason why von Däniken's books have been so successful is a distinct *absence* of critical thinking.

As much as some may hate to admit, the public is gullible. We have a penchant for believing a good deal of what we read and see on television. If you disagree with this point then ask yourself the following question: Which magazine has a larger reading audience? *Time* or the *National Enquirer*? If you picked *Time*, you're wrong. Next to *TV Guide*, *National Enquirer* is the most widely read magazine in the United States! Now if this doesn't say something about the reading habits of the populace, I don't know what else does.

The public accepts what it reads as being for the most part true. And when you have such books as Gary Kinder's *Light Years* being deliberately labeled and marketed by his publisher as a work of "nonfiction," then the truth is even more difficult to distinguish unless the unsuspecting reader decides to independently check the data presented in such works.

The public accepts the *National Enquirer*'s stories of Holly-

wood's affairs and scandals, President Clinton's alleged repeated consultations with ETs, and stories of werewolves and
vampires just as they accepted von Däniken's ancient astro-
naut stories.

But the public is not alone, for some of the "experts"
(UFOlogists in this case) have fallen victim to subjectivity as
well. For example, a significant number of my colleagues
(among my associates are all of the well-known names in this
field) tell me UFOs are unquestionably real.

Since the term "UFO" stands for Unidentified Flying
Object, I have no quarrel with this. As long as there are people on this planet there will always be sightings of objects
which are unidentified. So, from this standpoint, UFOs cannot
be anything else *but* "real." However, when some of these
same colleagues point to the mounds of "scientific evidence"
as a means of justifying their beliefs I feel compelled to ask
them (quite seriously) to which evidence do they refer? I certainly know of none. And in theory, I should, having been a
UFOlogist myself for more than twenty-two years now and
having investigated thousands of cases.

More often than not I'll get a reply like: "Well, you know,
Kal, the millions of sightings, all of those photographs, the
landings, the abductions, the government memos we now
have; all these people can't be lying." While I certainly agree,
such a statement conveys, in my opinion, a fundamental lack
of understanding as to the true nature of the UFO "evidence."

All UFO cases can be broken down into four general categories, the first of which is a sighting, when a person sees a
UFO. UFO photos and films are also included in this category
since they, too, are supposed to depict what it was that the wit-
ness(es) allegedly saw.

The second category includes the radar-visual cases, instances where a UFO is seen and tracked on radar as well.

The third category covers the landing-track cases, incidents where a UFO hovers above or near the ground or lands,

and produces some sort of *physical* evidence to show that it has been there. Examples of such physical evidence are landing-gear impressions, radioactivity, so-called burnt circular rings, flattened grass, and so on.

The fourth and final category of UFO data covers the alien being/occupant or abduction cases: instances in which the actual *pilots* are seen in or about their craft, or have forcibly taken on board their ship one or more human beings. Usually, these people claim they are subjected to some sort of physical examination or interrogation and are then released.

Surely the existence of literally *millions* of reports world-wide proves *something,* doesn't it? Of course it does, but unlike a good deal of my colleagues *I don't profess to have the answer(s)!* The reason for my cautious stand rests with the *very nature* of this so-called evidence. Unfortunately, almost all of it is *scientifically worthless!*

Consider if you will the first category of UFO data: the sightings. In truth, a sighting is nothing more than a story. You can't prove that it actually happened. Unless glaring evidence of a hoax is detected, all you can do is accept the person's *word* that what he or she is telling you is the truth. After you've gotten this far, you have another problem: How can you prove that the incident actually occurred precisely the way the witness(es) describes? Practically speaking, you cannot.

UFO photos and films fare only slightly better, because even if absolutely no evidence of a hoax is detected, you cannot prove that the object in question is an extraterrestrial spacecraft. There's always the possibility that the "UFO" could be either a secret military aircraft, or even a large, thirty-five-foot model dropped out of an airplane.

What about the second category of UFO reports: the radar-visual cases? Once again we're left with the same problem in that you cannot prove that the object(s) in question is an extraterrestrial spacecraft.

The landing-track cases offer theoretically the largest

potential for scientific paydirt. But while there are more than 4,500 such reports on record,[2] a truly unexplainable physical trace or irrefutably extraterrestrial artifact has yet to be uncovered, even in the Meier case!

The "creature" and abduction reports bring us full circle to the same, fundamental problem once again: they are also nothing more than stories, perhaps genuine, perhaps not.

So, where's the plethora of "scientific evidence" to which many of my fellow UFO colleagues often refer? To use a popular addage: Where's the UFO "beef"? Well, it's located entirely throughout the four categories of data just reviewed. At least that's what a good many appear to believe. However, as we have shown above and for the reasons described, the truth unfortunately isn't always that simple.

Again, this is due to a lack of critical thinking.

On the other side of the coin, getting back to the issue of the general public: How many of you remember a book by the title of *Guardians of the Universe* by Ronald Story? How about *The Space Gods Revealed*, also written by the same author? These two books conclusively prove that Erich von Däniken does not have a case, and that von Däniken even *manufactured* some of his "evidence," particularly the material cited in his bestselling book *Gold of the Gods*. If neither of these two titles strike a cord of familiarity, I am not the least bit surprised. For, unlike the books of von Däniken, they were never runaway bestsellers. The masses didn't flock to the book stores by the millions to read the true story that these works told. Their minds were made up: von Däniken is right, let reality be damned. Again, there is a lack of critical thinking.

People seem to *want* UFOs and ancient astronauts to be real. They seem to *want* to believe in ESP, ghosts, and reincarnation. Historically, these phenomena have seemingly always held a special place in the minds and many cultures of humankind.

As our species rapidly approaches the end of this century,

uncritical acceptance of paranormal phenomena, as well as a rise in the membership of cults, is bound to increase several-fold. Historically, the end of every century has always brought forth scores of false prophets and self-proclaimed "Messiahs" who preach the gloom and doom of the impending end of our world, or the formation of some sort of "new world order."

Since the year 2000 is considered almost universally to be a significant, "special time" according to several of the world's major religions, as well as to the millions of people who comprise the very real but ill-defined "New Age" movement, one must be careful, especially during this unique era of time.

The topic of UFO phenomena, which are composed of numerous and diverse claims, is an area certainly worthy of scientific study. However, professing to know just *what* UFOs are, and claiming that there is "hard, quantifiable, scientific evidence" for their existence, is another matter entirely. While a priori belief in paranormal phenomena, or any other subject for that matter, is everyone's individual right, one should always exercise caution against those who mislead and misinform.

Remember, con men and pseudoscientists exist in just about *every* field of study and are *not* unique to the world of UFOlogy.

Will *you* be their next victim?

Notes

1. Ronald Story, *Guardians of the Universe?* (London: New English Library, 1980), p. 9.
2. Stanton T. Friedman, personal telephone conversation with Kal K. Korff, Fredericton, New Brunswick, Canada, October 10, 1994.

Appendix

Page 1 of Neil Davis's Analysis

DESIGN TECHNOLOGY

P. O. BOX 611   POWAY, CALIFORNIA 92064

<u>Preliminary Photo Analysis</u>

<u>Subject</u> 3"X4½" color print of UFO submitted for analysis by W.C. Stevens.

<u>Supporting Information supplied by W.C. Stevens</u>

Location of scene — East of Lake Zurich, Switzerland in rolling hills.
Nearest town is Hinwell.

Data and time — 3 August 1975, 1720 local time.

Camera — Olympus ECR 35 mm, S/N 200519, 42mm focal length Rokkor lens.

Camera settings — 1/100 second, F/2.8

Film — Kodak 18 DIN negative film.

Number of photos taken — 6

Photographer's estimate of object diameter — 7 meters.

<u>Test results</u>

The print was visually examined microscopically to qualitatively evaluate the sharpness of the image of the object and of the scene. There is no discernable difference in image sharpness.

Color separation black and white negatives were made at magnifications of 1 and 10. The resulting negatives were processed by a scanning microdensitometer yielding density contour plots. Examination of these plots did not reveal any details which would cast doubt upon the authenticity of the photograph.

The print, color copy negatives, and color separation black and white negatives were carefully examined for evidence of double exposure, photo paste-up, model at short range suspended on a string, etc. Nothing was found to indicate a hoax.

Examination of the location of the shadows and highlights in the photograph verifies that the object and the scene were apparently taken under the same conditions of illumination.

419

Page 2 of Neil Davis's Analysis

DESIGN TECHNOLOGY

P. O. BOX 611   POWAY, CALIFORNIA 92064

Many small black specks, apparently caused by dirt on the previous positive, were found on the print. Their presence indicates that this print is either a 2nd generation print from a color negative original or that the original is a positive transparency not a negative as was stated in the supporting data.

Conclusion: Nothing was found in the examination of the print which could cause me to believe that the object in the photo is anything other than a large object photographed a distance from the camera.

Recommendations:

1. These results are preliminary and qualititive in nature because of the unknown processing history of the print, and its presumed inferior quality to the original negative. A more detailed, quantitative analysis of this photo can only properly be made on the original film. It is most desirable that all 6 original photos be examined. It is possible to optically or digitally superimpose the several images of the object resulting in an image with increased resolution.

2. With the original photo available it should be possible to compute the distance from the camera to the object using the decrease in contrast due to haze at greater distances. To perform this calculation it is necessary to know the distances from the camera to features in the scene such as the near trees and the increasingly distant hills. If it is not possible to obtain these measurements at the site then an aerial photograph or topographic map with those features identified would be needed.

Analysis performed by

Neil M. Davis
Physicist
13 March 1978

Bibliography

Adamski, George. *Inside the Spaceships.* London and New York: Abelard-Schuman, 1955. Also published in paperback as *Inside the Flying Saucers* (New York: Warner Paperback Library, 1967; 1974).
———. *Flying Saucers Farewell.* London and New York: Abelard-Schuman, 1961. Also published in paperback as *Behind the Flying Saucer Mystery* (New York: Warner Paperback Library, 1967; 1974).
Adler, Bill, ed. *Letters to the Air Force on UFOs.* New York: Dell Publishing Company, 1967.
Allingham, Cedric. *Flying Saucers from Mars.* New York: British Book Centre, 1955.
Arnold, Kenneth, and Ray Palmer. *The Coming of the Saucers.* Amherst, Wis.: Amherst Press, 1952.

Babcock, Edward J., and Timothy G. Beckley. *UFOs Around the World.* New York: Global Communications, 1978.
Baker, Robert M. L. *Investigations of Anomalistic Observational Phenomena.* El Segundo, Calif.: Robert M. L. Baker, 1968.
Ballester-Olmos, Vicente-Juan. *A Catalogue of 200 Type-1 UFO Events in Spain and Portugal.* Evanston, Ill.: Center for UFO Studies, 1976.
Barker, Gray. *They Knew Too Much About Flying Saucers.* New York: University Books, 1956.
———. *The Strange Case of Morris K. Jessup.* Clarksburg, W. Va.: Saucerian Press, 1963.
———. *Gray Barker's Book of Saucers.* Clarksburg, W. Va.: Saucerian Press, 1965.

Barker, Gray. *Gray Barker's Book of Adarnski*. Clarksburg, W. Va.: Saucerian Press, 1967.

Beckley, Timothy Green. *UFOs Around the World*. New York: Global Communications, 1968.

Bergier, Jacques. *Extraterrestrial Visitations from Prehistoric Times to the Present*. Chicago: Henry Regnery Company, 1973.

Berlitz, Charles. *The Mystery of Atlantis*. New York: Grosset and Dunlap, 1969.

————. *The Bermuda Triangle*. Garden City, N.Y.: Doubleday and Company, 1974.

Bernard, Raymond. *The Hollow Earth*. Mokelumne Hill, Calif.: Health Research, 1963.

Bethurum, Truman. *Aboard a Flying Saucer*. Los Angeles: DeVorss and Company, 1954.

Binder, Otto O. *Flying Saucers Are Watching Us*. New York: Larchmont Books, 1968.

Bloecher, Ted. *Report on the UFO Wave of 1947*. Washington, D.C.: Ted Bloecher, 1967.

Blum, Ralph, and Judy Blum. *Beyond Earth—Man's Contact with UFOs*. New York: Bantam Books, 1974.

Blumrich, Josef F. *The Spaceships of Ezekiel*. New York: Bantam Books, 1974.

Bowen, Charles, ed. *The Humanoids*. Chicago: Henry Regnery Company, 1974.

Byrne, Peter. *The Search For Bigfoot—Monster, Myth or Man?* Washington, D.C.: Acropolis Books, 1975.

Clark, Jerome, and Loren Coleman. *The Unidentified: Notes Toward Solving the UFO Mystery*. New York: Warner Paperback Library, 1975.

Cohen, Daniel. *Myths of the Space Age*. New York: Dodd, Mead and Company, 1967.

Condon, Edward, ed. *Scientific Study of Unidentified Flying Objects*. New York: E. P. Dutton, 1969.

Constable, Trevor James. *They Live in the Sky*. Los Angeles: New Age Publishing Company, 1958.

————. *Sky Creatures—Living UFOs*. New York: Pocket Book Library, 1978.

David, Jay. *The Flying Saucer Reader*. New York: New American Library, 1967.

Davidson, Leon. *Flying Saucers: An Analysis of the Air Force Project Blue Book Special Report No. 14*. White Plains, N.Y.: Blue-Book Publishers, 1976.

Dione, R. L. *God Drives a Flying Saucer.* New York: Exposition Press, 1969.

Downing, Barry. *The Bible and Flying Saucers.* Philadelphia: J. B. Lippincott Company, 1967.

Drake, W. Raymond. *Gods or Spacemen?* Amherst, Wis.: Amherst Press, 1964.

———. *Gods and Spacemen in the Ancient East.* London: Neville Spearman, 1973.

Edwards, Frank. *Stranger Than Science.* New York: Lyle Stuart, 1959.

———. *Flying Saucers—Serious Business.* New York: Lyle Stuart, 1966.

Emenegger, Robert. *UFOs: Past, Present and Future.* New York: Ballantine Books, 1974.

Flammonde, Paris. *UFOs Exist!* New York: G. P. Putnam's Sons, 1976.

Flindt, Max, and Otto Binder. *Mankind: Child of the Stars.* New York: Fawcett Publications, 1974.

Fort, Charles. *The Book of the Damned.* New York: Boni and Liveright, 1919.

———. *New Lands.* New York: Boni and Liveright, 1923.

———. *Lo!* New York: Claude H. Kendall, 1931.

Fowler, Raymond E. *UFOs—Interplanetary Visitors.* New York: Exposition Press, 1974.

———. *The Andreasson Affair.* Englewood Cliffs, N.J.: Prentice-Hall, 1979.

Fry, Daniel W. *The White Sands Incident.* Los Angeles: New Age Publishing Company, 1954.

Fuller, John G. *Incident at Exeter.* New York: G. P. Putnam's Sons, 1966.

———. *The Interrupted Journey.* New York: Dial Press, 1966.

———. *Aliens in the Skies.* New York: G. P. Putnam's Sons, 1969.

Gardner, Marshall. *Journey to the Interior of the Earth.* Aurora, Ill.: Marshall Gardner, 1913.

Geller, Uri. *Uri Geller: My Story.* New York: Praeger, 1975.

Genesis III Productions Ltd. *UFO . . . Contact from the Pleiades, Volume I,* 1st ed. Phoenix, Ariz.: Genesis III Productions, Ltd., 1979.

———. *UFO . . . Contact from the Pleiades, Volume II.* Phoenix, Ariz.: Genesis III Productions, Ltd., 1983.

Girvin, Calvin C. *The Night Has a Thousand Saucers.* El Monte, Calif.: Understanding Publishing Company, 1958.

Haines, Richard F. *Project Delta: A Study of Multiple UFO.* Los Altos, Calif.: L.D.A. Press, 1994.

Hall, Richard H., ed. *The UFO Evidence*. Washington, D.C.: National Investigations Committee on Aerial Phenomena, 1964.

Hendry, Allan. *The UFO Handbook*. Garden City, N.Y.: Doubleday and Company, 1979.

Hewes, Hayden. *The Aliens*. Edmond, Okla.: International UFO Bureau Press, 1970.

———. *The Intruders*. Edmond, Okla.: International UFO Bureau Press, 1970.

Hobana, Ion, and Julien Weverbergh. *UFOs from Behind the Iron Curtain*. New York: Bantam Books, 1975.

Hynek, J. Allen. *The UFO Experience: A Scientific Inquiry*. Chicago: Henry Regnery Company, 1972.

———. *The Hynek UFO Report*. New York: Dell Publishing Company, 1977.

Hynek, J. Allen, and Jacques Vallee. *The Edge of Reality*. Chicago: Henry Regnery Company, 1975.

Jacobs, David Michael. *The UFO Controversy in America*. Bloomington, Ind.: Indiana University Press, 1975.

Jung, Carl G. *Flying Saucers: A Modern Myth of Things Seen in the Sky*. New York: Harcourt, Brace and Company, 1959.

Keyhoe, Donald E. *Flying Saucers Are Real*. New York Fawcett Publications, 1950.

———. *Flying Saucers from Outer Space*. New York: Henry Holt, 1953.

———. *Aliens From Space*. Garden City, N.Y.: Doubleday and Company, 1973.

Kinder, Gary. *Light Years: An Investigation into the Extraterrestrial Experiences of Eduard Meier*. New York: The Atlantic Monthly Press, 1987.

Klass, Philip J. *UFOs Identified*. New York: Random House 1968.

———. *UFOs Explained*. New York: Random House, 1974.

———. *UFOs The Public Deceived*. Amherst, N.Y.: Prometheus Books, 1989.

Korff, Kal K. *A Comprehensive Review of UFO Motion Picture Films*. UFO Report, October 1980.

———. *The Meier Photographs: Hoax from the Pleiades*. UFO Report, December 1980.

———. *The Billy Meier Hoax*. Washington D.C.: *Frontiers of Science*, March–April 1981.

———. *The Meier Incident—The Most Infamous Hoax in UFOlogy*. Prescott, Ariz.: Townescribe Press, 1981.

Kusche, Lawrence D. *The Bermuda Triangle Mystery—Solved*. Amherst, N.Y.: Prometheus Books, 1986.

Landsburg, Alan, and Sally Landsburg. *In Search of Ancient Mysteries*. New York: Bantam Books, 1974.

Levitt, Zola, and John Weldon. *UFOs: What on Earth Is Happening?* Montreal, Canada: Harvest House, 1975.

Lorenzen, Coral E. *Flying Saucers—The Startling Evidence of the Invasion from Outer Space*. New York: New American Library, 1970.

Lorenzen, Coral, and Jim Lorenzen. *Flying Saucer Occupants*. New York: New American Library, 1967.

———. *Encounters with UFO Occupants*. New York: Berkley Publishing Corporation, 1976.

Meier, Eduard Albert. *Stimme der Wassermannzeit*. Hinterschmidrüti, Switzerland, 1976.

Menzel, Donald H., and Lyle G. Boyd. *The World of Flying Saucers*. Garden City, N.Y.: Doubleday and Company, 1963.

Menzel, Donald, and Ernest H. Taves. *The UFO Enigma*. Garden City, N.Y.: Doubleday and Company, 1977.

Michel, Aime. *Flying Saucers and the Straight Line Mystery*. New York: Criterion Books, 1958.

Moosbrugger, Guido. *...und sie fliegen doch! UFOs: Die größte Herausforderung des 20 Jahrhunderts*. München, Germany: Michael Hesemann Verlag, 1991.

Ostrander, Sheila, and Lynn Schroeder. *Psychic Discoveries Behind the Iron Curtain*. Englewood Cliffs, N.J.: Prentice-Hall, Inc., 1971.

Philips, Ted. *Physical Traces Associated with UFO Sightings: A Preliminary Catalog*. Northfield, Ill.: Center for UFO Studies, 1975.

Randi, James. *Flim-Flam!* Amherst, N.Y.: Prometheus Books, 1982.

Ruppelt, Edward J. *The Report on Unidentified Flying Objects*. Garden City, N.Y.: Doubleday and Company, 1956; revised edition, 1959.

Sagan, Carl, and Thornton Page, eds. *UFOs—A Scientific Debate* . Ithaca, N.Y.: Cornell University Press, 1972.

Salisbury, Frank B. *The Utah UFO Display: A Biologist's Report*. Old Greenwich, Conn.: Devin-Adair Company, 1974.

Sanderson, Ivan T. *Uninvited Visitors: A Biologist Looks at UFOs*. New York: Cowles Education Corporation, 1967.

———. *Invisible Residents*. New York: World Publishing Company, 1970.

Saunders, David, and R. Roger Harkins. *UFOs: Yes!* New York: New American Library, 1968.

Spencer, John Wallace. *Limbo of the Lost.* New York: Bantam Books, 1973.

———. *No Earthly Explanation.* Springfield, Mass.: Phillips Publishing Company, 1974.

Stanford, Ray. *Socorro "Saucer" in a Pentagon Pantry.* Austin, Tex.: Blueapple Books, 1976.

Stevens, Wendelle C. *UFO . . . Contact from the Pleiades: A Preliminary Investigation Report—The Report of an Ongoing Contact.* Tucson, Ariz.: Wendelle Stevens, 1983.

———. *UFO . . . Contact from the Pleiades: A Supplementary Investigation Report—The Report of an Ongoing Contact.* Tucson, Ariz.: Wendelle Stevens, 1989.

———. *Message from the Pleiades, the Contact Notes of Eduard "Billy" Meier, Volume I.* Phoenix, Ariz.: Wendelle C. Stevens and Genesis III Publishing, 1988.

———. *Message from the Pleiades, the Contact Notes of Eduard "Billy" Meier, Volume II.* Phoenix, Ariz.: Wendelle C. Stevens and Genesis III Publishing, 1991.

Story, Ronald. *The Space Gods Revealed: A Close Look at the Theories of Erich von Däniken.* New York: Harper and Row, 1976.

———. *Guardians of the Universe?* London: New English Library, 1979.

Stringfield, Leonard H. *Situation Red: The UFO Siege.* Garden City, N. Y.: Doubleday and Company, 1977.

Tacker, Lawrence J. *Flying Saucers and the U.S. Air Force.* Princeton, N.J.: D. Vam Nostrand Company, 1960.

Temple, Robert K. G. *The Sirius Mystery.* New York: St. Martin's Press, 1976.

Thompson, Keith. *Angels and Aliens: UFOs and the Mythic Imagination.* Menlo Park, Calif.: Addison-Wesley, 1991.

U.S. Congress, House of Representatives. *Committee on Armed Services, Unidentified Flying Objects, Hearings, 89th Congress, 2nd Session, April 5, 1966.* Washington, D.C.: U.S. Government Printing Office, 1966.

———. *Committee on Science and Astronautics, Symposium on Unidentified Flying Objects, 90th Congress, 2nd Session, July 29, 1968.* Washington, D.C.: U.S. Government Printing Office, 1968.

Vallee, Jacques. *Anatomy of a Phenomenon: Unidentified Objects in Space—A Scientific Appraisal.* Chicago: Henry Regnery Company, 1965.